PRAISE FOR WINNING DIGITAL CUSTOMERS

"Howard and his team have been applying their transformation methods here at Barnes & Noble Education for the last several years with outstanding results. I've seen first-hand just how effective the methods outlined in this book can be and would recommend it as a go-to guide for any organization involved in digital offerings."

Michael Huseby
Chairman and CEO
Barnes & Noble Education, Inc.

"I've worked with Howard Tiersky for years and have seen his practices in action. They work! If you are in charge of any aspect of digital, this book is your road-map. Howard and his team have been applying the principles in this book at The Avis-Budget Group for over five years with spectacular results. No matter what industry you are in, I highly recommend using this book as a guide to your digital transformation."

Gerard Insall
Chief Information Officer
Avis Budget Group

"This book will teach you exactly how to drive your company's digital transformation to victory. It is a treasure chest of techniques coupled with an online archive of lessons and tactics that will help you out-market and out-innovate your competitors."

Jeremy Gutsche
CEO of Trend Hunter and *New York Times* Bestselling Author

"The relationship we build with our customers, especially online, is more important than the products and services we sell them. Howard will show you how to transform your business from simply meeting a need to developing a true digital relationship with people so that they genuinely care about what you do to help them."

David Meerman Scott
Wall Street Journal* bestselling author of *Fanocracy

"A smart, highly accessible, deeply practical guide to truly understanding today's consumers and how to design products and experiences they will love."

Thomas Gewecke
Chief Digital Officer and EVP, Strategy and Business Development
Warner Bros. Entertainment

"*Winning Digital Customers* is the rare business book with a demonstrable ROI. Buy one for every member of your team. It will help you grow your business."

Shelly Palmer
LinkedIn's Top Voice in Technology
CNN Contributor, CEO of The Palmer Group

"A must-have guide to saving your company. For me, as a seasoned CXO who has played a part in many digital transformations, this easy and practical read is now my go-to guide."

Tony Doye
Chief Strategy Officer, Girl Scouts of America
Former CEO, Fujitsu Americas

"This book will drive you through the complexity of digital transformation in such a way that every step will look simple. By applying these 5 rules, you could win more than customers' money; you could win their heart."

Jean-François Ségrestaa
Head of Marketing
Airbus Defence & Space – Intelligence

"A fascinating and highly accessible primer on the steps to succeed at digital transformation. No matter how experienced you are, you will learn something important from this book!"

Rob Roy
Chief Digital Officer
Sprint

WINNING DIGITAL CUSTOMERS

THE ANTIDOTE TO IRRELEVANCE

....

HOWARD TIERSKY

Project Supervisor: Connor Gundersen
Cover Design: Damon Freeman
Internal Design: Juan Diaz R.
Illustrator: Lubov Babaeva
Editors: Marilyn Freedman, Caryn Pine, Tami Brehse

Printed in the United States of America
ISBN: 978-1-7345585-3-1

Spiral Press is an imprint of Cranberry Press and is available at a special discount for bulk purchases in the U.S. through its distributor National Book Network (NBN). For more information, please contact the special market department at NBN 15200 NBN Way, Blue Ridge Summit, PA17214, or call 1-800-462-6420 or email custser@nbnbooks.com

TABLE OF CONTENTS

MICHELLE MCKENNA
SVP & CHIEF INFORMATION OFFICER OF
THE NATIONAL FOOTBALL LEAGUE

I've been fortunate to have had the opportunity to serve as a transformational change agent at some amazing companies—brands like Disney, Universal Studios, Constellation Energy and most recently, The National Football League, where I was delighted to be asked to become The League's first Chief Information Officer. All of these companies were "best in class" in their business sectors *before* I arrived, but all needed significant digital transformation.

Howard Tiersky has been one of my secret weapons in each place I've led meaningful change. He is one of the brightest, most collaborative and best creative thinkers I've ever worked with. It's made a huge difference in my career that he was a partner to me in many of my accomplishments, and I'm happy that he's now written his methods all down so that others can now know what works.

I met Howard before people were even using the term "digital transformation," but we knew the world was changing and that necessitated re-thinking the way businesses interacted with their customers.

Since then, Howard has significantly and repeatedly helped me to break down "change" into manageable chunks, provided real, *practical* advice, and worked with me to craft road-maps to make it happen. That's what this book does, as well.

It's a very readable but detailed, pragmatic guide about how to drive digital transformation in the "real world," including both the specific steps to follow and many anecdotes to put them in context.

I'd like to briefly mention three of the key themes that Howard covers in depth in the book that I think are especially critical to your success as a leader or stakeholder of digital transformation.

UNDERSTANDING YOUR CUSTOMER

First, I couldn't agree more with the core premise of this book that it all begins with understanding your customers, whatever term you may use for them. At the NFL, they are called "fans." At Walt Disney World, where I started on this journey, we called them "guests."

I remember when I began applying the principles outlined in this book to improving how Disney's guests experienced "vacation booking." As we conducted research to understand their emotional decision-making and then created customer personas using the techniques Howard describes, we ended up empathizing with guests in a far more profound way.

That led us to do things like changing the name of our "Vacation Booking Process" to "Dreaming." It seems so simple to just name a process something different, but once you do that, you begin to put yourself in the mind of a mom sitting at home on her computer, *dreaming* about taking her daughter to Walt Disney World for the first time. All of a sudden, how you serve up content, how you structure the steps to go through the actual booking, what tools you provide for planning—it changes how you think about all of that.

And that changed thinking eventually has a huge financial impact on your business results, as we saw at Disney.

JOURNEY MAPPING AND DESIGN THINKING

Secondly, this book describes how to integrate Customer Journey Mapping and Design Thinking to form the core of your digital transformation process, an approach that has been critical to the many successful transformations I've had the opportunity to lead.

2

For example, at Universal Studios Theme Parks, we went out with Howard's team and got amazing customer insight, and it led us to a clear vision of the experience we needed to create for our guests. But it also led us to momentarily panic, thinking, "Oh my God, this means we've got to rip out our entire reservation system. It means we've got to totally re-engineer our marketing database!"

This book documents an approach that helps you plan ambitious but *rationally-paced* change—starting with quick wins—helping you discover which pain points *don't* have to wait until your entire platform is fixed, begin with those, and *then* build larger change consistent with your long-term vision.

LEADERSHIP AND ALIGNMENT

Being a champion of change can make you popular in the beginning.

But if you exclusively focus on what has to be done and forget about the need to bring people along, you will most certainly not last in your job.

I've learned the "shelf life" of executives that drive transformation is usually eighteen months to three years. At the NFL, this is my eighth season. In each of those eight seasons, my goal has been to transform or evolve some process that's been in place for many years.

I don't think I would have had the long career that I've had doing this work if I didn't find ways to get large numbers of stakeholders fully aligned. This book is filled with creative "change management" approaches that Howard has used to support me over many transformations with many challenges, and no doubt some he has had to invent while doing so.

For example, when I met Howard, he had begun to perfect an approach to intensive brainstorming and decision-making workshops, which I've since utilized a great deal. Using techniques described in this book, we would accelerate in a few days what would typically have taken weeks and weeks and weeks. I have used these ideation processes many times at the NFL as well as Universal Studios to great benefit, and I've also had many successful workshops at Howard's creative facility in New York, The Innovation Loft.

His process definitely expands your thinking. It definitely creates new products. It definitely helps you get there faster.

But the thing that is often the most valuable is that it's authored by everyone. There's not a CIO or a Chief Digital Officer or a CMO that's coming and saying, "These are the ten things we're going to do."

And that has much more staying power than a top-down directed approach. So much so that I had Howard and his team set up and operate a permanent innovation space for me at Constellation Energy when I was CIO there because we were having to literally change the entire company to go from being a monopoly to consumer choice—where you, as a customer, got to decide who provided your energy. That required completely renovating every system, and it was so intense that we couldn't just go away to a workshop for a couple of days. We literally had to *live* in the workshop approach, and it worked amazingly well.

In this book, Howard reveals how he achieves these kinds of results. You will find many methodologies, techniques, and top-secret tricks that can make a huge difference for you.

Even if you've already hired the most prestigious consulting company or agency out there, reading this book and applying its principles will help you achieve real, sustainable change that can survive and thrive long after the last consultant leaves the building.

Michelle McKenna
CIO, National Football League
May 17, 2020, New York City

COVID NOTE:

This book was written before Coronavirus changed life as we know it. And it's going to print amidst quarantine. As the window to make changes was closing, our editor called to ask us if we wanted to make any updates to the text given how much the *world* has changed in the last few months. Upon reflection, we didn't revise anything. Here's why.

At its core, digital transformation is about anticipating, responding to, and leading change. As we discuss in the book, the companies that are struggling today are those who have either not understood how their customers' needs have changed for a digital world or who have failed to change rapidly enough to keep up with them.

COVID-19 is simply *more* change and *faster* change than we've seen before, and it's change that is driving customers even more to digital experiences. So "dealing with" COVID-19 as a business is about doing the exact things outlined in this book—taking a fresh look at your customers' needs and then adapting your customer experience and supporting technology/processes to best meet those needs.

Of course, we never anticipated the pandemic and its impact on the world, but because this is a book about adapting to a changing world, it's actually just what you need in this time.

HALF OF THE VALUE OF THIS BOOK IS ONLINE

We have many resources and tools to offer that we couldn't fit in this book. That's why we've compiled a large collection of supplementary material at the book website **WinningDigitalCustomers.com**. Just enter the passcode, **CustomerLove**, to access a trove of materials that can help you as you embark on your digital transformation efforts. Look for callouts throughout the book marking materials available on the book website. You'll see icons along with short links to the content. We've also included QR codes that you can scan with your phone. If you need instructions on how to do that, we've provided a quick explainer video at `wdc.ht/QR`. Some examples of the supplemental material available on-line include:

 Bonus videos that will give you extra assistance in putting this book into action.

 Pre-formatted spreadsheets that you can use for various activities and deliverables described throughout the book.

 PowerPoint slides summarizing each chapter of the book with additional diagrams and statistics that can be used in your presentations.

 Templates for many of the deliverables described throughout the book.

 *eBooks that provide **additional techniques useful when applying the book's five-part methodology**.*

These tools are invaluable for putting the book into action, and we hope you'll take advantage of them. Make sure you go to **WinningDigitalCustomers.com** and enter the book passcode:

CustomerLove

to access all of the bonus content now!

Dedicated to everyone striving to unleash

the massive potential of "digital"

as a force for good in the world.

WINNING IN AN ERA OF TRANSFORMATION

. . . .

CHAPTER ONE

WINNING IN AN ERA OF TRANSFORMATION

YOU HAVE A PROBLEM

I f you are trying to make a legacy brand successful in today's digital world, you've got a problem. But this book is going to tell you exactly what to do about it.

My 7-year-old son, Joseph, likes to text our family group chat with news stories that *he* thinks we need to know about, such as the recent sightings of giant squids off the coast of Japan.

One evening last year, my phone dinged with a group text from Joseph sharing the announcement that very soon, every single Toys"R"Us in America would be closing.

"FOREVER 🪦" Joe added for emphasis in a follow-up text.

I was well aware of the problems the company faced. In fact, Toys"R"Us executives had recently visited our offices to talk about bringing in my firm to help improve their customer experience, but time just ran out.

I was disappointed that I wasn't going to be consulting on a Toys"R"Us turnaround, but little Joe's text prompted me to imagine how truly

devastated I would have been had Toys"R"Us disappeared when I was *his* age.

I figured I should probably check in. I headed downstairs and approached Joe, who was still at the kitchen computer. I gently asked how he was feeling about the news of the chain's closure.

He thought for a second, and then answered with a cheerful shrug, "I don't care!"

Seeing my surprised reaction, he gestured back at the screen and reassured me, "Dad, don't worry. We can just order whatever we need from Amazon!"

Some say Toys"R"Us "went under" because they had too much leveraged debt, and it's true that *was* a genuine problem. Others say that downloadable video games reduced the demand for physical toys, and they have—a bit. But Toys"R"Us died from something more profound—a lack of love. They just no longer mattered as they once did. If 7-year-old boys don't care whether your toy store stays or goes, you're done for.

At Joe's age, I *did* love Toys"R"Us. I also loved my Kodak camera with its flashbulbs, Speed Racer, my Timex digital watch, my Atari and IHOP. A few decades later in life, I loved Borders Bookstores, *Melrose Place* and my Blackberry.

Today, I love my Mac, Google Slides, Alexa, and Game of Thrones. And, I'm back to loving IHOP again. How about you? What do you love? Disney World? Chipotle? Fortnite? Lululemon? Snapchat?

MORE IMPORTANTLY, DO YOUR CUSTOMERS LOVE YOUR BUSINESS?

This book is a blueprint for earning love from today's customers, who I like to call "digital customers," and it's a treatise on the idea that obtaining that customer love is the single most important factor in the success of your business.

· ·

WHAT IS LOVE?

Of course, there are many meanings of the word "love." I *love* my wife and I *love* my Ford Mustang, but not in precisely the same way.

When my firm polls consumers and asks if they love Citibank, most say "No." When we ask if they love Starbucks, many say "Yes." *They* know what we mean.

In this context, love is shorthand for the desire to be *connected* with a given brand and the strong faith that the brand will give you what you need.

In fact, our research shows that consumers think of brands on a continuum, as shown in the diagram.

The world has been changing rapidly, and once-loved brands have been falling down that scale. As they become irrelevant, they disappear. Meanwhile, new brands keep appearing and moving *up* the scale. You may have noticed that many of today's *most* loved brands are fairly young, like Amazon, Uber, Google, and Instagram.

But *some* of today's beloved brands *aren't* new—they are brands that have succeeded in remaining

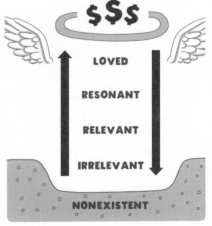

Brand-Love Continuum

‹ wdc.ht/LOVE

loved through the changing times, such as Nike, Disney, Whole Foods, and UPS.

So, old or new, what does it take to be loved? It doesn't require being perfect, or nobody would ever receive love. Analysis of our research reveals that there are three primary factors that are common across "loved brands."

 wdc.ht/FACTORS

- They meet the needs of their target customers extremely consistently.
- They periodically do things that delight customers beyond their expectations and needs.
- They "stand for" something that resonates with their customers.

When we say "stand for something," that doesn't necessarily, or even primarily, mean politically. While there *are* loved brands whose formula includes a social stance, such as Ben and Jerry's (environmentalism) or Chick-fil-A (conservative social values), other brands "stand for" apolitical values or philosophies: Apple stands for empowering individualism; Häagen-Dazs stands for the joy of indulgence; Nike stands for achieving your personal best; Walmart stands for the idea that you deserve low prices.

But many brands don't really stand for *anything*, or at least nothing the customer believes is sincere, and that limits their ability to inspire customer love. "Standing for" something doesn't just mean you have a slogan or an ad campaign. In order for cynical customers today to *love* a brand for what it "stands for," they need to see those values *in action,* whether through philanthropy, policies, products or service.

Test the formula for yourself on the brands you love and, experimentally, even the people you love. Consider it for your own company.

. . . .

ISN'T THAT THE SAME AS "LOYALTY"?

You may ask, isn't the "love" I'm talking about just another term for "loyalty"? You can call it that if you like, but I don't.

Love is a feeling.

In the English language, "loyalty" *can* also be a feeling, but it's not used that way in business today. It's used to refer to a specific behavior: repeated transactions.

You might book the same airline every week because they fly where you need to go, or eat at the same coffee shop every day because it's near your home. These companies consider you "loyal," but you may not *feel* either love or loyalty for their brands. Nevertheless, you have your *reasons* for continuing to do business with them—to *behave* "loyally"—at least for now.

We certainly *want* the behavior that is called "customer loyalty," but let's not mix that up with a *feeling* like love.

The term "customer loyalty" is also very often used in the context of loyalty *programs*—point-based accounts that give the customer "free stuff" if they engage in repeat transactions. Loyalty programs can be very effective. *However,* they represent a much narrower approach to achieving repeat business than the idea of customer love. With limited exceptions, loyalty programs are really just a form of discounting. You pay $300 for a flight, but you get points back that are worth, perhaps, $25 toward future travel. Maybe you also get coupons for a couple of free drinks.

It's a solid move to improve the value proposition in this way, but it's really just a way to offer the customer a better deal. It may stimulate sales, but it's transactional; it doesn't generate love.

. . . .

MEETING YOUR CUSTOMERS' CHANGING NEEDS

You can't buy love. But you can *inspire* it by ensuring that you follow the love formula—meet and occasionally exceed the needs of your customer (including, but by no means limited to, giving them a great deal) and stand for something they care about.

Of course, the devil is in the details. What *are* the most important needs of your customers? How do you determine if you *are* meeting them consistently? What "extra" things *would* delight your customers? What are the values that your customers find attractive?

It may sound like a puzzle, but if it is, there's an answer key in this book. There are *proven methods* to answer all these questions, and we will cover them in detail.

And these are questions that must also be studied on an *ongoing* basis because the answers are not static. That's why so many once-beloved brands are now gone. At one point, they *were* meeting and exceeding their customer's needs, and they stood for something customers cared about. That's how they *became* beloved. But when their customers' needs or values transformed, the brand didn't change, or didn't change enough, and that *broke* their "customer love" formula.

WHAT'S CHANGING? IT'S DIGITAL

To *keep* the love, you have to change with the times.

What's changing? No matter what industry you are in, the most significant change influencing customers over the past decade has been the massive increase in the role "digital" plays in their lives.

Customers today consume digital experiences via PCs, game systems, smart TVs, kiosks, voice-controlled appliances, and a host of other connected devices, but clearly the *most* prevalent access point to the digital world today is the smartphone.

How important are smartphones in your customer's life?

A few years ago, when my daughter, Jessica, was in 8th grade, she kept oversleeping and missing the school bus, and I would have to drive her to school.

One day, she did it *again*, and as I was driving her, I told her that from now on, any morning that she missed the bus, she would lose her iPhone for the day. Then, I told her to hand over the device.

That afternoon, I got home from work a little early and found Jessica in the living room despite the fact that she had previously planned to spend the afternoon at the mall with her friends.

I asked her what happened. She said, "Well, you took away my phone!" Not seeing the connection, I asked what that had to do with going to the mall. She lectured me, "There's no point in going to the mall with my friends if I don't have my iPhone!" As if it were the most obvious thing in the world.

Perhaps you believe this is just an example of a dramatic teenager trying to inflict parental guilt. I'll concede this as a likely contributing factor. But consider these stats from several different research studies that looked at how attached *your* customers are to their smartphones:

- There are 265 million smartphones in the U.S. today, covering more than 80% of the population over the age of 10.[1]

- The average smartphone user checks their phone 80 to 150 times a day; 71% typically sleep beside their mobile phone.[2]

When asked if they had to choose between their smartphone and other things important to them:

- 64% of Americans said they wouldn't dine out for a year if they had to give that up to keep their phone.[3]

- 50% reported that they'd skip vacation rather than relinquish their phone.[4]

- Nearly half of Americans said they'd work an extra day each week if they had to in order to keep their phone.[5]

- And more than one in three reported that they'd give up sex for a year versus giving up their phone.[6]

While digital may not be the *only* thing that matters, for most businesses, if you aren't delivering on digital, you absolutely aren't meeting your customers' needs.

This is why I call today's customers "digital customers" as a reminder that no matter what business you are in, the vast majority of your customers today are living a lifestyle that has digital at the center.

Digital is *so* important to customers' lives today that if you aren't delivering an excellent digital experience, you are also quite likely not aligned with their *values.* This is because the empowerment of being able to access the brands they love whenever they want and however they want has now transcended being just a "need" for many of today's consumers. It's so core to their lifestyle that if it appears that you don't care deeply about it, not only are you not meeting their needs, you are in conflict with their fundamental values and worldview. It doesn't mean they won't ever buy from you, but it's very hard for them to love a brand that doesn't appear to value something so important to them.

. . . .

DO WE EVEN NEED THIS TERM "DIGITAL" ANYMORE?

There's an old joke: one fish asks another fish, "How's the water?" And the second fish responds, "Water? What the heck is water?"

Along those same lines, I hear more and more debates about whether we should even still be using the word "digital" because, "Aren't *all* businesses pretty much 'digital' today?"

To me, it's not a question of having a *digital* businesses or *non-digital* businesses. Yes, *nearly* all businesses today, even the ones that are "behind the curve," have significant digital operations, and most *also* have aspects of their customer experience that are not particularly focused on "digital." That's all fine, but...

IF A COMPANY IS SUCCESSFUL TODAY, IT'S NOT BECAUSE THEY ARE A DIGITAL BUSINESS BUT BECAUSE THEY ARE RESONATING WITH AN AUDIENCE OF DIGITAL CUSTOMERS.

. . . .

IT'S NOT GOING WELL

Although many companies are *trying* to get to digital resonance, research shows that most aren't where they need to be. A Gartner survey found that, across industries, digital experiences did not live up to expectations for 84% of customers.[7]

This isn't necessarily for lack of trying.

- A KPMG survey found that 96% of organizations were embarking on some phase of digital transformation.[8]
- But Forbes reported that 84% of transformation efforts have failed.[9]
- Further, a Capgemini study found that only 39% of organizations report having the digital capabilities needed to turn their investments in digital into business success.[10]

THAT'S THE LOVE DILEMMA

To deliver "digital" at the increasingly elegant level today's customers expect, most companies need to reinvent themselves in a variety of ways, and quickly.

But enterprises are just not *designed* for rapid change. Digital transformations at large organizations are often riddled with problems such as the absence of an aligned vision, organizational resistance, byzantine technology, and a lack of customer centric thinking.

The consequences are playing out all around us. In prior decades, we saw the demise of companies like Borders, Western Union, and Kodak. More recently, it's Sports Authority, Linens and Things, Circuit City, and many others.

And of course, there are a great many "legacy" brands who are still *surviving* but find themselves financially challenged and shrinking as they struggle to stay relevant in a digital age.

IT DOESN'T HAVE TO BE THAT WAY

Tenured companies, or what my colleague Bob Taylor likes to call "analog classics," *can* transform successfully and earn love in a digital age. HBO, Walmart, FedEx, 1-800-Flowers, and *The New York Times* are all companies that are successfully transforming.

My 25-year career as a consultant has given me the opportunity to study *what works* for enterprises re-inventing themselves for a world filled with digital customers and to codify it into methodologies that my team and I use to help clients everyday.

This book is a consolidation of those learnings into a conceptually simple five-step process with sufficient detail to empower you and your team to apply it in the real world.

This "Customer Love" Digital Transformation Formula integrates leading methodologies, such as LEAN, Design Thinking, and customer journey mapping with modifications and extensions we have developed over the years to optimize them to work at large enterprises. The formula presented in this book is not academic; its principles have been proven at a wide range of companies from GM to Universal Studios to Avis to Exelon—companies where we have helped to drive all or part of a major transformation.

. . . .

THE STRUCTURE OF THIS BOOK: 6 SECTIONS

The book is broken into six sections. This first section, "Winning in an Era of Transformation," explains what digital transformation *is*, why it's essential, and what some of the key challenges are when driving change, as well as revealing the most important success factors to winning in a digital age.

There are many methodologies to approach digital transformation, and based on the statistics previously cited, it appears that some of them don't work all that well. That's why the remainder of the book will provide you a tested and proven *formula* for how to transform in order to win the love of your customers.

The formula has five activities, and each of the remaining five sections of the book goes into step-by-step details on one of these activities.

The Customer Love Digital Transformation Formula

❶ UNDERSTAND YOUR CUSTOMER

The first activity in the formula is to "Understand Your Customer." That section of the book will detail why customer centricity is essential, then give you a rich set of tools to gather the insights you will need to understand your customer in an actionable way—proven tools that have been developed and curated during my 25 years of experience doing customer research.

❷ MAP THE CUSTOMER JOURNEY

The second activity is to "Map the Customer Journey," which consists of developing a vision for the future customer experience in the form of a customer journey *map*—a type of infographic that communicates the end-to-end customer experience you intend to create. I'll share the techniques we have used to do customer journey mapping for clients like NBC, Exelon and Airbus.

❸ BUILD THE FUTURE

The third activity is "Build the Future." This section of the book describes best-practice approaches to taking your customer journey map and making it a reality.

It reveals new, never-before-published updates to Design Thinking, the methodology used by Apple, Nike, Airbnb, and many other highly successful product development companies.

These first three activities are presented sequentially in the book and should also be approached more or less in order, although in the "real world" there will probably be some overlap or back and forth. The last two activities, however, occur in parallel with the first three.

❹ SHORT-TERM OPTIMIZATION

Building the future can take quite a while. But there are usually some areas where you are currently "letting the customer down" that you can fix quickly. This section of the book will explain how to get rapid results within your current circumstances, wherever you are in your transformation timeline.

❺ LEAD THE CHANGE

Perhaps most importantly, digital transformation requires bold, courageous, and determined leadership. The final section of the book will address the challenge of organizational resistance, and provide guidance on how to develop leadership teams and gain alignment. It will also go into detail about how to build and sell the case for large-scale transformation to your boss, CEO or board.

· ·

My inspiration for this book comes from all the legacy organizations that have tremendous talent, assets, and histories, but just haven't yet found a successful path to the customer love that they need in order to thrive. I'm also inspired thinking about the *customers* of these organizations who often desperately want them to adapt to meet modern needs and are waiting, less and less patiently, for it to happen.

Lastly, I am always in awe of the courageous *executives* at many of these companies who make it their personal mission to drive the innovation and transformation that are needed to win the love and increased business of digital customers. These leaders face enormous headwinds and often lay their jobs on the line in an effort to save their companies.

My message to these heroes is that you absolutely can succeed if you have sufficient determination and follow the right process. This book will give you a proven process. You will need to bring the determination.

CHAPTER TWO

WINNING IN AN ERA OF TRANSFORMATION

WHAT IS DIGITAL TRANSFORMATION?

My favorite restaurant is on the island of Cozumel, Mexico, a somewhat out-of-the-way destination primarily visited by SCUBA divers and cruise ships. One section of the island has small hotels and resorts, but most of it is made up of rugged beaches in their natural state, as they have been for thousands of years. It is on one of those beaches, on the out-of-the-way part of an out-of-the-way island, that you can find Coconuts Bar and Grill.

The restaurant's floor is sand, and tables are set up under palm trees and sky. There's a small, Jimmy-Buffet-esque shack where the food is prepared. Live chickens and parrots flap around. Don't expect air conditioning or even an electric fan since there is no power on this side of the island. If you are hot in the Mexican sun, have a hand-shaken margarita. Ice is brought daily from town in a cooler. The seafood is fresh because it's just been plucked out of the ocean. This business is doing just fine running a fantastic restaurant without electricity or running water, and I don't think they are in any hurry to change that.

But at Coconuts, you *can* pay with a credit card because they have Square connected to an iPhone. And, of course, they have a Yelp page so one can read reviews about their amazing cuisine and ambiance. Yes, they also have a website *and* a Facebook page.

Despite not needing electricity or running water, even Coconuts has adopted some key digital capabilities.

McKinsey & Company said back in 2016 that there is "nowhere to hide" from digital transformation, and apparently, this even applies at some level to "off-the-grid" beach shacks.

. . . .

"DIGITAL TRANSFORMATION" BEYOND THE BUZZWORD

The phrase "digital transformation" is trending hot on Google right now and it's popular to use it to describe just about any digital or technology initiative. But let's get *concrete* about what "digital transformation" *really* is and how to know it when you see it.

Indulge me for just a page or two of the brief history of digital. I promise it will be quick, and just a dash of context will give you clarity.

In the past 20 years or so, the business application of "digital" has gone through three main stages, as shown in this diagram:

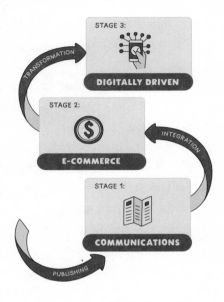

The Three Stages of Digital Evolution

‹ wdc.ht/EVOLUTION

Stage 1:
COMMUNICATIONS

It was the late nineties. The TV show *Friends* was in its heyday. Bill Clinton was hangin' with Monica at the White House, and AOL was littering the world with CD-ROMs.

Businesses then were leveraging "digital" to create "brochure-ware" by *publishing* content online to provide information to customers and prospects (and to employees via "intranet" sites). While this use of digital as an electronic communications platform remains one valuable application, today, most companies are doing more.

Stage 2:
E-COMMERCE

The second stage of digital was e-commerce. This involved enabling digital *transactions* such as through an online store or a self-service employee benefits portal.

In the year 2000, total U.S. e-commerce revenue was already a few billion dollars. By 2010, it was nearing $50 billion, and now, ten years later, it's over $600 billion.[1]

To go through the change from communications to an e-commerce model, companies had to undergo an *integration* effort. This entailed connecting their transactional systems and processes to digital interfaces such as websites and later, apps.

E-commerce enables you to "do business" in the digital realm, not just talk about it. But for many companies, e-commerce it is really just a *bridge* between a business built for a "pre-digital" world and customers who want to interact digitally. As the linguistics demonstrate, it's basically tacking an "e" onto the commerce they had been doing for decades.

While this is a step forward, few companies fundamentally change their brand, products or core value proposition simply by adding an "e" to their preexisting operations.

Stage 3:
DIGITALLY DRIVEN

There is a third stage that successful digital companies are playing at, but which many legacy brands have yet to embrace. This third stage entails what I call becoming a "digitally driven enterprise," and it requires another, much deeper level of change.

The journey to becoming a digitally driven enterprise is what "digital transformation" is all about.

Being digitally driven means far more than providing your customers with a good app. It means that you are aggressively creating products and customer experiences that take full advantage of the potential of digital—becoming a business that would probably be impossible outside of the digital world.

Most of the companies moving up the "customer love" ladder described in the previous chapter are either fully digitally driven or at least delivering many strong digitally driven capabilities.

Let's look at a few examples. AT&T enables you to do many digital things, but it is not primarily a digitally driven business. And it largely is not loved, I'm sorry to say. Skype (now owned by Microsoft) *is* a digitally driven business and earns its fair share of love, especially from customers who otherwise could not afford to speak regularly and at length to their distant families and friends.

Skype's fundamental business model would be impossible without the internet and digital devices that can connect "peer to peer," since they have offloaded the vast majority of the cost of telecommunications onto their customers' internet service providers. As a result, they are able to offer their services for free or very nearly free while generating billions of dollars of revenue per year.

When a company is *truly* digitally driven, they become tough for traditional enterprises to compete with. The telco industry estimates that the impact of Skype and similar services has cost them over $50 billion a year in lost revenue.[2]

Another example—Hertz will rent you a car to get from place to place. They have a nice app, an intuitive website, and helpful kiosks at their locations, but these are all e-commerce. Hertz's fundamental value proposition hasn't changed for the past 30 years. You go to the car rental facility, get the car, drive it around, and return it later to the same place, all the while getting charged by the day. Having an *e-commerce*-based digital reservation system is certainly beneficial because it saves the customer the effort of a phone call and saves the company money, as well.

But Zipcar (part of the Avis Budget Group) does it differently. They park their cars all over the city and use GPS to know where the cars are. They let you reserve a car "near you" on the street, unlock the car with your phone, drive where you need to go, and leave it possibly someplace else, where it can then be grabbed by another customer when they need it. This enables Zipcar to charge by the hour, with many customers potentially using the same car in the course of a single day. At its core, the business is digital. If the cars weren't connected to a wireless network and the customers did not have full touchscreen computers right in their pockets, the model would never work. While they still need *cars*, Zipcar does not need traditional rental centers, and they make car rental practical for a segment of customers for whom the traditional model does not make sense.

Uber takes this even further. Similar to Zipcar, you use an app to reserve an Uber. But Uber has leveraged a totally different model that uses 'digital' to mobilize individuals with a car, spare time, and a desire to earn a few bucks. They don't actually need to own any vehicles or employ any drivers. Instead, they act as a kind of "dating service" for people who want rides and people who want to provide them. Airbnb does something similar for hospitality.

These businesses are centrally reliant on digital experiences for their consumer value proposition and business models. Hence, they are "digitally driven" companies. In fact, Uber takes it so far that the digital infrastructure is nearly the *entire* capability of the company. The rest is effectively outsourced.

Other companies with inherently digital business models include Netflix, Google, Facebook, and eBay. Now, a contrarian might say, "Wait a minute, those are all 'internet tech' companies, so of course, they are 'digital.'"

But Google's fundamental value proposition is really that of a research library. eBay's is that of a giant store or swap meet. And Netflix's is that of a video rental store or a multiplex.

So, while it's true that digitally driven companies at times *feel* as though they are "tech companies," a close look often reveals that they are fundamentally fulfilling a long-standing product or service category, just in a new way. These example businesses aren't selling technology, like Cisco or Oracle. They are digitally driven manifestations of some other kind of company, such as entertainment, transportation, or telecommunications. *That's* what it looks like when businesses in those industries are digitally driven.

. . . .

WHY YOU NEED TRANSFORMATION

It may seem like your company is *far away* from that type of digitally driven experience. That's why you need "transformation."

"Transformation" *means* profound change, such as when a child goes through puberty and becomes an adult. After a transformation, as the Haddaway song often played at Tony Robbins seminars says, "Life will never be the same again." When Netflix's core business moved from mailing DVDs to streaming, that was a transformation.

Did your last digital initiative create a "Life will never be the same again" moment for your company? Or did business keep going on more or less "as usual?"
⟨ wdc.ht/LIFE

Of course, there are many great opportunities to engage in *non*-transformational change to the digital properties in your enterprise, and doing so may be a good starting point *towards* transformation. However, transformation *itself* is something more profound. Frankly, transformation also typically involves some level of discomfort, pain, and significant uncertainty. Another litmus test:

IF YOU AREN'T **FEELING PAIN,** YOU PROBABLY AREN'T TRANSFORMING.

< wdc.ht/PAIN

 **SOCIAL SHARING:** *Throughout the book, we've highlighted important points and quotations as shareable call outs. Next to these call outs, you'll see a link that you can use to share a graphical meme of the quote on social media. Scan the QR code or enter the short URL to choose what platform to share it to.*

 wdc.ht/MEMES

. . . .

And that brings us to perhaps the most important question about undertaking a digital transformation to become digitally driven: is all this pain really necessary for *your* enterprise? Sure, Uber and Netflix are great businesses, but does that mean becoming digitally driven is required for *every* business to achieve future success?

Will Coconuts, my favorite Cozumel beach bar, have to start serving IoT-enabled taquitos in order to avoid shutting its doors (despite not even having any doors)? Or can some companies continue just fine providing products like Frosted Flakes and dish detergent or services like accounting or roof repair without needing to transform? Can some businesses stay in "e-commerce" forever?

It's an important question that you need to answer for your own business, and we will delve into it more in the next chapter, "Is Digital Transformation Required?"

CHAPTER THREE

WINNING IN AN ERA OF TRANSFORMATION

IS DIGITAL TRANSFORMATION REQUIRED?

The Qing Dynasty ruled China during the 18th century, a time when each new emperor was selected from amongst the royal family based on merit. In 1736, it was the fifth son of the recently deceased ruler who won the competitive succession process and became known as the Qianlong Emperor.

What *merit* did the Qianlong Emperor possess that earned him the throne? Among other skills, he was an expert archer, winning many competitions with his longbow.

Flash forward 57 years. A diplomatic team from England, known as the Macartney Mission, is sent to China by the infamous King George III to negotiate trade agreements with the Qianlong Emperor. The delegation arrived with a proposal to trade large quantities of British guns in exchange for items that were desirable in the West.

Although China had *invented* gunpowder almost 1,000 years earlier, as of the 18th century, Chinese manufacturing of firearms was still primitive and their weapons far inferior to those made in England.

But that didn't matter much to the Qianlong Emperor, who was largely uninterested in guns and preferred to equip his armies  with his beloved longbows. In fact, he had discouraged divisions of his military that were experimenting with improving Chinese firearm design.

When shown a demonstration of how easily and reliably the British rifles being offered in trade could be aimed, fired, and reloaded, he is reported to have remarked that they seemed more like a weapon "for children," not for expert warfare.

At the end of the visit, the emperor wrote a letter to King George as a formal rejection of the British proposal. It stated:

"I set no value on your objects strange or ingenious and have no use for your country's manufactures."

Thirty years later, China was under near total British control, subdued by those childish European firearms during the Opium Wars.

Back at the time of the Macartney Mission, China's economy was the largest in the world. By the end of the Opium Wars, the Chinese had largely lost sovereignty over their own country. By ten years after *that*, the country's gross domestic product had fallen by half. As a consequence, the Qing Dynasty was the *last* of China's 12 imperial dynasties that had collectively ruled China for over 2,100 years.

IS CHANGE ALWAYS NECESSARY?

These days, board members across industries are demanding that their management outline plans for "digital transformation." However, the fact that this phrase is a hot buzzword in the boardroom is hardly a sufficient reason to rethink an entire company.

As explained in the previous chapter, digital transformation is about making your company "digitally driven." This means that your approach to selling and delivering your products and services becomes intrinsically tied to a digital world. We've discussed how companies such as Google, Amazon, and Netflix have benefited from this digitally driven approach, but is it really right for *your* company?

After all, change is risky. It's one thing if you are starting a *new* company, but if you already have a company that is *using* digital for marketing and e-commerce but is not necessarily "digitally driven," is it *truly necessary* to change? Can't the world still have *some* companies that are not digitally driven?

Sure, it can. Perhaps *you* have a traditional, non-digitally driven business that is healthy, growing steadily, nicely profitable, and not threatened in any significant way by "digital" competition or changing customer needs. Is that your situation?

If it is, then you should seriously consider *not* undergoing a major transformation. As we've said, it's risky, costly, and often painful. Many of your people will resist. As my grandmother would say, who needs that kind of *tumult*?

But if that describes you, you are a part of a teeny-tiny minority of businesses that are not threatened by a changing digital world. So just be careful you aren't misjudging the situation. This chapter will lay out the reasons why not just the majority of businesses but, in fact, *nearly* all businesses will need to become digitally driven to thrive.

. . . .

IT'S A NEW ERA

There have been *many* periods of time when businesses could operate in more or less the same manner for *decades*: updating their advertising campaign periodically, creating marginally "new and improved" products every few years, and incrementally implementing operational enhancements to keep cutting costs and drive profits higher.

But those "good old days" are gone for more than 90% of all industry sectors. Waves of disruptive digital change started in the travel and financial services industries in the late '90s, then hit the retail and media segments after that. Today, even industries as slow-moving as industrial manufacturing, higher education, and hospital operations require an increasing degree of digital centricity in order to be competitive.

Whether your business is window washing, restaurant supplies, maritime navigation, or podiatry, your customers' expectations are digital.

Your competitors, both traditional and "pure plays," are leveraging digital to drive better customer experiences and increased operational efficiencies—enabling them to offer a more compelling value propositions to customers at a lower price. If you aren't doing the same, it's going to be tough to remain relevant.

. . . .

SPEED IS ESSENTIAL

It's not just a matter of needing to change but needing to do it rapidly to keep up. Jack Welch, the former CEO of General Electric credited with increasing the value of GE by over 4,000%, said,

"IF THE RATE OF CHANGE ON THE OUTSIDE EXCEEDS THE RATE OF CHANGE ON THE INSIDE, THE END IS NEAR." [1]

< wdc.ht/CHANGE

Many great companies today are in just this situation, as is evidenced by the many shuttered or struggling brands already described.

· ·

DIGITAL TRANSFORMATION IS CUTTING ACROSS ALL INDUSTRIES

I used to observe that, while digital may have transformed travel, retail, and financial services, it isn't going to change much about the value proposition of a box of Corn Flakes. That may still *seem* true, but take a look at another "consumer packaged goods" product category—the razor industry—and how that has been disrupted.

In 2011, Michael Dubin observed that there was customer pain associated with both the price of razors and also the difficulty of purchasing them in many retail stores, where anti-shoplifting measures meant that in order to make a purchase, customers needed to track down a busy sales associate to unlock the protected "razor fortress." [2]

Dubin developed a competing razor utilizing digital design methods, engaged a third-party ecosystem of manufacturers to supply them, marketed them on-line, and fulfilled them directly through a subscription business model. He called his new company Dollar Shave Club, and it was so successful that, five years later, Unilever purchased Dollar Shave Club for around $1 billion.[3] The company has inspired a number of copycat businesses such as Harry's Razors, recently purchased by the owner of Schick for over $1.3 billion.[4]

Similarly, the food industry is starting to see some disruption not just from home delivery of groceries, but from services like Plated and Blue Apron delivering pre-measured ingredients with recipes.

Taxi drivers weren't particularly worried that "digital taxis" would take their jobs. But now that Uber and Lyft are at scale, the taxi business is in freefall. In 2013, a license to own a NYC yellow cab (called a medallion) could be sold for as much as $1.3 million. Today, the price has dropped to as low as $160,000, a decline of 88%.[5]

Staying with the theme of vehicles, how important is "digital" to manufacturers of cars—a clearly tangible "real world" product? Accenture conducted a consumer study that revealed that the "digital" elements of a vehicle such as its GPS and entertainment systems now rank higher in the decision-making process of new car buyers than driving performance.[6]

We can play this game for any industry—insurance, lawnmowers, construction. I just bought a garbage can that has an app that reorders custom-fitting garbage bags when I need them. It's great, *and* it creates recurring revenue for the manufacturer. They can sell the garbage can at a lower price because they know a good percentage of customers will subscribe for garbage bag refills.

THE THREE REASONS YOU MUST TRANSFORM

For the majority of businesses, digital transformation is essential for three reasons:

Reason 1:
REMAINING RELEVANT TO THE CUSTOMER

Customers today demand a superior digital experience, and, increasingly, if you don't provide it, you are irrelevant. A Salesforce study found that 80% of customers view "the experience" a company provides as equally important to its products and services.[7] Similarly, a PwC survey reported that 73% of people view customer experience as essential to their purchasing decisions and that 32% of customers say they'll stop patronizing a business if they have just *one* bad experience.[8]

But across industries, most experiences being offered today are simply not up to customers' expectations. For example, PwC also found that only 49% of U.S. consumers say that companies are providing a "good" customer experience today.[9]

Brands spend a lot of energy promoting online content *about* their products and how great they are. But consumers today have massive cynicism about what brands "say" about themselves. As Trinity Mirror and Ipsos Connect found in a study, almost half of consumers have a general distrust of brands and 69% specifically distrust their advertising.[10]

So how *do* consumers evaluate your brand and products if they assume most of what you *say* is a lie? Mostly, from their own digital *experience.* If your website is confusing and disorganized, *that* is the message people will take away. If your signup process is cumbersome, they assume that your product will be, as well. If your error messages are unfriendly, they intuit that your customer service will be similarly surly.

Reason 2:
GAINING THE EFFICIENCIES TO BE COST-COMPETITIVE

Companies that are winning in the digital economy are delivering a dramatically improved value proposition—offering customers more for less. How do they manage to do that? It helps to have investors who are patient about whether the company operates at a profit. But more long-term, these companies are able to offer more for less because they leverage digital efficiencies to operate in a different way—harnessing tools like crowdsourcing, AI and process automation.

If you don't have access to these types of opportunities to increase efficiency, it can be difficult or impossible to be price-competitive with those that do.

Reason 3:
ATTRACTING AND RETAINING TALENT

Millennials want to be part of companies that are digitally savvy. This might be the most important reason of all to ensure that your company has a high level of digital effectiveness—to be attractive to the next generation of employees.

A study by the market research firm Pen Schoen Berland found that 82% of millennials can be swayed in their career decisions by a digitally equipped office,[11] while 42% would leave a company due to "substandard technology."[12] Similarly, Microsoft found in a study that 93% of the millennials polled cited modern and up-to-date technology as one of the most important aspects of a workplace.[13]

· ·

STATS GET ATTENTION IN THE BOARDROOM

If none of these arguments has been enough to prove McKinsey's assertion that there is "no hiding from digital transformation," the bottom line is that digitally driven companies do better on universal business metrics: revenue growth, profit, and valuation.

Although each of the following studies uses a different methodology and terminology and arrives at slightly different numbers as a result, the trend is consistent.

BONUS STATISTICS: *Throughout this book, you'll find referenced statistics, such as the ones that follow, that may be helpful to you in making your case for digital transformation. Since these stats are ever-changing, we've created* Digital Stats Quarterly, *a periodical with all the latest digital transformation statistics. A one-year subscription is included with your book purchase, so make sure to follow the link here and harness our library of stats as you advocate for transformation.* wdc.ht/STATS

DIGITALLY DRIVEN COMPANIES HAVE GREATER REVENUE GROWTH

A study by the Aberdeen Group found that the top 20% of companies as measured by their "quality of digital customer experience" enjoyed an average year-over-year increase in revenue of over 35%, compared to a 7.7% average for the rest.[14]

"Digitally advanced" companies create 9% more revenue than their industry competitors, as reported in a study conducted by MIT.[15]

And digitally "mature" companies are almost three times likelier than lower-maturity organizations to report annual revenue growth significantly greater than their industry average, according to yet another study, this one by Deloitte.[16]

DIGITALLY DRIVEN COMPANIES HAVE BETTER PROFIT MARGINS

Despite the investments needed to transform, studies show that digitally driven companies deliver better returns.

A Harvard Business School study found that the three-year average profit for "digitally centric companies" was 5 percentage points higher than that of those "behind the curve." [17] A different study at MIT concluded that "digitally mature companies" are 26% more profitable overall than competitors.[18]

As we will address throughout this book, digitally effective companies tend to be highly customer centric. A KPMG study showed that "customer centric" companies saw a projected profit *growth* rate that was 3.6% greater than "non-customer centric" companies.[19]

DIGITALLY DRIVEN COMPANIES HAVE HIGHER VALUATIONS

Lastly, and perhaps most importantly, digitally driven companies have consistently higher valuations. According to MIT, more digitally "mature" companies achieve market valuations 12% higher than competitors.[20] Forrester calculated that in recent years, the stock price of "leaders in digital customer experience" grew by nearly 30% more than that of lagging brands.[21]

· ·

As these stats show, there's a strong business case for digital transformation. If you aren't sure what it would look like if your organization were transformed, *we will examine that question in the next chapter.*

CHAPTER FOUR

WINNING IN AN ERA OF TRANSFORMATION

WHAT DOES BEING DIGITALLY TRANSFORMED LOOK LIKE?

When my son Joseph was four years old, he was already an avid Netflix surfer, flying through the iconographic menus to find his favorite shows, despite not yet being able to read.

He was also a persistent question-asker. One day, when we were watching TV, he held up the remote control provided by our cable company and elbowed me. Pointing to the volume controls, he asked, "Daddy, these buttons make the sound get louder and softer, right?"

I responded, "Right."

Then he pointed to a very similar set of up-down buttons just adjacent to the volume, asking, "Do these *also* change how loud the TV is?"

"No," I said, "those buttons change the channel."

Joe, who already watched hours of "TV" every week, furrowed his brow, then looked at me confused and asked, "What's a channel?"

I realized there wasn't much point in explaining it to him, as the concept of a channel wasn't going to be a part of his life any more than rotary phones or 8-track tapes.

THREE PATTERNS OF SUCCESSFUL DIGITAL BRANDS

Companies that are digitally transformed deliver their products or services in a way that's *built* for the digital age. Going back to Joe's question, what *is* a TV channel anyway? It represents a certain frequency used for terrestrial broadcasting—an outdated technology that offers an experience far inferior to that of today's home entertainment options.

Companies that are digitally driven have dropped or marginalized legacy products and services and reinvented what they do for the digital world. They have replaced waiting lines with apps, call centers with chatbots, and channels with on-demand videos on any device, and it's all in the service of improving the customer experience by meeting their needs in a better way.

That doesn't mean, by the way, that *everything* these companies do is digital or that they have abandoned the idea of a physical presence. Amazon has recently started opening retail locations, E*TRADE has physical branches, and many "pure play" apparel brands born online have created "pop up" stores as an alternative way for customers to learn about their products.

Of course, in all these cases, their physical presence as compared to their digital footprint is of quite a different ratio, and the in-person experience is highly digitally enabled. But nevertheless, they recognize that physical experiences are a valuable part of the customer journey.

As we said in Chapter 1, it's not about making your company *entirely* digital, but rather about reshaping your brand experience to resonate with an audience of digital *customers*—customers who are living a lifestyle with digital at the center.

So, what would it look like if *your* company were digitally driven?

In studying a large number of successful digital brands, we've observed three key patterns that they all have in common, and these patterns account for a lot of their success in generating customer love. The three patterns are:

HYPER-
CONVENIENCE

PROACTIVE
PERSONALIZATION

MASSIVE
VALUE SHIFT

The Three Patterns of Successful Digital Brands

 wdc.ht/PATTERNS

Digital Success Pattern One:
HYPERCONVENIENCE

Uber eliminates the "inconvenience" of taking 30 seconds to pay the driver when you arrive at your destination. Netflix auto-starts the next episode of *Stranger Things* so you can binge-watch for hours without lifting a finger. Alexa will check your Amazon package delivery status if you just ask it three words: "Where's my stuff?" No doubt they are working on getting that down to one. Digital leaders obsess over removing every little bit of unnecessary effort that they possibly can.

One day, I was having a few after-work beers with a client, Neal Zamore, the SVP responsible for digital at Avis and Budget rental cars. We were brainstorming how to make the car rental experience even more appealing for customers, and he coined the term "hyperconvenience" to describe the extremely high level of ease that today's consumers expect and often receive from those winning the digital race. I've been using that term ever since.

Digitally driven companies allow customers to do things like deposit a check just by taking a picture, as Chase does, or order their favorite configuration of pizza simply by texting a pizza emoji, like Domino's does. Companies that are resonating with today's customers are taking the effort out of the interaction at every point possible. Meanwhile, many legacy brands still ask their customers to stand in line, wait on hold, navigate byzantine voice menu prompts, fill out forms, repeat themselves, or sort through merchandise to find their size.

IF YOU USE THE PHRASE "THANK YOU FOR YOUR PATIENCE" WITH YOUR CUSTOMERS, YOU ARE DOING IT WRONG.

‹ wdc.ht/PATIENCE

But hyperconvenience isn't just about removing steps; it also means making it easy for customers to see, understand, and engage with everything your brand has to offer, providing customers what they want, when and where they want it.

Uber offers all its different services, from basic cars to town cars to delivery, within the same app and the same interface. Netflix is available on just about every platform known to man, from smart TVs to computers to phones to watches, and a quick login anywhere connects you to their massive volumes of content.

In fact, in many Marriott hotels, when you turn on the TV, you are prompted to log in to your Netflix account, and they will deliver your subscription to you right in your hotel room. Try that with Cablevision!

Hyperconvenience can be further broken down into three primary attributes.

HYPER CONVENIENCE

SPEED

ACCESSIBILITY

EASE

3 Attributes of Hyperconvenience

‹ wdc.ht/HYPERCONVENIENCE

Three Core Attributes of Hyperconvenience

(1) SPEED: Hyperconvenience reduces the time from start to completion. How does your offering compare to your competitors in this regard? Amazon, for example, has gone from free 2-day shipping to 1-day and now same-day deliveries in some markets.

(2) EASE: The amount of customer effort, either physical or mental, is reduced. Users don't have to work to "figure things out." If ordering an Uber is a 10 out of 10 in terms of ease, where is your brand?

(3) ACCESSIBILITY: Digital leaders make it possible for you to access their capabilities wherever and whenever you want. This might mean through a website, app, SMS, chatbot, virtual assistant, or whatever method is handy at the moment. Do you give your customers the kind of flexibility Gmail does? They let you check your messages in over a dozen ways including from the Gmail app on your phone, many other mobile mail apps, your web browser, an Apple or Android watch, many smart TVs, a Google Home device, desktop software like Outlook or Apple Mail, and even SMS.

Digital Success Pattern Two:
PROACTIVE PERSONALIZATION

Companies that are digitally driven know where their customers are located at any given moment, what they are likely to want, their payment preferences, and how they want to consume what they paid for.

In this age of Amazon and Netflix, customers expect recommendations as a basic feature of a relationship. Gmail suggests people you might want to add as senders to a message based on its content. Then, it "reads" your incoming email to suggest possible responses. Google's search engine tailors your results based not only on your current location but also on past searches and browsing behavior. Waze notices the address of your next calendar appointment, checks traffic based on where you are at the moment and alerts you when it's time to leave to be on time.

How does your company's personalization compare to these leaders who are "setting the bar" in your customer's mind?

 ## Digital Success Pattern Three:
MASSIVE VALUE SHIFT

Wikipedia replaces the multi-volume encyclopedia set. It offers thousands of times more content and is constantly updated—all for free. Craigslist replaces the classified ads in the newspaper with a solution that is far easier to search, more comprehensive and also free, at least for most listings. Google's broad range of services, from maps to search to spreadsheets, are not only free, but the breadth of their capabilities exceeds the capacity of a hundred libraries and thousands of dollars in software. Evernote, Dropbox, and so many more digital services offer free versions that fully meet the needs of many customers, along with paid versions that are disruptive in their low pricing. Amazon provides more selection than any mall, free shipping, and, in many cases, lower prices. Digital winners present what are fundamentally "better deals" to the customer.

How Is This Possible?

1. **BY STREAMLINING COST:** For example, Amazon simply does not have the real estate investments that a traditional retailer of its size would have, and they use AI and robotics to enable massive scale at a fraction of the handling cost per order that large legacy companies typically incur. Skype is so inexpensive because all the processing is done by the customers' computers. They don't actually carry the voice conversation the way a traditional telco does—they simply connect customers.

2. **VIA ECOSYSTEMS:** Digitally driven companies often use technology to connect suppliers directly to customers—avoiding the need to own assets or inventory. Examples include Uber, Airbnb, eBay, and Amazon Marketplace.

(3) **WITH SCALE:** By operating globally (with a limited geographic footprint), digital winners grow their customer base, further driving down their costs per user.

(4) **BY SHIFTING BUSINESS MODELS:** Gmail is free because it's supported by advertising. Dropbox is free because it has an upgrade path to a paid version. Amazon makes very little money from some of its product categories but makes a fortune on data and hosting services.

How Can You Improve Value for YOUR Customer?

Think of customer value as an equation—how much you give your customer in exchange for how much you ask them to give you.

CUSTOMER VALUE = BENEFIT − COST

Disrupters are innovating on both components of that equation, and you can too.

The most obvious part of "cost" to customers is, of course, the money they spend, but consumers also measure cost in time, convenience, and level of effort. When customers have to work harder to extract the value from your offering, they perceive it as an increase in "cost."

There are also many ways to increase the benefits of a product or service, including adding features, making the product more flexible or extensible, improving ease-of-use, and extending the longevity of a product.

BONUS TRAINING VIDEO: *Login to the book website to access a video that describes five approaches to reducing cost and another five methods to increase benefits. It also provides an exercise you can use with your team to apply them to your company.*

▶ wdc.ht/MOREVALUE

. . . .

You might be thinking that these categories cover a lot of ground, and you're right. It would be overwhelming to focus on implementing *all* of these methods to reduce cost, increase benefits, add hyperconvenience and proactive personalization and you don't need to. You just need to pick the ones that will have maximum impact in terms of *your* customers' thoughts, feelings, and, ultimately, behaviors.

Knowing which those are is the key to success, and it's why companies that are successful in the digital world are adopting "customer centricity" as a core mantra. In the next chapter, we'll delve more deeply into the idea of customer centricity and why it is so profoundly important.

CHAPTER FIVE

WINNING IN AN ERA OF TRANSFORMATION

CUSTOMER CENTRICITY IS THE KEY TO BUSINESS RESULTS

E arly in my career, I was given the opportunity to lead a product development team assigned to create a new digital communication platform for accounting firms. Our target users were auditors and tax consultants. Since we had worked with those types of people periodically, and thought we were pretty smart, we felt we knew what they needed.

We went into the project with some big ideas and quickly landed on a vision for the product that we loved. It was innovative, creative, and exciting. The image of the user interface still brings a smile to my face as I write this; it was so cool. The team was devoted to the product and its potential. We worked 18-hour days for months on our mission. I barely saw my wife during that time. When I did, I told her passionately about the progress we were making and how awesome the platform was going to be. In retrospect, I'm pretty sure she got tired of hearing about it.

Finally, the product launched! We were so excited to share it with the world. What happened?

The features we thought were so fantastic just weren't important to our users. And in our passion to deliver *those* innovative features, we had overlooked some of their more basic, critical needs. Also, because we didn't fully understand the circumstances under  which the product would be used, it had some major usability problems. It worked great for *us* on the product development team, but the users weren't like us.

In short, it was a disaster. In less than a week, we went from visions of world domination to our sponsors telling us they were "pulling the plug." I still remember that meeting as one of the low moments of my life. While we couldn't believe it at the time, it was entirely predictable.

We fell in love with *our idea* instead of our users. We wanted our *product* to fulfill its potential instead of thinking about how to help our customers fulfill theirs.

We held a common misconception about how customer experience works.

THE COMMON MISCONCEPTION ABOUT CUSTOMER EXPERIENCE

Here is how I thought customer experience innovation worked when I was developing the product for the accounting firm.

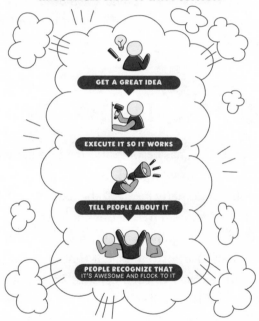

MISCONCEPTION OF INNOVATION

GET A GREAT IDEA

EXECUTE IT SO IT WORKS

TELL PEOPLE ABOUT IT

PEOPLE RECOGNIZE THAT
IT'S AWESOME AND FLOCK TO IT

THIS (ALMOST) NEVER WORKS

< wdc.ht/MISCONCEPTION

This approach *almost never succeeds*. It's based on the assumption that the user will love whatever your creative mind dreams up. That's how art works (when it works), but that's not how business works. That's not the recipe that makes customers love your products or brands. If we recall the love formula, the first thing we must do is to *meet our customers' needs* consistently—not bring to life the fruits of our imagination.

That doesn't mean there isn't room for a lot of creativity in designing new customer experiences. In fact, it's essential. But a different *process* needs to be followed. Thinking back to my accounting product, had we poured all our passion, long hours, and skill into the *right* process instead of expecting customers to love the product of our intuition, who knows what we could have achieved? Even though it was over twenty years ago, I am filled with regret just thinking about it.

So, what *is* the right process? It's a *customer-centric approach*.

WHAT DOES IT MEAN TO BE CUSTOMER CENTRIC?

"Customer centric" has become another popular term that many organizations like to throw around. But let's get past the buzzword and drill into what it actually *means* to be "customer centric," versus not. Clearly, all businesses *have* customers; that's where the money comes from. How can a business *not* be customer centric?

All businesses *have* customers, but that does not mean that the customers are at the *center* of the business. Putting the customer at the center means that the whole strategy of the business *orbits* around the customer.

Orbiting is visible as motion over time. If you looked at a snapshot of the solar system, it might not be obvious which objects were orbiting around others. But if you look at a video, it becomes easy to see.

Every company has products or services that are distributed along one or more channels to one or more types of customers. Sometimes things are fairly static, and we don't have enough motion to detect whether customers are really at the center. But eventually, things change;

for example, customers' needs or buying patterns shift, and the business has to make a move. That's when we'll see where the center is.

PRODUCT-CENTRIC COMPANIES

If a company is a product-centric business and things need to change, the business might say, "Hmmm...we make this product and our existing customer doesn't seem to want it anymore, so let's find a *new customer*." And, of course, depending on how different the new type of customer is, it may be appropriate to target that customer via a different distribution channel, as well. The key measure is that the product *stays* while the other dimensions change.

Kodak is an example of this. It was a film company from the start, and you may be surprised to learn that it still exists, although it's a tiny fraction of what it once was. What do they sell in this age of digital cameras? Film. To whom do they sell it?

Once upon a time, they mainly sold it to consumers at drug stores, supermarkets, gas stations—basically everywhere. Today, few consumers want it, so no mass-market store wants to sell it. But it turns out there are still niche applications for film. Certain medical imaging devices and other industrial products continue to use film for various esoteric reasons. So, Kodak keeps scouring the planet for customers who will buy *film* and uses the distribution channels most appropriate to those types of typically commercial customers.[1] You have to give them credit, they are a *dedicated* "product-centric" company.

DISTRIBUTION-CENTRIC COMPANIES

Another option is being a *distribution*-centric company. For example, if you are a catalog retailer and the products you are selling in your catalog no longer interest the customers to whom you're sending your catalog, you either find a new customer base to send your catalogs to, put different products in your catalog to interest your customers, or maybe both. You figure out what you need to change on the customer and/or product dimensions to make the *catalog* part work because you are a "catalog" company.

Of course, no company operates on only a single strategy at a time, but the "centricity" of a company will dictate the focus of its dominant strategies in times of change.

CUSTOMER-CENTRIC COMPANIES

So, of course, a company that *is* customer-focused centers on what the *customer* needs and how they can deliver their core value proposition to their target customer.

For example, I think most people would intuitively agree that Apple is a customer centric company. Let's look at its history and apply this same method of analysis.

Two decades ago, Apple primarily sold computers and developed software *for* computers. Then, for a time, music players and music eclipsed computers as their primary product focus. Now smartphones dwarf the company's businesses in computers or music players. In fact, they changed their name from "Apple Computer" to just "Apple" in recognition of this. In the same timeframe, Dell started as a computer company and, despite diversifying a bit, is basically still a computer company.

Apple has also radically shifted their distribution methods over the years. A few decades ago, the company's primary strategy was traditional retail distribution through electronics stores. They now primarily use a direct-to-consumer sales strategy, selling both physical and digital goods through their own stores and e-commerce channels. Their most important third-party points of distribution are no longer electronics stores. They are telecommunications companies like Verizon and Sprint.[2]

In the same time period as Apple's transformation, Sony launched a huge e-commerce store called Sony Style to distribute their products directly to consumers. It grew to over $1 billion in annual sales before Sony did an about-face because of pressure from "big box" retailers.[3] Now they have retrenched and are back to selling their products very much the same way they have sold them for decades.

Apple has clearly demonstrated that the other two dimensions of their business revolve and change as needed to keep the customer in the center. They are still selling to the same basic customer profile and selling the same core value proposition: digital tools that are easy to use, bring a smile to your face, and empower you to do the things you dream of doing.

. . . .

IS IT NECESSARY TO BE CUSTOMER CENTRIC?

So that's what it *means* to be customer centric. But do you *need* to be customer centric? I've "stacked the deck" a bit by talking about some companies that were *not* customer centric and who have struggled and then holding up Apple, the world's largest and arguably most successful company, as one that is. But you may not be convinced yet that it's critical that *your* business puts the customer in the center. That's why this chapter is not yet over; we're going to give you an even better reason than emulating Apple.

And even if you *are* already convinced and intuitively feel that it's important for your company to be customer centric, don't skip the rest of this chapter. You still need a strong business-minded answer as to *why*—because you will need to persuade others. Business leaders are often quick to give lip service to the idea of being customer centric, but many resist actually doing it.

Let's consider the typical "persuasion scenario" that must be overcome for a company's management to commit to becoming truly "customer centric," and then we'll move on to the killer argument that can win in those situations.

SENIOR EXECUTIVE MINDSET ON "CUSTOMER CENTRICITY"

The people who are responsible for a business' bottom line—CEOs, CFOs, boards of directors—tend to have a certain point of view about the customer, and it goes like this:

They *want* customers, absolutely. They always want more customers, bigger customers, and more "loyal" customers. Everyone agrees that customers are very, very important to the business.

And when you say you want to focus on improving the customer experience, you generally get a lot of agreement. After all, who can argue against that? The customer is critical. We want them to have a good experience. Sounds nice. You may even be able to convince the executives that a better experience will make customers love you more, which also sounds nice.

But when you *then* say that you need $2 million, or $20 million or $200 million to redo the apps, the e-commerce system, stores, whatever it may be, to *give* the customer a better experience, you often get a different response. You may hear something like:

"Hmmm, well as we said, we definitely care about the customer; we really do...But we are also running a business. Every dollar we spend comes right out of our profit. Customers are still doing business with us based on *today's* experience. Of course, it's *good* to make it better, but *how* good does it need to be? If we spend all this money improving the customer's 'experience,' how do we know if we will get that money back? Maybe if we leave it as it is, our customers will *still* give us their money. That would be cheaper, after all...

"Because if we *spend* all that money and make it better, customers will probably be *happier*, and they might love us more, but they might *not* give us *enough* more of their money to justify the cost of improving the customer experience. Maybe we are better off keeping the majority of that money as profit while just making a few token improvements."

It is this, only slightly caricatured, line of thinking that kills many potential beneficial investments in customer experience.

HOW TO PERSUADE THEM (OR YOURSELF)

In Chapter 3, we shared a variety of statistics showing that the companies that give their customers a better experience and are more digitally savvy are generating more revenue growth, more profit, and higher valuations. That data will be a useful start in making the case for funding. But those stats just show *correlations*; they don't necessarily explain *why* investing in better digital customer experience is worth it. Sometimes, when decision makers don't understand the logic, even statistics don't get you there.

Furthermore, it's important to deeply understand the *causality* between experience and business results because there are an infinite range of *ways* one could invest in improving the customer's experience—send customers gifts, carpet the store, create funny videos, offer them fresh coffee, give the app a facelift, add augmented reality, etc. You can't do it all. You'll need to figure out *which* ways of investing in customer experience will drive the greatest bottom line results.

If you tangibly understand exactly *why* a better customer experience results in better business—how one thing drives another and then leads to dollars—you are in a better position to figure out which changes will be the most worthwhile. When you understand how the machine works, you can optimize it. Let's look at how the machine works.

THE STRATEGIC CUSTOMER EXPERIENCE MODEL™

The executives who challenge customer experience budgets are not wrong. Any investment needs to make *business* sense. Giving the customer a better experience is not a moral obligation. And it's not the purpose of a business. Even getting customers to love you is not the purpose of a business. It's often *smart* business, but to achieve the benefits, you have to do it strategically.

By "strategically," I mean that improved customer experience is a means to an end. What is the end? Not to sound cynical, but in business, there is really only one end: money. In order to both justify customer experience investments beyond a token scale and ensure that those investments are applied with business impact, we need to show precisely how customer experience *connects* to money—to the business' bottom line. And it does.

Businesses generally exist commercially for two reasons: to generate a profit and to make the business more valuable, such as raising the stock price or raising the valuation that someone would use to buy or invest in a private business. So, increasing profit and business value have to be strategic goals of pretty much any investment.

You will misalign with the fundamental mindset of most executives if you make it seem like the *end* goal is to make customers happy. But, if we can effectively achieve our strategic goals *via* making customers happy and meeting their needs, then we have a wonderful ecosystem where we are doing good *and* doing well.

Personally, what gets me out of bed in the morning is creating great experiences for users, not raising the stock price of a company. But for customer experience investments to be justified and sustainable at for-profit companies, we need to be able to demonstrate that these two are connected.

So here's *how* they are connected. Consider what it is that drives share price: it's largely business profitability and beliefs about future profitability. The value of most traditional businesses is primarily calculated based on how much profit it's generating and how much it's expected to earn in the future.

So what drives business profit? Well, profit is simply revenue minus cost; so things that increase revenue and reduce cost are what drive profit. We often call these factors that increase revenue and reduce cost "business levers."

Common business levers that increase revenue include:

1. New customer acquisition
2. Customer retention and renewal
3. Upsell and cross-sell
4. Ability to increase price or reduce discounting

Common business levers that decrease cost include:

1. More cost-effective manufacturing
2. Reduction in customer service costs because customers are using self-service
3. Reduction in sales costs because customers are shopping or ordering digitally
4. Reduction in marketing costs due to customer advocacy
5. Getting customers to buy directly from you, avoiding distribution channel costs

Most business stakeholders will readily agree that moving these levers in a positive direction is how the company will increase its profit and, ultimately, its value. This part is not controversial.

But here is the critical link—a powerful idea to "connect the dots" for senior management. There is one key factor that cuts across *most* cost and revenue levers: customer behavior. If the customers do what we want them to do, we push the levers in the direction we need (more revenue, less cost). If the customers *don't* do what we want, or they do the opposite, we push the levers in the wrong direction.

Influencing the behavior of customers and prospects in a strategic direction is the single most impactful way to move business levers and, therefore, achieve business success.

So how do you do that? What is it that *causes* customers to behave in a certain way?

PEOPLE BEHAVE ONE WAY OR ANOTHER BECAUSE OF THEIR THOUGHTS AND FEELINGS.

< wdc.ht/FEELINGS

Let's take a customer who is considering buying a new car. He has feelings about certain brands or certain car dealerships. He has thoughts about how much he can afford to spend and feelings about how his *wife* will react to how much he spends. When he sits in the car, he has one feeling. When the salesperson sits him down at the desk and goes over the terms, he has various *other* thoughts and feelings.

The combination of his thoughts and feelings are 100% of what triggers his ultimate behavior. So, if we can figure out which thoughts and feelings will trigger the behaviors that we *want*—the ones that push our business levers in the right direction—that would presumably be very valuable. Maybe.

"Maybe," because it's only useful to know the thoughts and feelings that will drive desired customer behavior if you have some means to influence them. You might be asking yourself, "How do I *control* the thoughts and feelings of my customers? That stuff happens inside their heads."

While marketing technology has not advanced to the point where we can directly implant thoughts and feelings in our customer's consciousness (though someone is probably working on it), we do know what *creates* thoughts and feelings: *experiences*.

As a demonstration, think about a feeling you felt recently. Where did it come from? Did you see a puppy and feel happy? Did you stub your toe and feel angry? Did you watch a movie and feel scared? Did you *remember* a fight you had with your mother 30 years ago and feel remorse? Feelings come from *experiences* most of the time—either experiences in the moment or remembered experiences (or sometimes imagined experiences). Of course, not everyone responds with the same feelings to a given experience (more on that later), but the key point is that it's experiences that create feelings.

And where do *thoughts* come from? From things you learned, from things you saw, from things you heard or tasted. Thoughts largely *also* come from the amalgam of your experiences and the conclusions you have drawn from them.

USING THE STRATEGIC CUSTOMER EXPERIENCE MODEL

If experiences create thoughts and feelings, and thoughts and feelings ultimately connect to the behavior that drives business results, then getting the *experience* right is essential. Now, technically, we can't actually *create* experiences for people. People create their own experiences. But we can create *touchpoints*—a store, a website, a mobile app—and through their interactions with those touchpoints, people have experiences, and this is the root of the opportunity. *See this illustrated in the next diagram.*

STRATEGIC CUSTOMER EXPERIENCE MODEL

EXAMPLES:

BUSINESS RESULTS
INCREASED SHARE PRICE
REDUCED COST
INCREASED REVENUE

CUSTOMER **BEHAVIORS**
BUY MORE/BUY DIRECT
SELF SERVICE
REFERRAL/RENEWAL

CUSTOMER **MINDSETS**
THOUGHTS
FEELINGS

CUSTOMER
EXPERIENCES/TOUCHPOINTS
DIGITAL
LIVE/PHONE
PRODUCT USE

‹ wdc.ht/MODEL

Of course, not everyone has the same experience when interacting with the same touchpoint. One person goes to a store to buy dishes, finds a set he loves, has an easy checkout experience, and is happy. Another person can't find what she likes, feels the prices are too high, and talks to a rude salesperson.

In both cases, thoughts and feelings from their experiences at these touchpoints ripple forward to their behavior, some of which will push the store's business levers, which will then lead to positive or negative consequences for the business' results.

So, when we talk about creating a "user experience" or a "customer experience," we are generally talking about creating the touchpoints, the interaction with which will result in the user having an "experience."

Or even *more* accurately, customers will usually interact with a *series* of touchpoints over time. They might go to your website and then drive to your store. While in the store, they may use your mobile app, and perhaps, a kiosk. When they get home, if they have a problem, they may call your call center or use your chat feature. Later, you may email them, text them, or send them something in the mail, and one of those experiences may inspire them to come back to the store or shop on the website, and the cycle continues. This series of interactions is what we mean when we speak of a customer journey, which we will unpack in detail later in the book.

When a customer journey results in far more positive emotions than negative ones, when the customer *thinks* and *feels* that the brand is meeting their needs consistently and even occasionally giving them that delightful feeling of surprise when their expectations are exceeded, and when the experience is aligned with the customer's values, then we have the right ingredients to inspire the love that is so valuable to long-term business results.

But while having a strategically engineered customer experience is the most important factor for business success, it begs a critical question not answered in this chapter: How do you know what *specific* customer experiences will ripple through the chain of thoughts/feelings/behaviors and, ultimately, business levers and profit in *your* business? Figuring this out is the key to everything.

Before you can design experiences that will drive *your* desired customer behaviors, you need to understand *your* customer—what they care about, what kind of pain they are in, and what their unmet needs are.

. . . .

In the next section of the book, we will get very specific about how to do that as we begin the first activity of the five-part Customer Love Digital Transformation Formula.

ACTIVITY 1:

UNDERSTAND YOUR CUSTOMER

STEP 1:

RESEARCH
QUESTIONS

 CH. 6

STEP 2:

INDIRECT
CUSTOMER
RESEARCH

 CH. 7

STEP 3:

DIRECT
CUSTOMER
RESEARCH

 CH. 8

STEP 4:

SYNTHESIS
OF RESEARCH
INTO CUSTOMER
PERSONAS

 CH. 9

The previous chapter described how business objectives are achieved. We said it's by giving customers the *experiences* that trigger *thoughts and feelings* which motivate *behaviors* that are aligned with our business goals.

A retail store might offer a nursing mother a special room to take care of her baby, which makes her *feel* understood and makes her *think* the store cares about her. As a result, the next time she needs something that the store carries, she may make a point of going to that store.

An airline might launch a new app that allows the traveler to manage their entire itinerary with just a couple of taps, and as a result some customers may *think* the airline is easier to fly and may *feel* that the airline is "cool," and as a result, the next time they have the opportunity to choose which airline to fly, they go with the "easy and cool" one.

But of course, there are so many things a business could do with an eye toward improving the customer's experience, and most of them cost money. How do you know what specific experiences will actually lead to beneficial behavioral triggers for your company?

How do you know what your spouse might like for their birthday? *Understanding* your customer thoroughly is foundational to being able to anticipate what experiential changes will move their behavior in the right direction. It's *also* foundational for the Design Thinking 2.0 process, which we will detail later in the book. These are the reasons "Understand Your Customer" is the first activity in our five-part Customer Love Digital Transformation Formula.

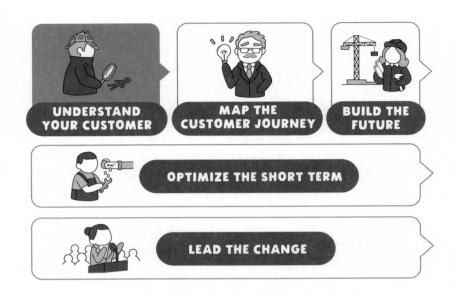

The Customer Love Digital Transformation Formula

How do you go about understanding your customer? Through research—a variety of different types of research. This section of the book will describe a detailed approach to identifying who your customers are and then gathering and synthesizing research insights to yield a rich, actionable understanding of them.

In future sections of the book, we will focus on how to *leverage* that understanding to create fantastically successful customer experiences that drive business results. *This* section will walk you through four steps to understanding your customer, one per chapter.

FOUR STEPS TO UNDERSTANDING YOUR CUSTOMER

RESEARCH QUESTIONS (CH. 6): The first chapter will describe the beginning of the research process in which you will create a first-pass segmentation of your customers and identify a strategic set of questions that your research will seek to answer.

INDIRECT CUSTOMER RESEARCH (CH. 7): Chapter 7 will describe how to identify potential sources of customer insight that may already exist, either at your enterprise (such as historical transaction data) or out in the world (such as third-party studies) and how to leverage them effectively.

 DIRECT CUSTOMER RESEARCH (CH. 8): The next chapter will provide a methodology for conducting structured research interactions directly *with* your customers that generate volumes of insight with good accuracy and in an efficient manner.

 SYNTHESIS OF RESEARCH INTO CUSTOMER PERSONAS (CH. 9): The last chapter of this section will describe how to take all of your learnings from both direct and indirect research and synthesize them into highly digestible infographics that communicate key insights about each type of customer.

• •

By going through these steps, you will gain the concrete, actionable understanding of your customers that you need to design an experience that inspires the behaviors that align with business success.

CHAPTER SIX

UNDERSTAND YOUR CUSTOMER

RESEARCH QUESTIONS

A t age 62, a Florida woman named Unni Haskell decided she wanted to start playing golf—a deceptively tough game to learn. She drove to a nearby course, rented some clubs, and psyched herself up for what was to be her *very first game.*

Unni piloted her golf cart to hole number one and stepped onto the tee-off area. She unwrapped a brand-new ball and stuck it on a tee. She took a driver out of 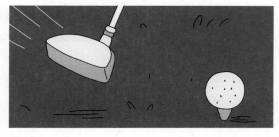 her rented bag, raised the club and swung at that darn ball as hard and as fast as she could.

What do you think happened?

Despite her novice form, The ball traveled a respectable 75 yards. It actually landed on the green. It bounced a couple of times. Then it rolled quite a ways...*right into the hole.*

Yep! She hit a *hole in one* on the very first stroke...of the very first hole...of her very *first* game of golf. This made her a minor internet celebrity for a time. You can Google her.[1] Experts say the odds *against* an "amateur golfer" hitting a hole in one are 12,500 to 1, let alone an amateur *who's never played before.*

Want to know how she did it?

Dumb luck.

Try it 100,000 times and it will probably never happen again.

I mention this story because it has certain similarities to the strategy that a surprising number of companies use when trying to build products and experiences they hope their customers will love.

It is, of course, *possible* that you could conceive, design, and build a new product, retail experience, or digital property, do absolutely no meaningful customer research, and still hit a hole in one, driving the exact customer behavior you are hoping for...*if* you are supremely lucky.

Perhaps you have already tried applying the "Unni Haskell" approach to product development at your company and discovered that you aren't blessed with 12,500 to 1 luck. If so, you are not alone. According to Nielsen, 85% of new consumer products fail in the marketplace.[2]

Those who "pooh pooh" customer research often have an anecdotal story of a successful product that was launched based purely on intuition and grit. Well, now *you* have Unni's anecdotal story to further prove an inspiring point—anything is *possible.*

Anything is possible, but the real question in business is what is predictable. Products driven by a research-based understanding of the customer are far, far more predictable in their adoption and overall success than those that are not. ◂ wdc.ht/POSSIBLE

So let's do it *that* way. There are four steps to the process of "understanding the customer."

In this chapter, we will focus on the first step: research questions.

¿?¿
WHAT ARE RESEARCH QUESTIONS?

The term "research" describes a set of activities conducted to gather information for the purpose of answering specific *questions*. While they may be broad or narrow, any research activity should be in response to a clear set of questions that define the its goals.

What are the questions you should be asking in doing research to understand your customer? Customer research questions exist along two primary axes: *Who* are your customers? And what do we want to know about them?

WHO ARE YOUR CUSTOMERS?

Before you start the research, it's important to be clear about what defines your customers. You need to know *who* you are gathering information about. There may be certain characteristics that put someone inside or outside the circle of your target customers. For example, you may have products only for women, or you may exclusively sell in North America, or perhaps you provide services primarily to large corporations or to startups.

Most businesses target a variety of different types and flavors of customers. We call each "type" of customer a "segment."

Review the different categories of customers that your business serves or would like to serve, and then determine which are in scope for any given research effort.

It may seem backward to create these types of customer segments *before* doing research, but you need some general idea of who you are targeting in order to *structure* the research. Once the insights are gathered, you will create more refined customer personas that might change these high-level segments. Think of them as an initial scaffold that we will use to frame out our understanding of the customer.

START WITH THE SIMPLE AND OBVIOUS

Here's a simple example to demonstrate what defining customer segments looks like. If you're Microsoft, your customers might fall into three categories:

HOME USERS   **BUSINESS USERS**   **PC MANUFACTURERS**

Three Categories of Microsoft Customers

‹ wdc.ht/CATEGORIES

Microsoft sells products to individual consumers, such as Surface Tablets and XBoxes. They also develop and market enterprise software and cloud services for the business market, and then there are PC manufacturers like Dell who pay Microsoft on a wholesale basis for installing MS Windows on the computers they sell.

Each of these high-level segments can most likely be broken down into some more discrete subcategories as shown below.

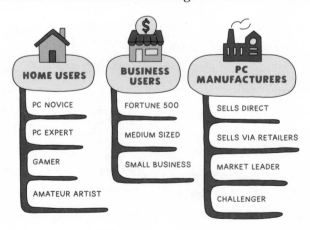

Subcategories of Microsoft Customers

‹ wdc.ht/SUBCATEGORIES

Create an equivalent model for your business. At this prepara-
tory stage, don't worry if your model is not 100% complete. Focus on
documenting the simple distinctions between customers that your
company is already aware of. Also include any segments that you are
not selling to today but that are a near-term target.

DIMENSIONS OF CUSTOMER SEGMENTATION

Creating that basic segmentation model is the first step, but it's
just a starting point. Customer traits don't really exist in a strict hierarchy, so it's more precise to think of customers as having a variety
of dimensions.

For example, in the "Home Users" top-level category above, some
of the sub-options shown relate to the customer's experience with
Microsoft products (PC novice versus expert). That's one dimension.

The other options relate to a different factor. Sub-segments of
"gamer" and "amateur artist" are more indicative of *how* the user will
utilize the product and are another dimension. And of course many
customers will possess multiple of these characteristics.

And your customers have a variety of *other* qualities that distinguish them from one another, as well. For example, you most likely
have both male and female customers. Your customers are of different
ages. They may live in different geographic areas. They might speak
different languages.

Some of these may be very important to understanding the
differences between the types of customers *your* business serves, and
some of them may not be very important. How many dimensions are
there? The theoretical list is unlimited.

Here are some common categories of customer dimensions that are relevant to different types of business:

Common Categories of Customer Dimensions

DIMENSION CATEGORY	EXAMPLE DIMENSIONS
Demographic	Age, gender, marital status
Economic	Income, savings, debt, home ownership
Psychographic	Political tendencies; environmental awareness; feelings toward money, health, or spirituality
Firmographic	For B2B businesses, company characteristics such as size, industry, structure, valuation and revenue.
Location	Where the person lives, works, or travels, as well as languages spoken
Interaction Preferences	How they prefer to interact: web vs. store vs. phone, etc.
Relationship Status with Your Company	Are they already your customer? If so, how big a customer? Or are they a former customer? Are they a customer of a competitor?
Buying Stage & Timing	Where is the customer in the lifecycle of a purchase decision (awareness, evaluation, consideration, contracting, post-purchase, or renewal consideration)? What is the urgency of their purchase?
Affinities	Tastes in music, food, culture, hobbies, sports teams, celebrities
Trigger	What has put them into the market at this moment?
Category Specific	Information that affects how you might serve that customer which is specific to your type of business. For example, an energy company might segment customers by whether their home is heated by oil or natural gas.

WHICH DIMENSIONS REALLY MATTER?

Of course, trying to create a segmentation model based on all of these categories would be overwhelming, and this is just a list of examples.

You'll need to prioritize—to decide which categories and dimensions are most *relevant* to your business. We have generally found it best to focus on 5-10 significant dimensions to maintain a balance between insight and action.

For example, gender is a far more important variable when selling lingerie than it is when selling office supplies. Dietary restrictions don't impact car sales, and political party affiliations are rarely relevant when selling breakfast cereal.

Although the research you will do next will refine or perhaps even completely transform your initial model, take a stab at identifying the dimensions and characteristics that are the most significant for your business. You will use them to ensure that you are finding the right diversity of subjects for your research.

In other words, if the way you interact with your customer varies in important ways based on whether they own a home, then your research probably needs to include both renters and homeowners. In contrast, if geographic location is unimportant, then there's no point in worrying about getting customers from every different region of the country to participate in the study.

To be clear about the terminology, the dimensions are the domains that matter, like gender or age. "Characteristics" are the choices that exist within each dimension. For example, within the dimension of gender, female and male are characteristics. Within certain dimensions such as age, use characteristic *groupings* like 18-25 years old, 26-40 years old, etc.

For each dimension that you preliminarily prioritize for your business, create a map of its key characteristics and identify which ones are most important.

For example, for Rolex, wealth is a very important dimension. Below a certain level, an individual is probably outside the Rolex target customer group. Above that level, Rolex knows they want you as a customer, but they are still interested in understanding the specific *level* of wealth of any given customer because it may impact which products are most likely to resonate. Rolex has watches that cost a "mere" $5,000 and others over $400,000.

BONUS TEMPLATES: *If you want to learn more about customer dimensions and what they look like in action, check out the book website, where we've created downloadable, full-color, editable samples of customer dimension infographics. You can use these as templates to create attractive slides or as posters for the dimensions you define.*

 wdc.ht/DIMENSION

WHAT DO WE WANT TO KNOW ABOUT OUR CUSTOMERS?

Now that we know *who* we are researching, the second part of defining research questions is to determine what it is we want to know *about* them. For example, we might want to know, "How satisfied are our customers with our current mobile shopping experience?" Or, "What are the most important factors to our customers when deciding whether or not to do business with us?" Or a hundred other things.

These *research* questions are *not* the literal questions you ask the customer; they are the *things you want to know.* In a subsequent chapter, we will discuss how to craft these into a script for interacting with test subjects in a research session.

Some research questions may relate to *all* customer types, while others may be specific to only one. Of course, even questions that are the same for all customer types may have very different answers depending on the segment. For example, building on the earlier Microsoft example, you may decide that it's helpful to understand how all three segments of Microsoft customers make the decision to buy Microsoft products. However, the way a Fortune 500 company decides to buy a six-figure license for enterprise software is probably quite different from how a teenager decides to buy an Xbox.

SOME COMMON THEMES OF RESEARCH QUESTIONS

What knowledge about the customer would be helpful in crafting a delightful and strategically effective customer experience for your business?

The answers will vary somewhat based on your industry, but here is a starter set. It's rare to be conducting customer research and not be interested in many of these themes.

For each type of customer:

1. What are their goals and desires?

2. What are their fears and pet peeves?

3. What unmet needs do they have in their life?

4. Have they ever heard of your brand? What do they think of you?

5. How do they feel about your competitors? Your industry overall?

6. Why do they buy your products or services today compared to alternatives? Or why do they not buy?

(7) What is their experience and level of satisfaction through each stage of the lifecycle of a purchase (gaining awareness, shopping, buying, using your product, getting support, etc.)?

(8) What are their preferences in terms of channels of interaction (web, mobile, phone, in-person, etc.)?

Start with this list, customize the questions, and add any others that may be specific to your situation or industry. Or work with a firm that does market research (such as mine) to use their experience to help you.

COMPANY MYTHOLOGY

Most companies have apocryphal beliefs about their customers which are widely accepted because employees have heard them so many times, even though nobody may know where the information actually came from. Your company's may be, "Our top customers are not price-sensitive," or, "Our older customers are not interested in interacting with us digitally. They prefer the call center." Or, "Our mid-tier products are only used by home users, and our top-tier line is used only by professionals."

Very often, these passed-along beliefs *sound* logical, but are they *true*? And even if they were *once* proved to be true, are they *still* true? Customers change over time. Corporate beliefs tend to change much more slowly. Customer research is an opportunity to validate accurate assumptions and update any false ones.

RESEARCH TECHNIQUES

Now that you know *what* you want to know and you have identified the different segments of customers from whom you want to collect answers, let's take a high-level look at the *techniques* you can use to get the actual answers.

There are many dozens of different potential research techniques, and they fall into two primary buckets: indirect and direct customer research. Each of the buckets have their own strengths and weaknesses.

INDIRECT CUSTOMER RESEARCH

This category consists of a variety of methods for gathering customer insights *without* needing to directly interact with customers, mostly by leveraging already existing materials and data.

The methods in this category can be quite efficient since you are building on prior analysis and analyzing information previously collected. The downsides of this category are that what is available to you may be incomplete, and it doesn't give you the same level of deep insight you get by interacting directly with the customer.

But it's good to *start* with these indirect methods because you can very efficiently gather insights from indirect sources. Then, what gaps remain can be filled through more direct research with customers.

The very next chapter in this section of the book is dedicated to providing detail on five categories of *indirect* customer research techniques.

DIRECT CUSTOMER RESEARCH

This second category of customer research contains various methods where data is collected *directly* from representative customers. We'll be going into detail on direct customer research in Chapter 8. It's very powerful to get information "right from the source," so try to include some direct research methods whenever possible. However, it can also be more time consuming, and at times logistically challenging, depending on how difficult it is to reach a given customer segment. Customers for Corn Flakes are easy to find. Those with experience procuring luxury jet aircraft, as we needed to find for one client, can be trickier to recruit.

Chapter 8 will dive into detailed methods and best practices for conducting direct customer research.

. . . .

A COMPREHENSIVE TOOLBOX

There are additional research methods not included in this book simply for space, however using only the techniques in the next two chapters should give you more than enough insight to synthesize a rich, detailed, and actionable understanding of your customer.

CHAPTER SEVEN

UNDERSTAND YOUR CUSTOMER

INDIRECT CUSTOMER RESEARCH

I led a workshop a number of years ago for one of the world's largest credit card issuers. The session was about improving the cardholder experience. While planning the workshop, we asked, as we usually do, who on the attendee list could act as the "voice of the customer." There were a number of *very* senior executives scheduled to participate. We inquired, "Roughly how much time do you estimate that these executives spend with cardholders?" Unsurprisingly, the answer was, "Not very much."

To address this gap, we added to the attendee list of senior executives an equal number of experienced agents pulled out of the company's call center, all of whom had spent at least five years interacting with customers. We had quite an interesting three-day session in New York, mixing twenty of the company's top leaders with twenty "working Joes" (and Josephines) who normally spend the whole day on the phone with cardholders.

After using a few "ice breaker" exercises to ease both sides' initial shyness to mix and mingle, they were soon all laughing and collaborating together.

Over the course of the three days, it was inspiring to see how often the representatives from the call center would respond to questions from the executives with fascinating and rich detail about the existing customer experience—providing deep insight into the customers' mindsets and priorities. The executives would often pull out their journals and take detailed notes.

This is the power of getting the voices of *real* customer experts in the room, even if they aren't dressed as fancily as executives.

It's also emblematic of this chapter's theme—these types of "customer experts" are one source of *indirect* customer research, which is step two of the process of understanding your customer.

. . . .

WHAT IS INDIRECT CUSTOMER RESEARCH?

As we described in Chapter 6, indirect customer research is a set of methods used to gain insight into your targeted customers without necessarily interacting with them personally.

You probably already have a wealth of customer insight tucked away in various, disparate places within your enterprise, from databases to PDFs to the knowledge in the brains of your customer-facing teams. It can be very fruitful to start aggregating it and analyzing it to understand what it means and how it relates to the research questions you defined in the previous chapter.

Begin by looking at those research questions and then map them to the different methods described in this chapter. You may well find that some of your questions can be answered, at least to some level of precision, without ever talking to customers. Of course, those insights may also raise other questions not as easily answered through indirect research, and some of your initial research questions may *not* be possible to answer indirectly, depending on the data available. It is for this reason, among others, that we almost always recommend combining indirect customer research with direct customer research.

In this chapter, we will talk about five specific methods for indirect customer research.

5 INDIRECT CUSTOMER RESEARCH METHODS

DATA ANALYSIS   **SECONDARY RESEARCH**   **COMPETITIVE RESEARCH**   **CUSTOMER EXPERTS**   **SOCIAL LISTENING**

 wdc.ht/INDIRECT

 Indirect Research Method 1:
DATA ANALYSIS

There is probably a lot of information about your customers stashed away in different databases, spreadsheets, and Dropbox folders at your company. The key is to find out about it, get your hands on it, and then use it to help answer your research questions. It may well be incomplete, but you'll have many more research techniques after this one to fill in the gaps.

What data do you need to look for, and where can you find it? Described below are a number of "typical" data sources you may find at a large company.

DIGITAL
METRICS

**DATA
ANALYSIS**

BRANDING &
MARKETING
STUDIES

SALES &
INQUIRY
DATA

CALL CENTER
RECORDS &
RECORDINGS

CUSTOMER
FEEDBACK
MECHANISMS

Five Sources of Data Analysis

‹ wdc.ht/DATAANALYSIS

In each category of data, you'll probably need to do a little digging to find the right owners. Then, approach them with your list of research questions. This is important, as many of these data sets can be vast. Having the research questions in hand means that you are not just asking the owners asking for gigabytes of data (which you probably wouldn't be able to do anything with), but rather requesting that they can help you *leverage* their data to answer specific questions.

For example, if you ask the digital operations team if they have data about web interactions, they almost certainly do. But they can't just "send" you that. It's probably in multiple systems, and there are a variety of different types of data. And even if they did, it's not at all obvious what this data *means*. If they were to send you a log of every user who went to the website in the last month and the specific pages they looked at, what would you do with that? Alternatively, they could send you the current reports they generate regularly *from* that data, which would probably be useful to review; however, those reports may not be designed to slice the data in a way that specifically answers *your* research questions.

Data analysis is the process of taking data sources and *using* them to answer the *research questions* you've defined. The answer may be easy to find, or it might require clever digging. And sometimes the answers are inconclusive, or one answer just raises five other questions. That's fine—that's part of the fun. Just gather the insights you gain, compare them with those you get from other research methods, and add any new questions to the list.

The *method* by which you analyze a data source will be quite different depending on what kind of data it is. For example, web traffic information tends to be logs of interactions, typically with some kind of tool at the front end, like Omniture or Google Analytics. There are people trained in using these tools. You need to get access to one of them, either inside your company or a consultant, who can query the data set based on your research questions.

Other data sources might require quite different processes to analyze. For example, if you are reviewing branding studies conducted by your marketing group, the "data" from *these* studies might be survey results or videos of focus groups. In that last case, one technique is to send the video files to a transcription service such as Rev.com. Once the videos are in text format, you can search them for topics relevant to your research questions and either just read the transcripts or jump to the parts of the video that are most pertinent.

In every case, you will look to the data source with your list of research questions in hand to determine which questions are potentially answered by it.

What's different is that in one case you may need to review a PowerPoint presentation or watch some videos, while in another you may be number crunching in Excel or using proprietary tools like Tealeaf or Cognos to do the analysis, with aid from appropriately trained individuals. Don't be afraid of data sources that require skills that you don't possess in order to be analyzed. You are a leader, not necessarily the "doer" of everything. Your job is to *focus* these potentially diverse analysis activities by using and iterating your set of research questions.

BONUS EBOOK: *There's a lot more to say about how to analyze and benchmark each of these discrete types of data. We've gone into more detail in your bonus eBook,* Studying Customers: Secret Techniques to Find Out What Customers REALLY Need. wdc.ht/STUDYING

THE PROS AND CONS OF NUMBERS

Data is very often *numbers*, which have some advantages and drawbacks. Very often, numbers tell you *what* happened but not necessarily why, *yet the why is the most important part.* If I only know my car won't start, it's hard to know what to do about it. If I know it won't start *because* it's out of gas, or *because* the battery is dead, or *because* I don't have the key, then I know what to do.

For example, site metrics may tell you that 30% of the people that reach the last step of your e-commerce "check out" process abandon without completing their order, but the numbers probably won't tell you *why* they are leaving. So, you'll then harness other research tools that can help clarify the "why." We'll talk about some specific techniques to do this in the next chapter.

But the big *advantage* of numbers is that they can be easily compared. Some of the comparisons you'll want to do will be *within* the data sets at your company. For example, you might compare the sales of your larger stores versus smaller ones, or the level of customer satisfaction of one of your products versus another.

It's also often beneficial to look at numbers over time. How do *this* quarter's satisfaction levels compare to the last? If they are down, there may be a new problem. Let's find it. If they are up, it suggests we might have done something good. What was it? Can we do more of it?

In addition, you may want to "benchmark" your results against competitors or industry standards. If you find that 10% of the people you send emails open them, is that good? Is that terrible? It's helpful to know that because it gives you a sense of whether there's likely to be substantially more upside if you make changes or whether you are brushing up to the top of the range.

Sometimes there are reference sources available that you can use to benchmark your internal results. But be aware of the *caveat* that many metrics are measured differently by different companies.

 BONUS VIDEO: *To learn more about comparing digital benchmarking data, check out the bonus video* 5 Key Factors to Consider When Comparing Digital Benchmarking Data *on the book website. This video goes into more detail than we do here, making it an an invaluable resource for anyone conducting data analysis.*

▶ wdc.ht/BENCHMARKS

 ### Indirect Research Method 2:
SECONDARY RESEARCH

The term "secondary research" simply means reviewing the research others have already done. Perhaps someone else has studied the very same questions you are focused on and has already found some of the answers for you. There are five primary sources we suggest turning to for secondary research:

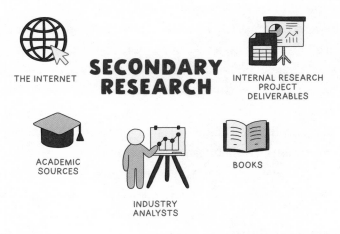

  wdc.ht/SECONDARY

Secondary Research Source 1:
THE INTERNET

What do most of us do today when we have a question? We Google it. Do that with your research questions. Of course, Google probably won't have results specific to your company's customers; however, it might still yield some helpful results. For example, if you want to know whether older customers are using *your* bank's app as much as the younger customers, that information is probably not on the internet; however, you *will* find trends on how different aged customers adopt financial services apps in general.

Of course, as with anything you find on the internet, "consider the source" and don't rely on it exclusively. For example, it's common for vendors who are trying to sell software to conduct market research to prove that the problem their product solves is an important one. A SaaS company that makes chatbots may publish a study that says that "75% of all consumers say they prefer using a chatbot to calling or using a website." The fact that the sponsor of the study *benefits* from the findings doesn't mean that the data is invalid, but use your judgment. And remember, our goal in research is not to be "right," it's to find out the truth, so avoid the temptation to give more credibility to data because it supports your hypothesis. Rather, evaluate it on its own merits, and look for multiple independent sources with similar findings.

Secondary Research Source 2:
ACADEMIC SOURCES

A lot of research, including research on customer trends, is done in a university setting and published in journals such as the *Harvard Business Review.* While *some* of this may come up in a general internet search, some of it won't. There are additional search tools such as RefSeek, JStor, Google Scholar, and Questia that can help you find this content.

Secondary Research Source 3:
INDUSTRY ANALYSTS

There are many companies that regularly publish analytics and research on factors that may be on your list of questions.

Some of these companies provide this information for free because they sell consulting or other services and want to promote their "thought leadership" to build their brand. Companies like Accenture, McKinsey, Bain, IBM, BCG, Deloitte, Capgemini and my company, FROM.Digital, do this. Searching their sites can often lead you to PDFs that combine professional insight with researched data, and these tend to be fairly credible sources. We've cited many such studies throughout this book.

Another class of analysts are paid analysts. Companies like Forrester, Gartner, IDG, and eMarketer sell fairly expensive subscriptions, mostly to large companies and, in exchange, provide well-researched articles on a wide range of topics, some of which may intersect with your research questions.

There are also a number of industry-specific analyst companies that follow this model but focus more narrowly. For example, PhoCusWright publishes analytics only on the travel industry.

These reports can be expensive, so you might want to check out this video:

BONUS TRAINING VIDEO: *To help you gather as much relevant information as possible, we've created a short bonus video with "Killer Tips to Get Expensive Analyst Reports for Free." This will teach you some ways to obtain valuable, well-researched, premium information without paying for any pricey subscriptions.*

▶ wdc.ht/GETREPORTS

Secondary Research Source 4:
BOOKS

Amazon is the third largest search engine on the internet[1] (after Google and YouTube). There may be useful books that address one or more of your research questions. Find them.

Buy the Kindle version so you can search the book for your desired topic more effectively. You don't even need a physical Kindle to read eBooks anymore. Amazon provides a web reader, as well as free mobile apps. If you find some books that even *might* be relevant, buy them and check them out; both printed and Amazon eBooks are returnable.

Secondary Research Source 5:
INTERNAL RESEARCH PROJECT DELIVERABLES

Lastly, since secondary research simply means *prior* research, if you scout around, you may even find that there was past analysis or a study done by your own company, possibly with an outside agency, that already examined some of the same issues that are on your list of research questions. If so, you definitely want that. But if your company is similar to many with which I've worked, it may take some digging. Ask around.

If you are leveraging past analyses, be careful to ensure that any analysis in which you put stock is reasonably recent and that the methodology used is explained clearly and seems legitimate. Ideally, speak to whoever did the analysis, as well.

Indirect Research Method 3:
COMPETITIVE RESEARCH

Find out what your competitors are doing. While it may not give you *definitive* information about your customers, if competitors are doing something that surprises you, *there is probably a reason*. Of course, it might not be a *good* reason, but consider the insight to be a tip that they *may* know something about the customer and their needs that you don't. Then, you can potentially use this insight to generate additional research questions.

For example, if you are an airline and discover that your competitor is offering gluten-free meals. That may seem like a lot of trouble for what you *assume* is a small percentage of customers likely to be interested in that. But it may raise the question, "How many customers *do* care about it?" And if the answer is "I don't know," then maybe you need to find out. Your competitor seems to think it's significant.

Indirect Research Method 4:
CUSTOMER "EXPERTS"

Customer Experts are people who know a lot about your customers and whose knowledge you can leverage, like the call center representatives in the credit card story at the start of this chapter.

I put the word "experts" in quotes for several reasons. First, some people who *think* they are customer experts may not possess fully accurate information. And second, the people that really *do* have firsthand knowledge about your customers may not always behave or look like "experts." We will expand on this paradox shortly.

Why are we talking to these "experts" instead of just going to actual customers? Well, you definitely *do* want to talk to actual customers, and the next chapter will go into that in great detail. However, usually, we interview the "experts" first and *then* the customers.

Customers, of course are completely authoritative about their own thoughts and feelings. However, they only know about themselves as individuals, or possibly the small group of other customers that form their family and friends. The accuracy is high, but the sample size is small.

With customer "experts," you are speaking to people who may have experience with large *numbers* of customers or who have spent *years* immersed in data about customers. They can leverage that broad mental database to see patterns/trends or answer questions about a variety of different customer segments. So that's valuable in a different way, although, of course, it's one step removed.

There are key three categories of customer experts: executives, frontline employees and outside specialists. Let's dive a little deeper into each category.

CUSTOMER EXPERTS

EXECUTIVES

FRONTLINE
EMPLOYEES

OUTSIDE
SPECIALISTS

‹ wdc.ht/EXPERTS

 Customer Expert Type 1:
EXECUTIVES

At most companies, there are executives who have confidence that they understand the customer. It's good to talk to these executives for multiple reasons, but, not to sound cynical, just remember that *confidence* is not the same as accuracy.

Now, I have spoken to many VPs of Insights and CMOs who are supremely knowledgeable about different customer segments and whose perspective is extremely valuable and accurate. One hour with them is an incredibly efficient schooling in their company's customers.

However, at least equally often, I have spoken to executives who offer commonly repeated beliefs about what the customer thinks and cares about, many of which are eventually shown to be over-simplifications, out of date, or just flat out wrong by the subsequent direct customer research. In fact, a key *benefit* of doing comprehensive customer research is to *help* those executives, and the wider team, get re-grounded in the reality of the customer's wants, needs, thoughts, and feelings.

So how can you tell whether you are getting good information when interviewing an executive? You may not be able to be *certain* until you compare the information received with data from other research techniques. But here's one test to start to assess the likely quality. As you interview the executive and they give you an answer to one of your research questions, an answer such as, "Our customers over 65 generally don't use the app," just ask with enthusiasm, "Oh, that's interesting. Out of curiosity, *how do we know that?*"

Tone is very important here; you don't want to sound like you are disagreeing or challenging but rather just trying to get "sources" for your study. The use of "we" in "how do *we* know that?" telegraphs that you *do* agree with them and are on their side.

You will usually get one of three types of responses. First, you may get some hemming and hawing. In that case, you know that this factoid is not "backed up" (which doesn't mean it's not true—it just means that what you are hearing is more rumor than expertise). The second possibility is a detailed answer referencing studies, data sources, etc. If so, great; you have a reasonable possibility that this individual knows what they are talking about and is pointing you to sources of verification. If these are sources you don't already have access to, ask for them. They could end up helping you answer additional research questions. That's good stuff.

And the third possibility is referral to another individual ("Oh, Paul, my VP of Customer Insights, covered that in his monthly briefing.") That's a perfectly respectable response from a senior executive. You probably then want to go and interview Paul and see if *he* knows what he is talking about. You may have just identified a great resource for additional insights.

Despite the variability in the quality of information, interviewing executives is a good practice. First of all, you may get one of the truly knowledgeable ones. Second, you may be pointed to some additional resources of value. And, lastly, from a political standpoint, it's good for people to feel included and respected, even if it turns out that some aren't contributing reliable substance.

Customer Expert Type 2:
FRONT LINE EMPLOYEES

The second category of customer experts are "front line employees." These are the people whose main job is to interact with your customers all day long. You probably have many that have been doing that 40-50 hours a week for *years*.

In his bestseller *Outliers*, Malcolm Gladwell says that becoming an "expert" at something, such as playing the piano professionally or being a champion soccer player, takes about 10,000 hours of practice.[2] So, if you have front line employees who have been interacting with customers for more than five years, 40 hours a week, 50 weeks a year, they qualify as "experts," at least to Gladwell.

Utilizing a combination of one-on-one interviews and surveys to seek out answers to your research questions from these front-line employees can be very, very rewarding.

Of course, any given employee expert may only see a piece of the story. Security personnel see a different side of your customers than your retail store associates do. Your call center engages with them at very different moments, as well. That's actually good because it gives you access to diverse perspectives, but it also means that you need to interact with a variety of them.

Customer Expert Type 3:
OUTSIDE EXPERTS

The last category of "customer experts" are external consultants who you may tap to provide insight into a specific type of customer. This can be particularly useful if you are targeting a new customer type with whom your organization doesn't have experience. For example, we once did a project for a company that wanted to expand into the sweepstakes market in Europe, where their presence was limited. We recruited an expert who wrote a very popular blog for sweepstakes enthusiasts in several European countries. She clearly knew the market and its customers quite well. We flew her over for a client workshop where she helped provide perspective on many of our research questions about that particular segment.

If you are in need of specialized outside expertise, search LinkedIn for someone with the right background or utilize a service that connects companies with individuals with specific expert knowledge, such as Maven or Clarity.fm.

Indirect Research Method 5:
SOCIAL LISTENING

If you are an organization of any significant size, customers are talking about you *right now* on social media. Many companies use "social listening software" to monitor social posts and respond to them for PR and customer service purposes.

But "social listening" is also very valuable as a research tool. Software platforms like Radian6, Awario, and Keyhole enable you to scan social sites and aggregate tens or hundreds of thousands of comments, tweets, and posts. Some tools will also scan blogs and even the subtitles of YouTube influencer videos—all with the goal of understanding *what people are saying about you* (or have said about you in the past). To save you from having to *read* all the posts, these tools extract key themes and summarize insights for you. Some also use artificial intelligence to conduct what is called "sentiment analysis"—assessing the *tone* of the posts to see whether people discussing the movie you just released or commenting on your accounting software are saying things that are largely positive, negative, or neutral.

The most high-end social listening platforms even build profiles of individual social posters based on *other* posts they have created, which can help you segment the feedback along different dimensions.

For example, social tools that analyze a poster's full Twitter feed can often come to a reasonably accurate determination about whether they have children or not (because, if they do, it will probably have been mentioned at some point in the feed). That then enables those tools to answer questions like, "Do people who have children post more positive or negative tweets about your store than those that don't?"

Naturally, you have to take a bunch of social posts with a grain of salt. People sometimes say things on the internet just to be controversial. Posters also tend to be at the edges of their satisfaction level—either very happy or very unhappy. And, while it's helpful to know this is how these people are feeling, social posts don't reflect the full range of customers. Nevertheless, the fact that thousands or even millions of customers are posting their thoughts and feelings about your brand and products is too great an opportunity for customer insight not to be utilized.

. . . .

So that gives you a pretty broad set of tools and places to find information about your customer without even needing to interact with them directly. Through indirect research, you can build a solid profile of the customer. But as we've said, it's most ideally used as the run-up to direct customer research. So, we'll look at that next. Hopefully, after learning so much about your customer using the techniques in this chapter, you will be excited to actually meet them.

CHAPTER EIGHT

UNDERSTAND YOUR CUSTOMER

DIRECT CUSTOMER RESEARCH

Carla, a 45-year-old social worker and mother of four from suburban Atlanta had agreed to participate in a market research my company was conducting. We'd been hired to study consumers who had not yet adopted online banking in order to understand what was holding them back and to identify ways to persuade them to try it.

We asked Carla some introductory questions, which she responded to with intelligence and humor. She described how she shopped online, Facetimed with her kids, and used many apps on her smartphone, including one that helped her coordinate a large church volunteer group that she ran. We then got around to the topic of online banking. She confirmed to us that she was pretty dead set-against it.

We probed as to what was holding her back. She explained her mindset with an analogy: "Have you ever been writing something in Microsoft Word," she asked, "And had the computer crash, and you lost everything you had written?"

I responded that yes, that *had* happened to me more than once and it's very frustrating. Sensing that I understood her, she connected the dots, explaining, "Honey, I just can't afford to let that happen to my money."

At that moment, a sound could be heard from behind the one-way mirror at the end of the room. It was one of my clients literally falling off her chair in the observation area. Thankfully she was not injured.

In my decades of direct customer research, the most universal theme I've seen is that when the research is structured correctly, you will learn things that you never could have thought of, even with years of conference room brainstorming. You will encounter people who have very different perspectives from yours and who see the world in a manner that is fundamentally distinct from the way you see it. You may realize that all the indirect data you have been analyzing up to that point has been interpreted through your own view of the world—your own knowledge, experiences, values, and beliefs.

Doing research on vacation planning for a major theme park, I observed that many families print out large numbers of web pages and sit down together to review the printouts—giving a huge advantage to those vacation destination websites that look good when printed. It's a common behavior. But I've never done that. Never even thought of doing it.

I've seen customers who couldn't sign up for a diet program because the program didn't provide the nutritional information they needed to determine if it would work with their allergies. I don't have any food allergies.

I've seen customers who didn't sign up for lower electricity rates because they worried falsely that their power would be restored more slowly in the event of a power outage if they signed up for the cheaper plan. My client never even considered this as an issue that customers might be concerned about because, based on how the industry works, it would never happen. The client knew that and I knew that, but clearly, lots of potential customers didn't. We started telling them and it boosted conversion rates.

In this chapter, we will continue to detail methods of customer research, focusing now on those that involve connecting to actual customers, which we call "direct" customer research.

· ·

RESEARCH TECHNIQUES MATTER

There is no substitute for spending time with customers and gaining a rich picture of their world. But *just* "spending time" with customers is not the most effective way to conduct direct research. The "customer experts" we talked about in the previous chapter may have seen enough customers over the years to piece together a detailed understanding just through natural interaction. But research needs to be much more efficient than that. Fortunately, there are specific methodologies that help ensure you talk to the right sample of customers and interact with them in ways that allow you to maximize the speed and accuracy of learning.

In 1985, Coca Cola brought "New Coke" to the market. It was a reformulation of the blockbuster product, making it sweeter, more like Pepsi, which had been gaining market share. The new flavor had been extensively tested using direct customer research—specifically "blind taste tests" in which subjects were asked to sip two generically labeled product samples and indicate which one they preferred. One sample was actually the existing Coke product and the other one was the "New Coke" formula, though the subjects weren't told that.

Customers overwhelmingly indicated they preferred the "New Coke" formula and so the researchers concluded it would be a blockbuster hit.

When the product was launched, the exact opposite happened. There was such a backlash that the company had to revive the original flavor as "Classic" Coke and eventually they discontinued the new formulation altogether, a very expensive mistake considering they had spent many millions of dollars to manufacture and market it.[1]

There are two morals to this story. The first is that no research is perfect. But the second is that the research techniques that are used matter a great deal. Coke had customers do blind taste tests, determined that they liked the taste compared to the original and concluded that they therefore would buy it. But it turned out that *taste* wasn't the only factor that influenced what product consumers would buy. To them, "their" Coke had a heritage and messing with the formula went against their brand loyalty. As we've said, customers engage in behaviors because of their thoughts and feelings. The idea of "*New* Coke" clearly did not inspire thoughts and feelings aligned with increased purchase. Had different techniques been used rather than blind taste tests, or at least had a greater *range* of techniques been applied, it would have quite likely generated insights that would have avoided the New Coke debacle.

In this chapter, we will review a variety of techniques for interacting with consumers. Specifically, we will discuss the following methods along with best-practice techniques that we have found increase the effectiveness of each method.

CUSTOMER INTERVIEWS

OBSERVATIONAL RESEARCH

STANDARDIZED MEASURES

SURVEYS

❮ wdc.ht/DIRECT

 Direct Research Method 1:
CUSTOMER INTERVIEWS

You probably have a good conception of what it means to interview someone, but there are a variety of specific practices that can help you to do this most effectively.

When planning any type of "real-time" customer research, such as interviews, there are a few steps to the process:

TARGET RESEARCH SUBJECTS

RECRUIT CUSTOMERS

DEVELOP A PROTOCOL

CONDUCT THE INTERVIEW

❮ wdc.ht/INTERVIEWPROCESS

 Customer Interviews Step 1:
TARGET RESEARCH SUBJECTS

A key first step in planning real-time customer research is getting clear on *who* you want to engage with. You will need to ensure that you speak to *enough* customers to make the findings reliable and that you have sufficient *diversity* of customers to cover the full range of dimensions and characteristics you defined earlier. For example, if you have a global business, you probably don't want to talk only to customers in New York City. If your law firm services a wide range of industries, you probably don't want to talk only to pharmaceutical clients. Depending on your research goals, there may also be some types of customers who you don't need to speak with at all.

A standard "rule of thumb" is to engage one-on-one with a *minimum* of 8-12 individuals "per segment." The number of segments depends on how deeply you want to dive. Let's look at a specific example. Say you're a bank. You could decide you have two segments: individuals and business customers. But you might then decide that businesses split up into large versus small, as well as into different industries. Individuals might be segmented based on net worth or life stage.

The more segments you define, the richer your research will be and the greater your ability to draw conclusions about customers with different characteristics. At the same time, the more individual research sessions you need to conduct, the more time and expense is added to the project—assuming the minimum 8-12 research subjects *per segment*—so you need to prioritize based on those tradeoffs of scope versus budget.

BONUS TOOL: *As you embark on segmenting your customers, make sure to visit the book website and download our Excel-based tool for defining and organizing your customer segments for research projects. It should help you hit the ground running.* wdc.ht/SUBJECTS

Customer Interviews Step 2:
RECRUIT CUSTOMERS

Once you know what types of customers you are seeking for the research, you need to get some of them "signed up" to participate.

There are many market research companies who are in the business of recruiting people to participate in studies. If you aren't experienced doing research, you may want to use one of them.

Subjects are typically recruited from email or phone lists. If you are looking to speak to *current* customers, you probably have or can generate a contact list. If you also want to speak to *prospective* customers, you will need to acquire a list that matches your customer profile.

 Customer Interviews Steps 3 & 4:
DEVELOP A PROTOCOL AND CONDUCT THE INTERVIEW

While getting your subjects signed up, you should be developing a "protocol" for the research activities—which is a cross between an agenda and a script. You will then use that protocol to *conduct* the sessions. Because these two are so intertwined, we'll discuss them together.

For interviews, it's common to engage with customers in one-on-one sessions lasting from 45 minutes to an hour. Ours generally consist of four stages.

INTRODUCTION AND LOGISTICS   **SUBJECT PROFILING**   **INSIGHT QUESTIONS**   **WRAP UP**

‹ wdc.ht/PROTOCOL

During the Introduction and Logistics portion, you will make the subject feel comfortable and go over any business details such as consent forms. During the Subject Profiling period, you will review their screening form and ask any additional background questions.

The third stage of customer interviews is typically the "meat" of the session—the Insight Questions. This is where you will unpack the core issues defined in your "research questions"—the things you really want to know. Your protocol should list out the items you want to ask about in chronological order. However, it's usually most productive to engage in a natural conversation with the subject, which may result in the flow of the discussion following a different sequence. That's fine. As you approach the end of this section, scan back over your list of questions and see whether you missed anything.

Generally, you'll need to adapt the research questions into a form more appropriate for speaking to subjects. For example, you may have a research question like, "Do customers really care whether our toys are made of higher quality materials than our competitors? Does it influence their purchase decisions?" You don't ask a subject, "Do customers care...?" because you aren't speaking to the subject as an "expert" on customers in general. You want to ask the subjects about *themselves* (and sometimes their family).

In fact, even when you word the question to be about them, sometimes subjects will drift into speaking about "people" in general rather than themselves. If they do, you should be very friendly but guide them by saying, "I'd really just love to hear about *you*."

I remember how one subject—a lovely woman we interviewed for a large bank in Cincinnati—was telling us how people make decisions about where to open checking accounts. She talked for several minutes about what "people" do and was so animated that we didn't want to interrupt her. But, when she finally took a breath, my associate said, "Awesome! Thanks for that description! So, I just want to confirm, when you say that's what 'people' do, is that also what *you* do?"

The subject laughed and replied, "Oh, no, darlin', not at all, but I'm an oddball." Of course, we then asked her what she did, and it was a totally different process. The truth is that a large percentage of people think of themselves as unique. Their *theoretical* idea of what "people" do is probably not accurate and therefore not useful. After all, they haven't studied it—that's what *you're* trying to do.

So questions need to be worded in such a way that the subject is answering about their own personal experience and generalizing as little as possible. We have *many* techniques to nuance the language of these questions and to drive how we ask follow-up questions. For safety reasons we've had to omit these details here (our editor was concerned that if the book became any longer it could injure readers if they dropped it on their toe). However, it's all laid out in your bonus eBook.

BONUS EBOOK: *There is so much more to say about how to run an effective interview, so we've put more guidance in your bonus eBook* Studying Customers: Secret Techniques to Find Out What Customers REALLY Need. *Make sure to download it now as it has tons of useful details for putting this section into action.*

 wdc.ht/STUDYING

 Direct Research Method 2:
OBSERVATIONAL RESEARCH

Our second form of direct research is called "Observational Research" and it covers a range of different techniques. During observational activities, instead of *asking* someone about their experience, you *observe* them engaged in an actual task in the moment (such as buying or using your product). When possible, you ask them to verbalize their "stream of conscious" inner dialogue so you can understand not just what they are doing but how it connects to their thoughts and feelings. This is by far the most accurate method of doing customer research. Subjects are telling you what they are thinking as they are thinking it, and you can observe their actions and generally their feelings, as well.

The primary downside of observational research is that it can be time-consuming, especially if you want to engage a large number of subjects. However, the level of insight gained from each session can be very significant.

If you want to observe a subject in action, you can either *ask* them to engage in a "real world" task in front of you in a research session (such as an interview), or you can place yourself at the time and place where subjects are *naturally* engaged in the activities you wish to observe (such as at a store, at a repair facility, in someone's living room, etc.) There are a variety of techniques based on this principle. The best one for your purposes will depend based on the type of subject you are researching and the type of task you wish to observe. In this chapter, we will discuss six observational techniques.

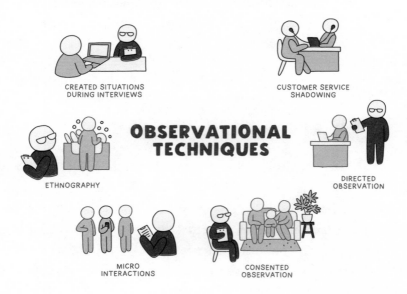

CREATED SITUATIONS
DURING INTERVIEWS

CUSTOMER SERVICE
SHADOWING

OBSERVATIONAL TECHNIQUES

ETHNOGRAPHY

DIRECTED
OBSERVATION

MICRO
INTERACTIONS

CONSENTED
OBSERVATION

 ‹ wdc.ht/OBSERVATION

Observational Research Technique 1:
CREATED SITUATIONS DURING INTERVIEWS

There are many types of tasks that a subject can effectively engage in *during* an interview, such as on-line shopping. For example, to study the process of booking rental cars for leisure travel, we recruited subjects to come in for an interview—targeting ones who said they had an upcoming vacation for which they had not yet booked a rental car.

When subjects arrived, after executing an interview protocol, we then asked them to tell us about their upcoming trip and to go ahead and engage in the process of shopping for and booking their rental car *in front of us,* using either a laptop we had available or their phone if they preferred.

The subjects were usually happy to get a "to-do" item out of the way during a paid market research session, and, of course, they knew they could always cancel the reservation if they changed their mind later.

We got to observe a variety of subjects who used differing shopping tactics. Some went to sites like Travelocity or Expedia that compare many rental car providers. Some logged into their employer's business travel portal even though it was a leisure trip because they wanted the corporate discount. Some Googled for rental car companies serving the city they were traveling to. And some went to the websites of specific car rental brands that they were interested in, such as Hertz, Avis or Enterprise. One subject just texted her assistant with the travel dates and told her to book whatever was a good deal. Seeing this kind of detail and "real world" activity is far more accurate than asking subjects about their prior experiences.

During these types of observational activities, we instruct subjects to "talk aloud" to let us know what they're thinking. It can feel strange to verbally share every thought one has, so we demonstrate playfully with an example such as, "Hmm, I need to find where to enter the date. Oh, there it is. Ok, so I'm putting in my departure date. Oh, I see I need to pick it from a calendar," and so on. Subjects generally "get it" pretty quickly and are usually willing to play along.

This method allows us not only to observe what they *do,* but based on their words, understand their *thoughts,* and based on their tone of voice and body language, infer their *emotions.*

In fact, some subjects *did* get emotional in our rental car study as they encountered obstacles and frustrations on various sites.

We also occasionally ask subjects questions during their task if we need more information. There may be a key moment where the subject does something or gets a certain expression on their face that seems important to understand, and sometimes subjects forget to keep verbalizing their thoughts. If you encounter this situation, and it seems like a good moment, it's ok to ask, "I'd love to know what you are thinking right now," or "Can I ask why you clicked on that? What were you expecting?" The most accurate information about what someone is thinking or feeling is always extracted *at that moment* rather than later when they need to reconstruct that moment from memory.

The downside is that asking questions does pose the risk of pulling the subject *out* of their task. So, try not to do it *too* often, and direct the subject back to the activity as quickly as possible.

Whether or not questions are asked, if the subject's "talk aloud" turns into an ongoing explanation *to the researcher* of why they are doing something rather than their natural "stream of conscious" thoughts, redirect the subject. Remind them, "Just focus on the task and verbalize whatever you are thinking and feeling as you'd hear it in your own head. Afterward, we can discuss anything else you'd like me to know."

Also, it may be hard, but when a user is engaged in a task, *don't help them.* It's a natural human reaction, if we see someone struggling, to want to provide assistance. After all, the person is experiencing some discomfort, and if we can take away that discomfort by giving them the answer, shouldn't we? Isn't it kind of *cruel* to just let them suffer—confused and frustrated? If you feel yourself burdened by this moral dilemma, remember the words of Mr. Spock from *Star Trek*:

"THE GOOD OF THE MANY OUTWEIGHS THE GOOD OF THE FEW."
-SPOCK < wdc.ht/SPOCK

As a researcher, you must be able to suppress the instinct to "save" the subject. You are trying to understand the experiences of customers, in general, through observing a small number of "representative users." The customers out in the "real world" don't have a researcher hovering over them ready to assist if they get confused. If we can use a few research subjects' pain to discover and then fix problems that are creating friction for thousands of real customers, then the research subjects have sacrificed their discomfort for the delight of a far greater group. Plus, they are getting paid.

But what if the subject asks you a question? They may say, "I can't seem to find the search feature, does this app have one?" A good response is, "We're really interested to see how you complete this task without assistance. I'd be happy to answer that question later, but please continue as if I wasn't here." You may get a few eye rolls from subjects when they realize you won't help them "cheat" their way out of pain, but they'll get over it.

OBSERVING "NATURAL" SITUATIONS

The logistics of these "created" situations are often more efficient than those of "real world" behavior since you control the timing of when subjects come and what tasks they engage in. It's hard to think of somewhere we could go and observe a bunch of people booking rental cars on-line. Another advantage of created situations is that

115

you can target the specific types of subjects you want to bring in, and you have a profile of them before they start.

That is not generally the case with natural or "real world" situations. Natural situations involve the researcher placing himself, as an observer, at the right time and place to witness subjects engaging in behaviors in their "natural habitat." These situations have some distinct advantages, like being even more realistic and, for certain types of activities, also being more efficient.

For example, if we wanted to observe subjects waiting in line at a supermarket, it would be difficult to recreate the experience in an interview. Simply going to a supermarket where there are dozens of people in line would be far easier.

The remaining techniques discussed in this chapter are variations of methods of "natural" observational research.

 Observational Research Technique 2:
ETHNOGRAPHY

The term "ethnography" comes from anthropology and originally referred to situations where researchers would go to live with, for example, native tribes, become a part of their world, and understand them from "the inside."

The reality TV show *Undercover Boss* is another example of ethnography. On each episode, a different CEO disguises him– or herself and gets an entry-level job in their own company. They then get to observe what it's "really" like to work there, seeing how customers, managers and others act when they think nobody important is watching.

Here's an example of applying the principles of ethnography for customer research. My team worked on a project for a large brokerage firm where we gathered insights about the types of account notifications brokers received and how they used them. We spent time in their branch offices posing as "temp" office assistants and basically just observing the brokers and their staff. After seeing the notifications (called "wires" in the brokerage biz) come in, we noted when brokers responded quickly and when they ignored them. We took pictures of stacks of notifications that were piled up, filling in-boxes and sometimes falling onto the floor. We tried to be a "fly on the wall" so as to get as realistic a sense as possible of how the office operated (and took a few phone messages to justify our presence).

Because, in this case, some of our observations related to employees who were not following the "head office" standard operating practices, if we had shown up to interview the brokers and their support staff, we almost certainly would have gotten a very different story from the one we observed surreptitiously.

However, you don't always need a fictional role. We did another project for a sports stadium client where we observed people entering the stadium with tickets, trying to find their seats, getting concessions, and buying merchandise. We documented how fans interacted with security personnel, how they left the stadium after the event, how they found their cars, and how they fared with traffic. In a crowded, public environment like that, you can basically just hang around and observe without needing any cover story.

However, when ethnography is executed in its purest form, you don't always get clarity on what people are thinking or feeling. In some cases, you can infer it from their reactions and body language, but it's not as transparent as having a subject verbalizing their thoughts and answering questions.

 Observational Research Technique 3:
MICRO INTERACTIONS

When engaged in ethnography, you can gain additional insight by selectively approaching people you have been subtly observing, revealing your purpose and asking if they'd be willing to briefly chat with you. For example, in the stadium research we did, we looked for people waiting in line for food or beverages who appeared frustrated or otherwise unhappy. After observing them from a distance, we approached them, identified that we were doing a research study for the venue and asked if they'd be willing to answer a couple of questions. If they agreed, we probed to understand what they were thinking and feeling and what experiences were leading to those thoughts and feelings. Our interactions were usually less than five minutes and happened while the subjects were waiting in line. This enabled us to combine initial fly-on-the-wall observations with some additional insight about the subject's intention and state of mind.

 Observational Research Technique 4:
CONSENTED OBSERVATION

Being a "fly on the wall" works fine when you are looking to observe people for relatively brief periods in crowded places. However, other activities occur in private. Also, in some cases, it's valuable to observe a single subject through a complete experience—like a restaurant meal from beginning to end—where it would be difficult to remain unnoticed for a long time (at least without CIA training).

"Consented observation" involves recruiting subjects that you target to participate in a research study, but then *you go to them* to observe them in their "natural habitat," with their permission and knowledge.

Part of the study for the theme park we discussed earlier falls into this category. We wanted to observe families engaged in vacation planning, which tends to occur in people's homes. The team recruited prospective customers with certain characteristics that matched our research goals, went to consenting subjects' homes, and observed them engaged in family discussions, at times lively debates, and even arguments about their family vacation plans. Sound like an interesting way to earn a living?

The families were asked to do their best to ignore our presence, but they were, of course, aware that they were being observed. Following each discussion (or all-out fight in one case), we interviewed participants alone to hear their individual perspectives and understand what they were thinking and feeling at key moments of the process. These one-on-one interviews enabled us to more deeply understand the priorities of different family members of different ages and genders.

We did another study for the Girl Scouts of America that involved visiting tweens and their parents at home to observe how the girls utilized social media apps to connect with friends. Spending some time observing the kids and their parents, we got to see where they would go in their home to use Instagram, how they would take pictures of themselves to post using a particular mirror in the house because it had good light, and how other environmental factors connected to their use of the technology.

We've done other studies in places like distribution centers or insurance agencies to understand how various digital tools are used in the "real world." Being able to see subjects at their actual desks and on their own computers, with their Post-it notes, arranged desktop icons and pre-created browser bookmarks gives a much deeper understanding of how a tool is really used than if we brought them to a conference room with an unfamiliar PC running the same software. I'll never forget observing a Merrill Lynch broker who had used an old fashioned Rolodex wheel to create alphabetically filed "cards" with instructions to himself about how to use the various features of the on-line account servicing platform. How to: open a new account, check balances, transfer money, etc.

Observational Research Technique 5:
DIRECTED OBSERVATION

A variation of *consented* observation is *directed* observation. In some cases, for the sake of efficiency, we visit people in their native habitats, but rather than wait for them to engage in natural behaviors, we prompt them to do so.

For example, we did a study for a company that manages disability insurance claims for large employers. We were asked to help improve the tools that the insurance company makes available to the HR and finance teams at their clients who review the status of multiple claims. So, we visited the offices of people in those roles at a number of their corporate disability insurance customers. The subjects told us about the various tasks they conduct in a typical week with the reports. We then asked them if they would be willing to go ahead and *do* those tasks while we were there, even though they may typically have done them sporadically throughout the week.

This is similar to how we ask subjects in "created situations" to engage in a real activity such as to shop for a rental car, but in this case, we're asking them to do the task in *their* environment (which is more realistic) but still "on-demand" rather than at its natural time.

It was fascinating to see one subject who printed the reports so he could use a ruler and marker to highlight certain rows. Another subject copy-pasted a PDF report into Excel so she could re-order the columns in a way that better suited her needs.

Using this research technique, we were able to see in an hour per subject what might otherwise have been four 15-minute tasks done on different days throughout the week.

All research entails some kind of tradeoff. Keeping the situation as "natural" as possible produces the most accurate observations, but practicality and efficiency also need to be considered. This means that in some cases we accept a reduction in the "naturalness" so that we can, for example, observe more subjects in the same amount of time and thereby increase the *aggregate* accuracy of our research.

Observational Research Technique 6:
CUSTOMER SERVICE SHADOWING

Whether we are specifically focused on improving the call center experience or not, whenever we are studying companies in industries where call centers are prevalent, we usually request to spend at least a few days *in* the call center observing live calls as a way to better understand customers. This typically involves sitting next to a customer service representative and, as they say in the call center industry, "jacking in," which means taking a second headset and plugging it into the same phone extension as the representative so that you can listen in on the call as it happens.

While this is somewhat similar to listening to call recordings, one of the data sources we identified as an "indirect" research source of customer data, it gives you the added benefit of being able to speak to the call center representative to debrief after each call, as well as see what they are doing on their screen.

And what makes this truly "direct" customer research is that if you are at a stage of your research where you are trying to answer very specific, still-open questions, you can use the call center shadowing for more *directed* research.

For example, in our work with one client, we knew that there were a large number of customers calling the call center because they had technical problems placing orders with the company's app. We listened to some of the recorded calls, but it was hard at times to understand exactly what the technical problem was. This was because the customer service reps were, rightfully so, focused less on the app *problem* and more on just helping the caller to get their order processed. They would usually just enter the order *for* the customer rather than try to

121

troubleshoot why the customer couldn't do it themselves in the app. This makes sense from a customer service perspective but was not especially helpful for our research.

So, we went to the call center and asked to be paired with some of their "top reps"—the ones with the best rapport with customers. We also asked the call center operations team to route calls having to do with app problems to the agents we were observing. Then, we explained to those agents exactly what we were trying to understand about the app situation. We wanted to know if the users were confused with the user interface (and if so, in what way) or if technical problems were occurring, or connectivity challenges, or whatever else would help us diagnose the root issues.

We coached the agents to use those calls as *both* customer service *and* a bit of market research. They would tell the customers, "I will definitely help you place your order, but I'd also like to be sure I understand why it's not working for you so we can fix it for the future." This approach allowed us to get our questions answered very efficiently. In less than a day, two researchers observed a total of 70 calls from customers with the target problem, and we gained clear insights into what the specific issues were.

This research technique was ideal for this type of problem. It would have been far more difficult to determine the cause of the app bug if we had simply recruited customers into a market research session because the "problem" only happened if the account had certain characteristics and the transaction being attempted had certain other characteristics, but we only understood that once we had diagnosed the issue. If we had recruited 20 customers and tried to have them replicate the problem, it might have only happened to one or two of them. Possibly none of them. But by limiting our research *only* to those customers who were already *having* the problem, we were able to find the pattern that caused it and then, fairly easily, fix it. Call centers are ideal for this type of issue-targeted research.

But customer service shadowing is not *limited* to call centers. On other projects, our team has shadowed top salespeople at car dealerships, observed interactions between the service desk and patrons at a shopping mall, and conducted "ride-alongs" on AAA tow trucks to observe how the drivers interacted with stranded motorists. In these cases, we adapt many of the same key principles of call center research.

The advantage of these in-person scenarios over call centers is that you have the opportunity to observe the customer's body language.

The added *complexity* is that you cannot be "invisible" the way you can when observing the call center interactions. You are standing right there, and the customer may wonder who you are.

That issue is typically solved in one of two ways. The first option is transparency—just very briefly introduce yourself and inform the customer that you are observing as part of a research program run by the company to understand customer needs. Most customers will be fine with this.

The quicker, simpler option is to tell the customer you are "in training," which, while a little misleading, is not entirely untrue. You are "in training" to better lead efforts to improve the customer experience.

BONUS EBOOK: *If you want to learn more about real-time customer research, there's more on that in your bonus eBook,* Studying Customers: Secret Techniques to Find Out What Customers REALLY Need. *It has answers to a list of common questions and more.*

 wdc.ht/STUDYING

Direct Research Method 3:
SURVEYS

Surveys are a valuable research tool because they allow you to reach a much larger number of subjects than would be practical with any sort of one-on-one activity. The downside of surveys is that they provide far, far less nuanced insight than in-person sessions.

That's why we primarily use them near the end of our research process. After doing 15, 30, or even 100 interviews or ethnography sessions, we generally have a lot of insights, but we really aren't sure about quantification. For example, if I interviewed 50 people and five of them have a certain concern about a product, that's 10%. But do 10% of *all* people have that concern? I really don't know because 50 people is far too small a sample size to generalize like that. A survey can get us a much larger data set cost-effectively.

We also like to put surveys last because very often in interviews, due to their open and exploratory nature, we learn about factors that we wouldn't have previously even thought to ask about in a survey. Surveys allow us to then investigate issues discovered using other research techniques and determine how prevalent they are. Doing a survey of 1,000 or even 5,000 subjects can be quite inexpensive, whereas interviewing, let alone observing, that many people would usually be cost-prohibitive.

Surveys help in another way, too. They can increase the diversity of your research sample. For example, I did a project recently where we interviewed about 30 people and then did a survey of 1,500 subjects. In the pool of 1,500 subjects, there were about 20 people who were actively serving in the military. In the interview pool, there were zero people in the military. The military was not a focused segment for this client, but through some of the responses we got from members of the military on the survey, we realized that they have some specialized needs, and there may be some specific business opportunities with that population that had not been apparent before. A larger sample allows for a greater diversity of age, ethnicity, background, and geography, which is very valuable.

BONUS EBOOK: *In your bonus eBook* Studying Customers: Secret Techniques to Find Out What Customers REALLY Need, *we've put together a list of critical considerations when planning a customer survey, so make sure to check it out at the link listed here.*

 wdc.ht/STUDYING

Direct Research Method 4: STANDARDIZED MEASURES

The last direct research technique we will cover is the use of standardized measures. The most widely known standard measure of customer satisfaction is called Net Promoter Score (or NPS).

NPS is based on the belief that the best way to find out if someone is satisfied with your product or service is *not* to ask them if they are satisfied, but rather to ask them about their likelihood of recommending your product/service to a family member or friend.

There are documented methods of gathering NPS so that the statistics can be compared across companies and more easily benchmarked. NPS should also be re-tested over time to determine whether a company is improving, declining, or flat-lining in terms of the satisfaction of their customer base as a whole, and within individual segments.

There are other standardized metrics, as well as other companies that provide standardized measurement via direct customer research. One such company is JD Power, which rates many facets of different companies within certain industries.

For example, JD Power measures customer satisfaction across all auto manufacturers each year. About 15 years ago, I worked with General Motors, which, when we were brought in, was ranked as the *worst* automaker in the industry by JD Power in terms of online customer satisfaction.

They were thrilled when, after less than two years of working with my team to develop and implement a new digital strategy, GM had climbed to become the *top* automaker ranked by JD Power in that area. Having a standardized index that not only measured GM, but also measured them against their competitors, helped to create a burning platform for improvement, track progress year-over-year, and prove the ultimate victory once the transformation was successful. General Motors actually published a research paper on some of the techniques we used. The abstract is available at `wdc.ht/GM`.

....

There are other methods you can use to engage directly with customers that haven't been covered in this chapter. Pair interviews, biometrics, remote user testing tools like UserTesting.com, and co-creation sessions are all methods we use but that we haven't had the space to address here. However, even if you stick only to the research methods described in the previous two chapters, you can get all the insight necessary to drive a massively successful transformation.

Of course, you will also wind up with a huge pile of information that then needs to be synthesized and made actionable. That process is the topic of the next chapter.

CHAPTER NINE

UNDERSTAND YOUR CUSTOMER

SYNTHESIS OF RESEARCH INTO CUSTOMER PERSONAS

When Gordon Bethune took over Continental Airlines as CEO in 1994, the carrier had just emerged from its second bankruptcy and appeared to be headed for a third and possibly final round. US Department of Transportation statistics from that year show that among the ten largest US airlines, Continental ranked dead last in every single customer service metric.[1]

In his book, *From Worst to First, Continental's Remarkable Comeback*, Bethune describes the challenges he faced when he first became CEO of the troubled carrier, including an overwhelming list of problems with the customer experience, both on the ground and in the air. It was too much to tackle all at once, and due to the company's poor recent financial performance, money was short. If the limited resources weren't prioritized properly, it could mean the end. He needed a simple method that the executives and managers in his organization could use as a litmus test for what was important when making decisions.

Bethune introduced the concept of "The Customer in Seat 9C"—a composite image of their best customer segment, business travelers—who were paying a premium fare and willing to pay more if their experience could be improved in meaningful ways.

Continental analyzed, then communicated, the key traits, preferences, and concerns of "The Customer in Seat 9C." When priorities had to be decided or choices made between alternate approaches, employees were trained to ask, "What would make a difference for the Customer in Seat 9C? What would make them prefer to fly with us? What would they be willing to pay more for?"

Over the next ten years, with this simple but disciplined focus, Bethune "piloted" Continental not only out of bankruptcy risk but to the title of "*Fortune's* #1 Most Admired Global Airline."[2]

Of course, the concept of what "The Customer in Seat 9C" wants is a massive generalization. On one flight, 9C could be occupied by a 60-year-old bank executive and by a 23-year-old entrepreneur running an organic farming business on the next. Surely, their needs are not identical.

LIKE SNOWFLAKES, EVERY ONE OF YOUR CUSTOMERS IS **COMPLETELY UNIQUE.** BUT ALSO LIKE SNOWFLAKES, MANY ARE EXTREMELY **SIMILAR.**

< wdc.ht/SNOWFLAKES

You may very well have noticed this during your direct customer research. After listening to 40 contact center interactions with customers calling to order parts or talking to 15 brides shopping for wedding dresses or speaking to a dozen owners of luxury cars, while you hear many unique stories, you also start to hear the same themes over and over.

Identifying these patterns is a key part of the analysis and synthesis that makes your customer research actionable.

If you recall, there were four steps to understanding your customer. The first was defining your research questions—both what you want to know and who you want to know it *about.* The second and third steps were all that research we talked about at length in Chapters 7 and 8, both direct and indirect. The final step is synthesizing the research and creating personas, which serve a similar purpose to Bethune's "Customer in Seat 9C" mantra—they are generalized composites of specific types of customers.

· ·

SYNTHESIS OF RESEARCH INTO CUSTOMER PERSONAS

If you engage in even a fraction of the research activities described in the previous two chapters, you'll have quite a wide range of information—insights from customer interviews, competitive examples, survey data, site analytics, and more. So how do you take all of the data gathered from customer research and turn it into personas or other actionable tools that can be used to drive decision-making? Here is a four-step process for doing just that.

 SYNTHESIS OF RESEARCH INTO CUSTOMER PERSONAS

| ANSWER THE RESEARCH QUESTIONS | DEFINE WHAT DIFFERENTIATES YOUR CUSTOMER SEGMENTS | DEFINE WHAT IS COMMON ACROSS YOUR CUSTOMER SEGMENTS | CREATE PERSONAS |

‹ wdc.ht/SYNTHESIS

Research Synthesis Step 1:
ANSWER THE RESEARCH QUESTIONS

Remember, we began this whole process to answer some research questions. The first thing to do as you work to answer them is really just structural. Initially, your research results will likely be organized by source—notes from different interviews, data from survey responses, various decks and reports, etc.

Start by putting all the information you have, no matter the source, together by research question. Notes from one interview or the various slides from one deck may pertain to five different questions—that's fine, break them apart that way.

We like to set up a "war room" where we print each research question in big type on a large piece of paper and tape them high on the walls all around the room. Then we grab printouts of all our research findings and start putting things on the wall under the questions to which they relate—quotes from customer interviews, slides from decks you found, charts summarizing your customer surveys.

Cut each out and paste them under the question they answer. Once these pieces start to physically occupy the same wall space, it's amazing how a picture starts to come together.

When we are examining multiple segments, we use colored tape to create bands going around the room. Between each line of tape are insights for a different type of customer. So, for example, under the research question of the customer's key goals, one band may contain information about the goals of our business customers and the next band about our individual B2C consumers.

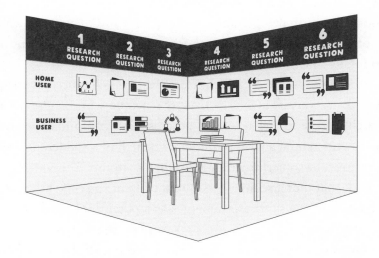

 wdc.ht/WARROOM

Once that is all set up, you can browse the room like an art gallery and consider the different, discrete pieces of information, ponder them individually and discuss them as a research team.

There is an aspect of research synthesis that is difficult to put into methodology. It involves simply looking at all the data, thinking of it in the context of the questions, and having dialogue amongst a team of researchers. A big part of success is setting up the environment

131

so that it's easy to see all the pieces, get the right people in there, and watch the sparks of insight start flying.

For some questions, the data from the different sources will all be saying the same thing, and you will feel that you have an authoritative answer to the question. In other cases, the outcome will probably be less consistent, and a deeper dive into the nuances of the data will be needed to try to sort it out.

You may also find that the answer to one question is really just the identification of a brand-new question and you need to do some additional research to answer it. Don't take this as a bad sign. If you've ever watched *Columbo* or an episode of *CSI*, you know that very often one clue leads to another clue and then another clue and then finally to the murderer!

Inevitably, not *every* insight from the research process is written down, so it's very valuable to have the people who conducted the research engage in the synthesis process. The group may be struggling to understand a pattern of data when all of a sudden one team member recalls something they heard in a customer interview or saw in a deck that didn't seem all that important at the time but now, in the context of the synthesis, emerges as a potential key piece in the puzzle. Write it on a Post-it and stick it up on the wall.

Synthesis should go on for at least a week or, ideally, a few weeks. Each day that you walk around that room, you may get a fresh insight or make a connection between data points in a new way.

Or your colleague might conceive of half of the answer to a question and tack it up on an index card. A few days after seeing the card, you may wake up in the middle of the night with a theory about the other half. It's part science and part inspiration.

CREATE A DELIVERABLE

Once the answers to the questions are largely in focus, create a deck that restates the goals of the research, the specific questions you sought to answer, and the methodology you used. Then, go through each question, answer the question, and provide the supporting data and its source so it's clear that the answer is research-based. Be honest about which questions have been decisively answered and where the data remains inconclusive. If you have a large amount of supporting material, you may find it's best to give a quick summary of the supporting data and then add an appendix with the gory details.

BONUS TEMPLATE: *To make presenting your customer research easier, we are offering a free PowerPoint template for research summary deliverables on the book website. It's a useful tool for summarizing your research results for a larger audience, so make sure to visit the link here to download it.*

 wdc.ht/RESEARCHPPT

These types of deliverables are invaluable for many purposes. At the same time, they can be somewhat dry and not necessarily a work product that everyone in the organization who needs to understand the customer will *read.* You will also want to produce something a bit more "snack sized" for the masses. In Step 4, we will create visually engaging, easy-to-read customer persona posters for this purpose, but first, we need to define a few more things.

Research Synthesis Step 2:
DEFINE WHAT DIFFERENTIATES
YOUR CUSTOMER SEGMENTS

Now that you have all this insight, it's a good time to ask a critical question: are there changes you want to make to your customer segmentation?

If you followed the approach that we defined at the start of this section on customer research, you identified a number of preliminary dimensions to segment your customers. They may have been age, gender, income, or dimensions specific to your industry, such as whether their business is cash or accrual based, whether their Diabetes is Type 1 or 2, or whether their kitchen countertops are granite or Formica.

As we discussed before, there are an unlimited number of *possible* dimensions, but take time now to revisit this question: what are the most important 5-10 dimensions for your business based on your customer research?

How do you *know* which dimensions are the most important? They are the ones where the answers to your key research questions are *different* depending on the characteristics of the customer on that dimension.

Look at the bands you created on the wall. If your research showed, for example, that people in rural vs urban vs suburban areas don't have any particular differences in how they relate to your research questions, then that dimension may just not be important in your business. But perhaps you discover that whether they rent or own their home is very important, meaning that homeowners have different needs vis-à-vis your customer experience than renters. If so, that sounds like a dimension you will need to focus on.

When we researched customers of theme parks, we learned that the ages of the children of our customers was important because if families had young children, they had very different needs than families with teenagers or families without children.

When we did research for a utility company, we discovered that families with pools in their backyard had some unique and important needs that should be addressed. But whether you have a pool in your backyard has very little bearing on your customer experience as a theme park visitor.

Use the insights you gathered to review the segmentation created prior to the research and modify it as needed. For each prioritized dimension, define the different characteristics you want to distinguish. In our theme park example, we defined the age ranges for children in a family: 0-3, 4-7, 8-12, and 13-18. We determined that a family could have one or more of these characteristics along this dimension since a given family might, for example, have both a 2-year-old and a 12-year-old.

 ## Research Synthesis Step 3: DEFINING WHAT IS COMMON ACROSS YOUR CUSTOMERS

The dimensions of segmentation define what is different across your customers, but it's also important to define what is *similar*.

Of course, all your customers are probably human, so there are many things they have in common. But in this step, we are looking for those characteristics that distinguish *your* customers, as a total population, from everybody else. For example, one might say that Rolex customers tend to be affluent. That's a characteristic that they mostly all share.

In contrast, some Rolex customers may have a more "classic" personal style while others are trendier, so personal style is a key dimension that Rolex needs to keep in mind as something that distinguishes between different segments of their customers. And, indeed, they make some traditional products that follow the Rolex heritage established 100+ years ago, and they make other watches with pictures of Marvel superheroes on them. But in all cases, it's a luxury experience targeting the affluent.

Research Synthesis Step 4:
CREATING A PERSONA

Now that you have defined what is common across your customers based on your research as well as the key differences *between* your customers, you are ready to start drafting personas.

A persona is a fictional character—a composite that represents one of several types of "typical" customers of your business. Each persona will share the characteristics that are common across all your customers and will then have assigned characteristics in each dimension that distinguish them from the other personas. This little family of characters is meant to represent the totality of your customer base and include prototypical combinations of dimensional characteristics.

SAM

AGE: **34**
LOCATION: **CALIFORNIA**
HOUSEHOLD INCOME: **$150K**
PROFESSION: **BUSINESS OWNER**
AVG. MONTHLY BILL: **$150**

ABOUT SAM:

"SAM STARTED RUNNING HIS OWN SEO CONSULTING BUSINESS A FEW YEARS AGO, AND IT IS DOING REALLY WELL. HE IS ALWAYS ON THE MOVE MEETING WITH CLIENTS AND POTENTIAL CLIENTS, AND HE RELIES A LOT ON HIS PHONE TO RESPOND TO EMAILS, CHECK APPOINTMENTS, AND HAVE TELECONFER- ENCES WITH CLIENTS. HE IS HAVING ISSUES WITH HIS CURRENT PROVIDER AND CALLS BEING DROPPED, WHICH IS UNACCEPTABLE FOR HIS BUSINESS."

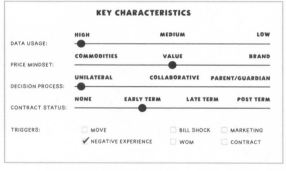

KEY CHARACTERISTICS

	HIGH	MEDIUM	LOW
DATA USAGE:	●		

	COMMODITIES	VALUE	BRAND
PRICE MINDSET:		●	

	UNILATERAL	COLLABORATIVE	PARENT/GUARDIAN
DECISION PROCESS:	●		

	NONE	EARLY TERM	LATE TERM	POST TERM
CONTRACT STATUS:		●		

TRIGGERS:
☐ MOVE   ☐ BILL SHOCK   ☐ MARKETING
✓ NEGATIVE EXPERIENCE   ☐ WOM   ☐ CONTRACT

CHANNEL PREFERENCES

INTERACTION	PREFERRED	SECONDARY
SALES/RENEWAL	FACE TO FACE	ONLINE
BILLING/PAYMENT	WEB	TELEPHONE
PROBLEM	TELEPHONE	WEB

Sample Customer Persona

 wdc.ht/PERSONA

Each persona should be given a memorable name, and the intention is that large numbers of employees can then be "introduced" to these characters to familiarize them with the different types of customers. Once these personas are known around your company, employees can use them as a shorthand. They may say that a given product is specifically "Targeting Tony," or that, "We have to look at the user interface of the checkout process to make sure it works not only for Frieda but also for Raul," who may be two personas with very different characteristics.

There is no magic number of personas, but most companies have ten or fewer. Six or seven is common. We want employees to remember them all.

Once you have defined your personas, it's good to create posters for each one that you can hang in conference rooms, hallways, or wherever employees congregate.

Each poster should show a picture of one of your fictitious characters (you can use a stock photo image) and describe some key findings of your research, such as this customer's needs, hopes, and fears. It can also show the dimensions of your segmentation model and indicate which characteristics of each dimension belong to that persona—the persona's "fingerprint." Your posters may include other bits of information that you decide are important for large groups of people to know, as well.

Some clients have gone as far as creating trading cards of all the personas, giving them out to all employees as a fun way to familiarize them.

You don't want the poster to get too complicated. Each one should be an easy 5-minute read—a gentle starting point for someone just beginning to understand the customer. Those who want to dive in more granularly can review the detailed research synthesis deck we discussed earlier, or even explore the research data itself.

BONUS TEMPLATES: *If you're generating personas, but not sure where to start, visit the book website at the link below to access a number of full-color sample user personas, as well as PowerPoint and Adobe InDesign templates.*

 wdc.ht/PERSONATEMPLATES

MAKING THE MOST OF CUSTOMER RESEARCH

In closing out this section on understanding your customer, I want to summarize a few overarching themes and offer some additional insights to make your research and synthesis as successful as possible.

HUMILITY

Have you ever purchased something expensive that you expected to use all the time, but once you bought it, you played with it only briefly and then never again? The reality is that we don't even know *ourselves* all that well. Acknowledge that it's no small feat to understand someone *else* well enough to predict their future behavior.

GET SPECIFIC

What do you need to know about the potential customers or users of your product that would *really* make a difference? The more precise you can be about what you want to know, the more insight you are likely to gather. Don't be afraid to be very specific; you can always gather insights that go *beyond* the language of your research questions.

BROAD INVOLVEMENT

It's not enough to have a few "market research" people who understand the customer. Ideally, everyone on the product, marketing,

IT and customer experience teams should have tangible insight into their products' users. Just reading someone else's PowerPoint overview doesn't impart a nuanced understanding. If at all possible, have everyone on these teams spend at least a couple of days trailing customers and watching them in their native habitats—or at least have them sit in on a few interviews. This allows the team to internalize the customer's world. Team members always come back from this type of experience full of inspiration and insights that they will keep with them for years.

ITERATION

The world is changing fast, and so are your customers. You have to keep studying them and learn how their needs are evolving or transforming. It never ends.

4D LISTENING

Lastly, when you're studying customers, try to see past the surface of what they're telling you they need. Henry Ford once said, "If I asked my customers what they wanted, they would have said 'faster horses.'" The moral of that story is *not* to avoid speaking to customers, but rather that your customers may not be able to envision the kind of solutions your product team can conceive. So, listen past their stated requests to fully understand their *underlying* concerns and needs. Your customers want to go *faster*, and it is your job to come up with a solution far more practical than breeding faster horses.

. . . .

That wraps up creating research-based personas and, more broadly, conducting customer research. Understanding your customer is foundational to everything you will do in digital transformation—that's why we covered it first and in so much detail.

139

In the next section, we will learn how to take these insights and use them to envision a future experience that will win the love of the customers you have so meticulously sought to understand.

CUSTOMER LOVE DIGITAL TRANSFORMATION FORMULA

ACTIVITY 2:
MAP THE CUSTOMER JOURNEY

CURRENT STATE JOURNEY MAPPING

CH. 10

COMPOSING YOUR FUTURE STATE JOURNEY

CH. 11

Abraham Lincoln once said, "If I had five minutes to chop down a tree, I would spend the first three sharpening my axe." More recently, the apparently more ambitious Albert Einstein said,

"Given one hour to save the planet,
I would spend 59 minutes understanding
the problem and one minute on the solution."

We aren't trying to save the planet here, but we may well be trying to save your company, and we have a little more "axe sharpening" to do. Shortly, we will start creating a vision of your future customer experience, but first we need to map out the *present* experience in some detail.

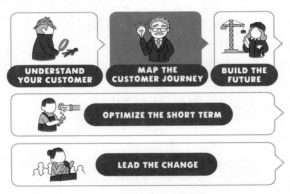

This section of the book presents an approach to customer journey mapping broken into two high-level steps.

 MAP THE CURRENT CUSTOMER JOURNEY (CH. 10): In this chapter we will document how to define the major steps customers go through in the course of their interactions with your brand and how to map out where customers' needs are and are not being met today.

 COMPOSE YOUR FUTURE STATE JOURNEY (CH. 11): Then in Chapter 11, we will draft a new vision of the step-by-step experience for customers, illustrating how previous customer pain points will be transformed and new delight created.

CHAPTER TEN

MAP THE CUSTOMER JOURNEY

CURRENT STATE JOURNEY MAPPING

I recently took an international flight from New York to Beijing. The day before I departed, I went to check in on-line, but I received an error from the airline's website that stated that because I was on an international flight, my passport needed to be verified before checking in, and that this had to be done in the app, not via the website. I decided to deal with it later.

The next morning, as I was Ubering to Newark Airport with my teenage daughter (and travel companion), Rachel, I figured it would be a good time to get it done.

I launched the app on my phone. It immediately recognized that I was about to take a flight and prompted me to check in. Great! Proactive personalization.

It told me that in order to check in, it needed to use my phone's camera to scan my passport. Sure! Cool.

Then, it instructed me to hold the passport so that it filled the window. I did as I was told and could see the passport on the screen, but the app didn't "recognize" the passport. I tried several times.

I held the passport farther away. I held it closer. I tried it sideways. I tried when the car was stopped at a light and not moving. I leaned away from the car window thinking maybe there was too much light. I shifted forward toward the windshield thinking maybe there wasn't *enough* light.

After about five minutes of fiddling, and for no particular reason I could discern, it finally "read" my passport. Hurrah! It then told me it had to "process" the passport image, which could take as much as five *more* minutes, and it gave me a progress bar.

Finally, it said my scan was accepted. Whew! It asked me if I wanted to save the passport to "my record" for future travel. "Yes!" I don't want to go through that again!

But since both my daughter and I were on the same reservation, I actually *did* have to go through that again. Next, it prompted me to scan *her* passport. I kind of hoped that maybe I'd "gotten the hang" of the scanning thing since I had finally succeeded in getting my own passport to scan. But I was giving myself too much credit. I had to spend the same 3-5 minutes showing the camera my daughter's passport from every angle before finally, mysteriously, it suddenly scanned hers. Same deal: 3-5 minute "processing time." "Yes," I wanted to save *her* passport information, as well. It seemed like victory was at hand.

The next screen said, "Please scan your visa for travel to China." (A visa is a piece of paperwork indicating you have official permission to visit a foreign country). Ugh, more scanning! But wait, I didn't *have* a visa for China. Why? Because we were only stopping in China on our way to Vietnam. Here's a fun trivia fact: you don't need an advance visa if you are going to be in China for less than six days. I was only going to be in Beijing for just over 24 hours: a quick visit to show my daughter the Great Wall and the Forbidden City and then on to Vietnam.

Thoughtfully, there was a button labeled, "I don't have a visa." I tapped that, and it told me that *if* I don't have a visa, I can't use the app to check in and have to visit the counter at the airport. The exact thing I was trying to avoid. Twenty minutes spent on this endeavor. Customer love level = low.

By now we were arriving at the airport. There was a line at the counter, but an open self-service kiosk. I entered my frequent flyer number to identify myself. It knew I was flying to China and told me that to check in, I need to...guess what? To scan my passport and my daughter's. So much for saving them to "my record" for future travel.

Then, of course, it asks me for a visa. I push a button indicating that I don't have one and that triggers a flashing light on the top of the kiosk and a caution symbol on the screen. I've been caught! My daughter looks nervous and is worried that we may be in trouble for not having a visa. A few moments later, an agent comes over in response to the warning light. I explain my situation, and she nods knowingly, waves her badge at the kiosk's sensor, and navigates to some top-secret admin screen. She overrides the problem, and it prints my boarding pass. Done. Rachel sighs with relief. Now hold that thought.

. . . .

WHAT IS CURRENT STATE JOURNEY MAPPING?

In 2017, Macy's posted their first year-over-year increase in financial results in eleven quarters following a major journey mapping project and associated implementation. Speaking at a conference at

145

the time, CEO Jeffrey Gennette said this about the process: "We did a forensic mapping of the customer journey. We looked at every step of the way. There were things [our customer] *did* love about Macy's, but there were things that they didn't. We had created major pain points all along the journey… What we heard from customers was a wake-up call. We broke down our journey. At each step, we identified what was working and what wasn't. This led us to the creation and launch of our [now successful]…strategy."[1]

All companies, including Macy's and my airline to China, have good experiences *and* points of pain as part of their current state customer journey. In the airline's case, following our check-in, things got much better. Rachel and I breezed through security, thanks in part to TSA Pre-Check, and we had the opportunity to have lunch at the airline's awesome business class lounge, where we were treated like kings. On the flight to Beijing, I streamed their on-demand entertainment options through that very same app on my iPad with no issues, and we arrived in China twenty minutes early and in great spirits.

Current state journey mapping is about getting clear on all these experiences: the awesome ones that wow your customers, the middle-of-the-road ones, and the bad ones, with all their warts, glitches, and points of frustration. Once this is done and analyzed, you will be in a position to start envisioning the *future,* which we will move on to in the next chapter.

Journey maps tell the story of how your customers are solving their needs today and reveal which needs are going unmet. They show how technology is impacting their experience, how they become aware of solutions like yours, how they shop, how they buy, and how they consume. They describe all the touchpoints that your customers use as part of their journey, such as: web, mobile, call centers, stores, printed materials, search engines, and social media. And they highlight where customers are being delighted and where they are being let down.

WHY DO WE WANT TO KNOW ALL THIS?

If we are going to completely redo the customer experience anyway, why is it so important to document and analyze it? Why don't we just "get going" on the future?

Well, for one reason, if your ultimate goal is to create a world-class customer experience, you will be creating it by transforming *from* what you have today into whatever that future vision is. If you want to plot a course, it's just as important to know where you are *now* as to know where you want to go.

But there are other reasons, as well. I remember once giving a major presentation to the CEO and top executives of a large vacation resort who had hired us to improve their customer experience. We presented the *future* vision of how the guest booking process should work. We explained how the guest would have the ability to search for rooms across all the properties, how their preferences would be remembered, how the transaction would be completed in just two clicks, and how they could return anytime and adjust their booking easily.

The CEO listened carefully and then, at the end, asked skeptically, "But isn't this pretty much how it works already?"

In fact, no. Not at all. The existing process at the time was clunky and disconnected. The search worked on only one property at a time, and the experience was not at all personalized. Once a booking was created, you could change it only via a call to the call center.

In the interest of being concise for the CEO, we had just "cut to the chase" of the future vision, but his question showed why that had been a mistake.

Of course, the pain of the "current state" was not the CEO's *personal* experience because when *he* wanted a room at one of his resorts, he just told his assistant, then she handled the rest. This isn't a criticism of him or any other CEO. Most senior executives simply don't "experience" the customer experience of their own brand, even when they *think* they are acting as a customer. In order to make good decisions, senior executives need to be educated. So, when creating a burning platform for change, it's important to be able to articulate clearly "how it works today."

And it's not just senior executives who don't understand the full customer experience. The truth is that in most companies, *nobody* does because even people who use the digital properties with regularity still do so in the context of their own individual situations.

For example, it could be that many employees of the airline I flew to China use the online check-in process all the time, but they just don't happen to be traveling to China without a visa. As a result, they aren't aware of the scenario described earlier. The check-in process may work just fine *for them*.

Even the people who are responsible for building and maintaining the customer experience rarely work on the *whole* customer experience. More often, people are working in one area—in ordering or fulfillment or marketing or inventory—so they don't have the holistic view either.

This is why, before beginning the future state work, we will document the current state journey.

. . . .

IT'S ALL ABOUT THE PAIN

It's important to understand what is *good* in your customer's current journey to ensure you don't "mess it up" as you create your new vision. But it's even more valuable to understand the areas where customers are having to exert a lot of effort or are experiencing "pain" in their current journeys. These areas of pain are the best opportunities for you to create a differentiated offering.

Look at any successful company today and you will see that they are in the "pain solving" business. Amazon solved the pain of not being able to find the book you want at your local bookstore, as well as the pain of having to drive to get it. Though they created a journey that added the pain of having to wait for the book to arrive in the mail. Now they are working hard to remove *that* pain by shortening the delivery times down to two days, then to one day, and, in some markets, they are now offering same-day delivery.

Google solved the pain of not being able to find things on the web. Uber solved the pain of not being able to hail a taxi or having a long wait for a car service. Facebook solved the pain of losing touch with friends. Skype solved the pain of expensive long-distance calls. The iPod solved the pain of having to decide what CDs to take with you.

If you can find the pain in your customer's current experience, you have identified a potential opportunity that, if you can solve it, might be a gold mine.

THE TWO TYPES OF PAIN

A useful way to distinguish the "points of pain" you discover is in terms of two categories that we call blame pain and accepted pain.

BLAME PAIN

Blame pain comes from failed expectations—negative experiences that customers have, which they "blame" on the brand with which they are interacting.

If I go to the store and the line to check out takes 30 minutes, that creates blame pain. I blame the store because I *believe* they shouldn't make me wait that long. If you are creating that kind of pain regularly for customers, you probably want to do something about it, since every minute that customers suffer and blame you creates negative emotions associated with your brand. Those negative feelings will drive future action and maybe even present action. I've occasionally walked out of stores that made me wait too long, leaving full shopping carts behind *with stuff I needed in them*.

ACCEPTED PAIN

In contrast, Amazon's new "brick & mortar" convenience stores—called Amazon Go—use optical sensors to detect what you put in your basket. Once you are done shopping, you can walk out of the store with *no check out whatsoever*. That goes the other direction. I have "accepted pain" that when I go to a store, I will need to check out. I *don't* "expect" it to take 30 minutes, but I "accept" that it will probably take 5-10 minutes. When, all of a sudden, it takes zero minutes, I am delighted. In fact, people will travel across town to buy a fairly ordinary sandwich at an Amazon Go store just for the "fun" of not having to check out. And that's the difference between the two types of pain.

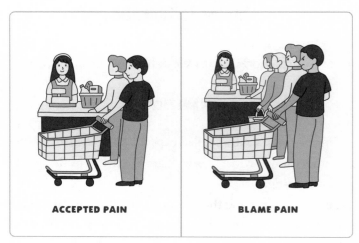

ACCEPTED PAIN   BLAME PAIN

wdc.ht/TWOTYPES

WHEN YOU **RELIEVE BLAME PAIN,** YOU AVOID NEGATIVE EMOTIONS. WHEN YOU **RELIEVE ACCEPTED PAIN,** YOU CREATE POSITIVE EMOTIONS.

‹ wdc.ht/POSITIVE

Which is more important? Well, in the recent book *The Power of Moments,* Chip and Dan Heath detail their studies on the impact of solving pain and creating delight. They conclude that, while businesses that are creating profound pain for customers need to deal with that first, in most cases, creating new "moments of delight" is more powerful at improving long-term satisfaction than removing inconveniences or annoyances.

But clearly, both are important, so before we start envisioning the future state, we want to be sure we have a good understanding of the current areas of pain because that's where a lot of the opportunities are.

 BONUS TRAINING VIDEO: *How you set your customer's expectations can have a lot to do with how they feel about any inconveniences or frustrations. On the book website, we've provided a video on how you can increase customer satisfaction by "Shifting Pain Perception." Check it out at the link provided.*

▶ wdc.ht/PERCEPTION

151

STEPS TO CURRENT STATE JOURNEY MAPPING

So, let's get started on our current state journey mapping. This chapter will provide an approach in four steps.

DEFINE EXPERIENCE STAGES

RESEARCH EXPERIENCES

DOCUMENT THE CURRENT JOURNEY

PRIORITIZE THE IMPACT

 wdc.ht/MAP

Current State Journey Mapping Step 1: DEFINE EXPERIENCE STAGES

The initial step of mapping out your customer's current experience is to break it down into a workable number of "stages." Most generically, customers go through a process of engaging with a brand that's something like this:

There is a *trigger*—something causes them to have a *need*. Their old car might break down, so they need a new one. Their granddaughter is turning four, so they need a gift. Their pants are too tight, so they need some new pants (or a treadmill).

What do they do next? They *search* for a solution. They may ask friends, use Google, browse a department store, read some advice blogs, etc. This typically leads them to some options.

Then they shift to *shopping*—they compare prices, features, and other factors of different alternatives they've identified in order to make a decision.

They then move into a *purchasing* experience. If it's a car, they may need to arrange financing. If it's a book, they may need to enter a credit card number. If it's life insurance, they may need to take a blood test.

The product is then fulfilled or delivered in some way and they "*use*" what they have purchased. Usage can have different sub-stages. For example, it may be a product that they need to assemble or learn to operate. If it's a cruise vacation, they may have usage sub-stages of the journey like embarking the ship, getting oriented, and departing.

"Using" can also include the need for *support* if they have a question or a problem.

And lastly, if they are happy with their experience, hopefully, they *share* their opinion with friends, either in person or on social media. These steps are shown in the diagram below.

Customer Experience Stages

 wdc.ht/STAGES

You might notice one additional element, which is the initial input, labeled "brand engagement" in the diagram. Brand engagement refers to the thoughts and feelings a customer has about a given

153

company prior to the triggered need. These thoughts and feelings influence the speed and manner with which the customer moves through the other stages of the cycle.

For example, my 25th wedding anniversary is approaching. I have a lot of trust and brand engagement with a particular jewelry store. That brand engagement gives me momentum coming into the process. I may do less searching and shopping because I go right to that store and take their recommendations.

Another part of that brand engagement is that I have an account set up at this jewelry store, so my transaction process is smooth and rapid. As a result, I move quickly to "using," whereas someone with limited brand engagement around jewelry might spend weeks looking at different stores trying to find a reliable source of advice.

This is why many companies spend a lot of money on advertising to get you enthusiastic about their brand, to get you to connect to them on Facebook, or set up an account, *even* if you aren't ready to buy anything from them right now. Their hope is that when a trigger occurs, you will immediately think of them and accelerate your journey to purchase.

This is epitomized by a billboard near my house advertising the excellent care available at the emergency room of a local hospital. Hopefully, very few people driving by on a given day are looking for an emergency room *at that moment*. But the hospital wants to create brand engagement so that when that trigger occurs—when you throw out your back or your kid gets bonked in the head at softball practice—you think of them first.

Now, of course, this set of journey stages is just a generic outline. It will vary by industry, and a first step in doing current state journey mapping is to draft out what the experiential stages are for *your* business.

For example, in the rental car industry, you might define a stage specific to returning the car. We worked with Gulfstream, a private jet manufacturer. Their customer journey typically involves a price negotiation process, a step that isn't present in most retail transactions. Then, after the contract is signed, there is a lengthy process of working with Gulfstream's amazing designers to select your aircraft's custom interior fixtures and furnishings—something that is a key journey stage for buying a private jet or a custom home but would clearly not apply to buying Froot Loops.

Renewal, repurchase, and loyalty should also fit into your experience stages. If you loved your last Nikon camera, then, when a trigger occurs indicating it's time for a new one—perhaps it accidentally takes a swim in the deep end of your pool—you are going to have a lot of momentum toward the latest Nikon model. But the sequence of that trigger being followed by a searching and shopping process work in pretty much the same way for repurchase as they do for an initial purchase.

In other industries, though, such as auto insurance or magazine subscriptions, you may want a specific stage relating to renewal because the renewal experience is fundamentally different from the *purchase* experience.

Take some time and map out what you believe the stages of *your* customer journey are. You probably have enough knowledge of your business to take a pretty good first stab, and you have the insights gathered from your customer research to help guide you, as well.

In the next step of the journey mapping process, you will conduct some additional research and use those additional insights to further refine your model of the journey stages.

Current State Journey Mapping Step 2:
RESEARCH THE EXPERIENCE

Once we have blocked out these large stages, it's time to map our customer's current experiences in each of them. How do we know what they are? Research.

In the previous section of the book, we talked at length about a wide range of research techniques. Thus, we won't discuss *specific* research techniques very much in this chapter since many of the same tools used to research customer personas can be applied to researching customer journeys. It's just that the research questions are different. For example, you will define questions like:

1. How are customers finding your company today?

2. What steps are they going through to make a decision about whether to do business with you (or someone else)?

3. How do they determine exactly which product or level of service to order?

4. What is their experience when actually placing an order? What problems do they encounter, and what do they do about them?

5. What happens when they experience your product or services? What is good or bad about it?

6. What occurs when they need help or support?

7. Do they advocate to others that they should do business with you? Why or why not?

Once you tailor these research questions to your company, you can apply the toolkit of research techniques described in Chapters 7-9 to answer them.

It may well be that, by the time you reach this stage, your prior customer research has already addressed many of these questions and all that is needed is to analyze the existing data in the context of this task. In which case, wonderful—less work.

You may also find that, once you set out to document the current journey in detail, there are some missing pieces and more research is warranted. That's fine too. The truth is that customer research is a never-ending process and there will always be new questions. That's why companies that are succeeding in winning their customers' love generally have standing research teams that are continuously looking at different aspects of the customer and their experience.

GATHERING CUSTOMER JOURNEY STORIES

"Journeys" are really just stories, like my international airline example. They have a hero or protagonist (the customer, generally) and a goal. Protagonists use different strategies to try to accomplish their objectives, hit different obstacles, and, in the end, are either successful or not.

A good strategy during customer journey research is to ask subjects to tell you *their* stories—to walk you through their recent experiences. Aggregating these examples of specific experiences will enable you to start drafting a set of maps that represent "typical" journeys. In many ways, it's like the personas you created in Chapter 9—you conducted quantitative and qualitative research and learned enough about a large pool of customers that you were able to construct a set of representative *characters* to summarize your learnings.

Now, we will create a set of *stories* that represent the most important, prototypical customer journeys that these characters experience.

BROADEN YOUR VIEW OF THE JOURNEY

A critical point to remember about journeys is that they are the *customer's* journey, not necessarily the story of the customer's journey with just your brand.

The way I prefer to think about it is that each of our customers and prospects are *already* on a journey (or a bunch of journeys focusing on different aspects of their life). Events occur in their lives that trigger goals and they then pursue those goals. Those are *their* journeys, whether your company exists or not. The purpose of a journey mapping exercise is to understand the journey that our customer is already on—what their current strategies and experiences are and how our current touchpoints do or don't fit into them effectively.

Our goal will ultimately be to figure out how we can add as much value as possible to that customer's journey, with the expectation that by doing so, we will be able to receive more value in return.

My company once conducted a study for a retail chain about how consumers shop for gifts. We learned about the methods customers use to determine *who* to give gifts to, how they figure out *what* to give, and the various sources they use to search for and acquire gifts, such as catalogs, stores, online, and their own closets as part of the practice of "re-gifting."

The journey we mapped went all the way through wrapping and presenting gifts. The brand we were working for played a part in that larger journey, but there were many parts where the brand was not involved. Nevertheless, understanding the full picture is very valuable for many reasons—for crafting resonant marketing messages, for enhancing the offer to better align with customers' larger needs, and for identifying new business opportunities.

The idea for the creation of the original iPod came out of a project focused on how the Macintosh computer could help customers organize their library of music files across various hard drives, CDs, and other media. Steve Jobs' insight into the larger customer journey helped him realize that there was an opportunity beyond the computer. While customers did not *expect* their Mac to put "10,000 songs in their pocket," it became clear that if Apple could solve the "music portability problem," they would be removing customer pain and creating new business opportunities.

So, if you are looking at the journey of ordering a birthday cake, consider also looking at the broader journey of planning a birthday party. If you are looking at the journey of filing taxes, consider looking at the broader journey of personal financial planning.

FOCUS ON UNDERSTANDING THE CUSTOMER'S EMOTIONAL LANDSCAPE

When researching, seek to uncover the *emotional* journeys customers are on, not just their actions. Emotions are the most important factor in driving behavior, including the behaviors that align with our business success, such as purchases, renewals, up-sells, or customer self-service.

As we have said, users begin their journey because they have a trigger that creates a need—they want to order a gift for their grandmother, pay a bill, download a movie, or post a photo to social media—and our objective should be to streamline their path to fulfilling this need.

But, if you really want to most effectively influence customer behavior, focus beyond just the raw "task" to the *feeling* the customer is *really* seeking to fulfill. Yes, they go to the vending machine to buy the candy bar, that's the task, but the *real* need—what the customer really wants—is the feeling of comfort they get from eating a candy bar, or perhaps the *feeling* of indulging themselves, or even just the pure sugar rush. But whichever it is, a *feeling* is the real goal.

AS THE BAND JOURNEY SINGS IN THE SONG "DON'T STOP BELIEVIN'," "PEOPLE ARE, "LIVING JUST TO FIND EMOTION."

Current State Journey Mapping Step 3:
DOCUMENT THE CUSTOMER JOURNEY

Current state journeys can be documented in various ways. One method is to use process flows that indicate typical paths and flag which parts of the experience work well and where there is pain. Some journeys flow in a straight path, but most have branching, like the example below.

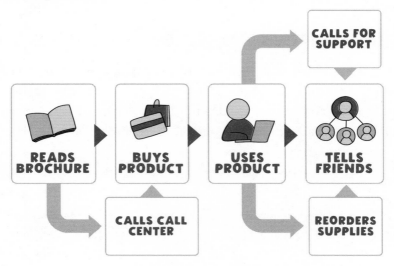

Customer Journey with Branching

‹ wdc.ht/BRANCHING

A richer style of documentation involves writing a set of narrative stories where the protagonists are your user personas. The stories then follow those characters as they move through a series of interactions that track to the stages of the customer journey you've defined (shopping, purchase, usage, etc.)

These stories can be presented as posters or banners to communicate the current state in a more engaging way than a dry flow diagram might.

One final format we find useful is what we call a "Pain Map." This is a banner divided into the stages of the customer journey, and it lists the top points of pain you discovered for each stage.

RESERVATION	DEPARTURE	FLYING
HAVING TO RE-ENTER FLIGHT DETAILS MULTIPLE TIMES	WAITING IN LINE TO CHECK IN	TURBULENC
HAVING TROUBLE FIGURING OUT LAYOVER TIMES	PAYING EXTRA TO CHECK BAGS	POOR SELEC
HAVING TROUBLE COMPARING PRICES	WAITING IN LINE AT GATE FOR A LONG TIME	NO LEGROOM
HAVING FREQUENT FLYER NUMBER REJECTED	BEING NOTIFIED OF DELAYS RIGHT BEFORE SCHEDULED DEPARTURE	CAN'T FIND THE
DECIPHERING HIDDEN FEES	HAVING NO ROOM FOR BAGS IN THE OVERHEAD	AISLES TOO SM

Example Pain Map (Partial)

 ‹ wdc.ht/PMAP

We created a Pain Map for one company, and their Global Head of Digital Customer Experience printed it as a banner that came out over 12 feet long. He hung it on his wall. When guests came to his corner office and asked what it was, he responded, "It's my 'to-do' list." And he meant it.

 BONUS TEMPLATES: *The diagrams that we show in the book don't give a full sense of what a complete pain map looks like. On the book website, we have provided a PDF of a full-size color example, as well as Microsoft PowerPoint and Adobe InDesign templates, to make it easier for you to create your own.* wdc.ht/PAINTEMPLATE

VISUALIZING OMNICHANNEL

Today, most customer journeys are omnichannel, meaning that customers engage with a brand in multiple ways, often even within the lifecycle of a single purchase.

They may learn about a product on their phone while swiping through Instagram, then go to their laptop and look up reviews. They might *then* show up at a store to see the item in person, order the exact color they want from an in-store kiosk, and have it delivered. While they wait for delivery, they might get updates via email or SMS. When they receive the product, they may have a question and use a Facebook bot, LivePerson chat or a call center to answer it. The number of ways companies interact with their customers seems to just keep growing, and customers are using them all.

It can be helpful to create visualizations to communicate what you have learned in your research about how different customer segments use different touchpoints and whether some touchpoints are more frequently used at different stages of the customer journey. Here is an example showing an analysis we did for one client.

	AWARENESS	SEARCHING	SHOPPING	PURCHASE	EXPERIENCING	SHARING
WEBSITE	●	●	●	●	●	●
APP	●	●	●	●	●	●
SOCIAL/ SF VIDEO	●	●	●		●	●
RETAIL STORE	●	●	●	●	●	
EXT. DISTRIB. RETAIL STORES	●	●	●	●	●	
EMAIL	●	●	●	●	●	●

Mapping Touchpoints to Journey Stages

 ‹ wdc.ht/CHANNELS

The diagram provides an "at-a-glance" way to understand to what degree each customer touchpoint is utilized at each step of the purchase process. The size of each circle indicates how popular that touchpoint is for customers in each stage of the buying lifecycle. This is useful in many ways. For example, when working on a given touchpoint, such as the website or catalog, it's helpful to know how customers are really using it, so you can focus content or capability improvements in a way that aligns with customer behavior.

 ## Current State Journey Mapping Step 4:
PRIORITIZE

Your current state map will no doubt highlight many opportunities for you to improve the customer's experience; that's the core goal. But in many cases, it seems to do its job a little too well, and the breadth of opportunity to make things better can feel overwhelming. You won't be able to fix every problem and pursue every avenue for customer delight all at once. So, you need a method to prioritize these points of pain and decide where to start.

We typically do analysis to measure each point of pain on three criteria and then use a scoring model to create an aggregate "pain score." That score is then plotted against an "effort" score which correlates to the level of cost and attention it will take to "fix" a given problem. Naturally, the most exciting opportunities are those that are creating a lot of pain and are easy to fix. There are usually a few of those; they're the "no brainers." The ones with high effort but relatively *low* impact are similarly easy to say "no" to. After that, it's a matter of deciding what level of ambition you want to undertake— whether to focus on some easier, medium-impact items, or to tackle the big hairy ones that have the potential to have a huge impact, or to look at a combination.

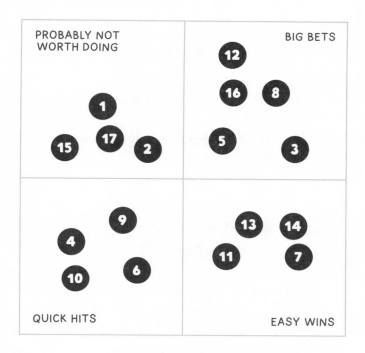

PLOTTING IMPACT vs EFFORT

IMPACT

Plotting Impact vs Effort

 < wdc.ht/MATRIX

THE THREE CRITERIA OF PAIN PRIORITIZATION

The three criteria we use to prioritize the potential "impact" of each item of pain are as follows:

- **CRITERIA 1:** SEVERITY
  How bad is the problem? Just a minor inconvenience? A major hassle? A relationship-ending crisis?

- **CRITERIA 2:** FREQUENCY
  How often does this problem actually occur? Is it something that happens to customers daily? Yearly? Does it impact all customers or only a percentage?

- **CRITERIA 3:** SEGMENT VALUE

  Does it impact any segment disproportionately? If so, what is the value of that segment? All things being equal, if you have two problems that each impact 10% of your customers, but one primarily impacts your *best* customers, that's going to make it a higher priority.

Other considerations include whether the issue might create any significant legal or reputation risk for the company, as well as what type of emotional reaction it prompts in customers. Earlier in this chapter, we discussed how customers "blame" brands differently for different problems. They can also have different emotional reactions ranging from confusion to frustration to anger. Different emotions influence behavior differently, and these considerations can also factor into prioritization.

Once you have scored each of the areas of pain or opportunity, you can visualize them using a four-quadrant chart like the example shown, or create a sorted list. Of course, there will always be more factors than can be included in a mathematical model, so final decisions should be made with human instinct, not by a sorting algorithm. However, the scoring is a supremely valuable tool to help decision makers better organize the key factors that should influence their decisions.

BONUS TOOL: *To help you prioritize your customer pain items, we've provided a free Excel spreadsheet with formulas that we use to score and sort customer pain items by cost and impact.*

wdc.ht/SORTPAIN

. . . .

*Once you complete the activities in this chapter, you should have a much clearer perspective on the current experience of your various customer segments as they move through the defined stages of your customer journey. You should also have a sense of their greatest points of pain and the priorities of these different problems. Your pain map will do a lot to help bring into focus what you do **not** want the customer experience to be. In the next chapter, we will focus on what we **do** want it to be.*

CHAPTER ELEVEN

MAP THE CUSTOMER JOURNEY

COMPOSING YOUR FUTURE STATE JOURNEY

I recently received an email offering 50% off photo prints at Walgreens. I had taken some cute pictures of my nine-year-old daughter Samantha's dance recital, and the offer persuaded me to have some 5x7s made. I tapped the email link on my phone, and it launched the Walgreens app, which was already installed because I use it to renew prescriptions.

I selected some ballet and tap dance shots from my phone's photo gallery, which was integrated right into the app. Easy. My credit card

was already on file. My closest Walgreens, based on my current coordinates, was defaulted as the pick-up location.

I received a text 45 minutes later confirming the prints were ready, and I drove the short distance to the store to pick them up. I parked right near the entrance. There was no line. The photos *were* ready. I reached for my credit card, but the clerk reminded me they were prepaid and handed them right to me with a smile. As I walked out of the store, I started paging through my photos and it was then that I noticed...they looked great.

A successful customer journey. If a friend asked me whether I'd recommend Walgreens to print their snapshots, I'd say absolutely. It was hyper-convenient, it was at a great price, and it was effectively personalized—they targeted me with a good offer and had my credit card and closest store saved. To be honest, short of making up for my photography skills, I'm not really sure what they could have done better.

So that's a great digital journey. And I have them *all the time*, with FedEx, with Dominos, and with HBO, among others. I mention these companies in particular because none of them were "born digital." There was a time when each *didn't* deliver a delightful digital journey. But they created a vision for the experience they wanted to deliver, they effectively aligned it with the needs of their customers, and they successfully executed it without being Google, Amazon, or Uber. If these large, legacy companies can do it, so can you.

In this chapter, we'll take the insights you gathered from your current state journey mapping work, as well as other sources of inspiration, and start envisioning and documenting your future.

WHAT IS A FUTURE STATE JOURNEY MAP?

In the previous chapter, we reviewed how to craft a *current state* journey map, and no doubt that process highlighted a variety of points of pain within your current customer journey.

BUT GREAT CUSTOMER JOURNEYS AREN'T JUST BAD CUSTOMER JOURNEYS WITH A BUNCH OF THINGS PATCHED UP.

 wdc.ht/PATCH

Most of the time, they involve transformational changes that deliver the customer a fundamentally different experience, at least in key respects.

Future state journey maps are a tool used to document the vision you want to move toward—a "North Star" ambition of the way the future customer should experience your brand through all the stages of your journey lifecycle, from awareness to shopping to purchase and beyond—the combination of which will inspire customer love.

Because, as we have said, today's consumers don't believe what you *say* about your brand. They believe in the experience your brand delivers. If your brand *can't* deliver a fantastic experience, it quickly becomes irrelevant to most of today's digital customers.

When you have a clear vision of what the future experience should be, you will be in a strong position to start determining what transformation is needed not only for user experience, but also for technology, data, business processes, and potentially your fundamental business model.

169

CUSTOMER JOURNEYS ARE TOOLS FOR STORYTELLING

As discussed in the previous chapter, customer journeys are stories. Stories start with a character and then quickly focus around a conflict or goal. In most journey stories, your customer (the main character) is *on* a journey because they have some sort of unmet need, which is a conflict for them. They have an upcoming work vacation and need to book a trip. The school year is starting, but their kids don't yet have back-to-school supplies. It's 90 degrees, and the air conditioner is not working correctly. While these might not seem as dramatic as Darth Vader powering up the Death Star to destroy the universe, they are very often just as important to your customers in the moment.

So, what *happens* in these customer journey stories as your hero tries to solve their dilemma? Well, the main character may view your ad, then browse your site, sign up for your social channels, and see a post that leads them to your retail store. Once there, they may interact with your salesperson and buy your product. When they get home, they may call your support center for help, access the product manual from their mobile phone, and reorder supplies for their purchase via Alexa voice commands. A thousand other variations are possible, but those are the types of "scenes" that make up your story.

When you created the *current state* customer journey in the previous chapter, you were acting as a sort of journalist, gathering the research, analyzing it, and documenting the current reality.

But now you have a chance to be a *novelist* and write the story the way you believe it *should* be. The story that will deliver an experience that inspires the thoughts and feelings that you know from your research are aligned with desired business outcomes. The story that will generate customer love.

All stories have a beginning, a middle, and an end. What happens at the end of *your* story? The end should be the resolution of the need, at least for now, hopefully via a great purchase and usage experience with a massive positive impact on the customer's perception of your brand.

And like many great movies, customer journeys often have sequels. After all, a customer's lifetime experience with a brand is hopefully a *series* of stories, each involving a problem and a ultimate resolution. On another day, another need arises. Another vacation to plan, another year of school supplies, another household appliance on the fritz, another car to trade in, another broken bone to have x-rayed. And, of course, if you gave them a great experience the last time around the circle, they are far more likely to just come right back to you again—what we referred to in Chapter 10 as "brand engagement."

. . . .

THE ACTUAL FUTURE STATE JOURNEY MAP DELIVERABLE

Let's start with the end in mind, as Stephen Covey advises in his classic book *The 7 Habits of Highly Effective People.* Then after we lay that out, we will walk through the process of getting there.

What will a set of future state journey maps look like when you are finished? Typically, we write 5-10 primary stories that represent the key customer experiences. In each of these stories, the main character will be one of your personas. However, that's not to say that the components of a given scenario will apply only to one persona; the persona is just the example protagonist in the story.

Each story is then composed of a series of interactions or "scenes." We usually find that 8-15 is a good range of scenes in a given story and is sufficient to describe an initial situation, the process the customer uses to look for alternatives, their experience making a final decision, transacting, receiving the product or service, using it, and ultimately resolving their need. Of course, not every story has those exact steps. Some stories may zoom in and focus on a very detailed customer service situation, for example, but the rule of thumb of 8-15 scenes is usually still applicable.

And even when a journey attempts to show a "full lifecycle," no one story can include every aspect of the total experience you offer customers. The range of possible interactions is too vast. But you should aim to showcase all the most important touchpoints and features somewhere across the complete set of stories. The most *important* ones are those that are transforming—the areas where you are either solving a current point of pain or creating some new experience of delight.

Of course, in the real world, each customer's experience and path will be unique. Not everyone will go through all the steps you describe. Some will move forward and then back. Some will exit partway through. The duration spent at each step can vary, and there will be many situations and circumstances not contemplated in the journey maps.

But the journey maps are not the only tools that document the requirements on which you will base your new experience. Rather, they represent a high-level vision articulated so that a broad group of people can get the "general idea" of the intended future experience.

Once the basic copywriting of each journey map is completed, add images to provide a visual component to the story and then print or plot a giant banner that shows the stages of the story with narration and pictures.

Sketch of a Future State Journey Map

⟨ wdc.ht/JMAP

When read, these journey maps should provide a clear description of how the customer interacts with your brand.

They should be specific. They should be visionary. They may also be a bit daunting, because the gap between where you are now and the vision you describe may be large. That's ok. The future state journey is meant to be your company's North Star.

 BONUS TEMPLATES: *The journey map example above is just a small portion of the final product you'll be creating. To see a full version of a journey map, check out the book website at the link below. You'll also find PowerPoint and InDesign Templates that you can use to jump start your own journey map creation.*

⤓ wdc.ht/FUTUREMAP

Ok, so that's *what* we are creating. *How* do we go about it? Here's a nine-step process to get it done.

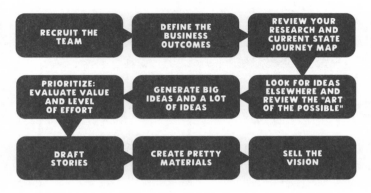

9 Steps to Create Future State Journey Maps

‹ wdc.ht/9STEPS

Future State Journey Mapping Step 1:
RECRUIT THE TEAM

It's important to have a group of at least 4-5 people assigned to draft the future state journey maps, and it's best to have much larger groups collaborate on them. We often run workshops with 30-40 people for several days to do this type of work.

The team should possess diverse skills, including user experience, operations, marketing, and IT. Preferably, involve some team members whose experience includes extensive face time with the customer, as well as those with a solid understanding of what it takes to implement new capabilities in your various touchpoints and systems.

While it can be very fruitful to use intense working sessions, such as a multi-day workshop, to draft journeys, you will most likely want to continue to iterate them over a period of at least a few weeks, depending on the complexity and the number of stakeholders.

Future State Journey Mapping Step 2:
DEFINE THE BUSINESS OUTCOMES

What outcomes are we seeking by transforming the customer's experience? Based on what we've discussed so far, you might assume that it's a reduction in customer pain or an increase in customer love. We *do want those,* but all that is just a means to an end. The ultimate outcome is some quantifiable *value,* which is what owners of businesses expect their investments to yield. Optimally, the way the business does that is by creating more value for their customers.

Therefore, before we start ideating, we should get very clear on the specific value-creating *behaviors* we want from our customers. This is because the task of designing the future state journey is really the task of engineering an experience that will drive the thoughts and feelings that will *lead* to those behaviors, so we need to know what our target is.

Even if you have a pretty good idea of what you want, for example, "More customers to buy more stuff," it's good to periodically review and make sure you are clear on *all* of the "value-creating behaviors" in which your customers could *potentially* engage.

Looking at this fresh allows you to identify possible new opportunities. It may be that you are focused on the most obvious value-creating behaviors but not on other more subtle behaviors, which, if increased, could amplify the total customer value to your enterprise. As you think through value-generating behaviors that you want to encourage, you may also find it helpful to consider any value-*destroying* behaviors that you want to *diminish,* since discouraging undesirable customer behavior can also create value for your business.

Here are four major categories and common subcategories of customer behaviors that create value. Of course, there may be variations within any given industry.

Behavioral Outcome Category 1:
MARKETING RELATED BEHAVIORS

We often think that generating value from the customer starts when the customer gives us their credit card, but the opportunity begins long before that. There are various behaviors that customers can engage in to make it easier or less expensive for us to market to them as we move them toward a sale. These include "opting in," connecting to your brand on social media, requesting free samples of your products, and visiting your locations.

Behavioral Outcome Category 2:
PURCHASE BEHAVIORS

Purchase behaviors are the ones we tend to think of first when it comes to creating value. However, there are several distinct subcategories that are important to consider, as they may need to be motivated differently from the basic buying behavior. Here are seven subcategories of purchase behaviors: becoming a customer, being upsold to a more expensive product, being cross-sold a related product, renewing, purchasing directly (versus via a higher cost channel), *not* returning or canceling the product, and *not* trying to "shop around" or haggle on price.

Behavioral Outcome Category 3:
PROMOTIONAL BEHAVIORS

The most powerful form of marketing is word of mouth. There are multiple ways your customers can create value by helping promote your brand and products. These can include referring friends, lobbying retailers to stock your product, and creating content or reviews for social sites or commerce properties.

Behavioral Outcome Category 4:
USAGE BEHAVIORS

Finally, customers can create value for your company in the course of using your product. Again, this will vary by industry, but here are a few common subcategories: ordering supplies, paying for services related to the initial purchase, paying invoices on time, and handling any support inquires through self-service channels.

Gather some colleagues together and brainstorm the matrix of value-creating customer behaviors in your business. You can use this list as a starting point. Remove or edit those that don't apply and add specialized ones. Then rank the value opportunity of each since some are larger than others. Finally, consider which ones you are currently focused on and which might be getting overlooked. This might generate some fresh ideas for how to move the needle of your business.

BONUS VIDEO: *There's much more to say about these four value-creating behaviors, so we've provided an infographic and video on the book website that goes into more detail.*

 ▶ wdc.ht/VALUE

Future State Journey Mapping Step 3:
REVIEW YOUR RESEARCH AND CURRENT STATE JOURNEY MAP

Your first point of inspiration for the future vision should be the current state journey map. To begin with, this tells you some of the things you are doing *well*; you can probably copy-paste those items directly from the present to the future. It also tells you where your customer is feeling pain. Being clear on where the customer is feeling the most pain is a powerful starting point for crafting an effective future state.

All this knowledge of the current state should be combined with the robust amount of insight into your customers' hopes, fears, wants and needs that you gathered while crafting your customer personas.

At this stage, you may be bringing new people into the project who may not have participated in creating the personas or the current state maps. Ensure they are fully up to speed on that material since it should be the basis for the brainstorming that comes next.

Future State Journey Mapping Step 4:
LOOK FOR IDEAS ELSEWHERE & REVIEW "THE ART OF THE POSSIBLE"

Ideas for possible solutions to your customers' points of pain are all around you. Take a look at how your competitors are solving the same types of problems that you documented on *your* current state journey map. They may well provide valuable points of inspiration.

Also, look at "comparative" customer experiences. By comparative, we mean brands that are not directly *competitive* with you but may have some elements of commonality. For example, in a recent project with a network of hospitals looking to improve patient experience, we leveraged best practices from Ritz Carlton and from cruise lines who have created world-class guest experiences. Similarly, a supermarket where people stand in line might have something to learn from Disney World; an automaker might be able to improve the purchase experience of a car by looking at the Apple Store sales experience, etc.

Also, ensure the team is immersed in "the art of the possible." Technology is offering a continuously widening palette of tools that can be leveraged to improve customer experience, from 3D printing to artificial intelligence to augmented reality to drones. Our goal should not be to just start throwing cool new toys into our customer experience, but rather to combine an awareness of what technology now makes possible with a focus on customer needs to see if there is some potential magic at the intersection.

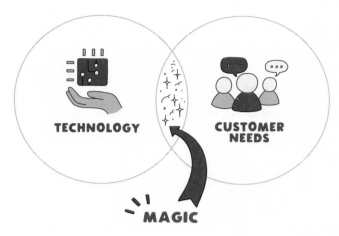

‹ wdc.ht/MAGIC

It can be fun to also look to what we call "the art of the imaginary." For example, in the 2002 film *Minority Report*, when Tom Cruise steps into a future version of "The Gap" clothing store, a camera uses eye recognition to automatically identify him, and digital signs immediately welcome him and start to market personalized offers based on his profile. This one moment in a science fiction movie has inspired many marketers to consider how to move toward a more personalized customer experience.

 FUN VIDEO: *If you haven't seen this clip, check it out on the book website using the link here.*

▶ wdc.ht/THEGAP

Imaginary visions of the future don't necessarily have to remain in the future. While the flying cars of *The Jetsons* haven't materialized, many of our modern conveniences were first envisioned on science fiction shows like *Star Trek* long before they were actually invented— the doors that automatically slide open when you walk toward them (now a supermarket staple), the tricorder (iPhone), computer voice recognition and more. What visions from the world of the imaginary are good points of inspiration for *your* journey?

Future State Journey Mapping Step 5:
GENERATE BIG IDEAS AND A LOT OF IDEAS

With all that inspiration, the ideas are probably already flowing. Let them out. Write them down.

One tactic that helps keep the ideas coming freely—in the initial brainstorming stage, try to avoid getting bogged down in implementation. That means not worrying if your back-end system is fast enough, if your customer service team has the right skills, if you have the budget, or if your legal department will let you "get away with it." These are all important considerations to be dealt with a little later, but initially, we want to allow the freedom to envision.

Also, encourage your team not to be afraid to put out half-baked ideas. Sometimes the mind of one person can generate an idea but also the realization that the idea has a fatal flaw. You can censor that idea out and not share it due to its flaws, but if you do that, you miss a major opportunity. Others on the team with different experiences may be inspired by your idea and offer variations on it that remove the flaws, or they might be aware of strategies to overcome the problems.

At this stage, don't feel that each idea needs to be a life-changing, complete, multipart journey. It's fine to have small ideas for optimizing individual interactions all the way up to holistic transformational ideas that seem wildly ambitious and would change the whole company.

Ideation is an activity which can be applied at many points in the Customer Love Digital Transformation Formula. Chapter 15 goes into great length on a wide range of ideation practices in the context of product development, and most of those practices can also be applied to the ideation of future state journey maps. When it's time to conduct your journey mapping sessions, you may want to refer to that chapter.

Future State Journey Mapping Step 6:
PRIORITIZE: EVALUATE VALUE AND LEVEL OF EFFORT

You may end up generating dozens or even hundreds of ideas from this process. Some may be for new products, others for ways to make it easier to access existing ones. Still *others* may be new ways of reaching customers through marketing or improved mechanisms to support customers. It now becomes necessary to prioritize which ideas will become part of your journey maps. Here are a few factors to consider:

Prioritization Factor 1:
OUTCOMES

The end goal of our new customer journey is to align with the key business outcomes we defined in Step 2. Go through each idea and consider what category of value-generating behavior it drives (sampling, sales, upsell, referrals, etc.) Of course, some will generate multiple types. An idea may help increase sales but also potentially influence repurchase or advocacy. While it may be a guesstimate at this stage, try to articulate what *degree* of impact each idea will have in each area. Part of that "degree of impact" should take into consideration what percentage of your overall customer base will benefit from the idea (some ideas apply only to a portion of your customers), as well as how meaningful the influence will be on those who benefit. If you want to be very precise, you can quantify both components and then multiply them and rank their products.

Prioritization Factor 2:
COST & LEVEL OF EFFORT

While you aren't necessarily trying to do a detailed budget at this point, score each idea based on how costly and difficult it will be to implement. At this stage we generally use the "T-shirt sizing" approach—small, medium, large, and extra large.

Prioritization Factor 3:
STORY VALUE

Some ideas are good ideas but just don't need to be part of an inspirational future North Star vision. Changing the color of the checkout button so that it stands out more might be the sort of thing you want to optimize, but not an important detail to include in the story.

Prioritization Factor 4:
MOMENTS OF TRUTH

The last factor is perhaps the most profound—prioritizing key moments of truth. What are the moments of truth? Your complete customer journey will be composed of a large number of interactions. Each time your customer uses your product, checks your site, views your social post, or does anything else to connect with your brand, these are the moments that make up the customer journey. But of course, you can't put *every* variation of how a customer might interact with your brand in the customer journey story. Just like when you tell someone the story of something that happened to you, you need to select which parts of the story are most important.

Moments of *truth* are those interactions where the customer has heightened receptivity to a reevaluation of the relationship, for better or for worse. When you handle them well and delight your customer, it goes a long way toward compensating for any other moments in the journey that are not yet totally optimized.

Multiple research studies confirm this idea that not all moments have the same importance to the relationship. Using the filter of "moments of *truth*" allows you to identify those that have a disproportionately large impact on the customer's long-term mindset about your brand. Then, you can invest more time, creativity, and money in those moments.

Here are three indicators that a moment in the customer journey may be a key "moment of truth."

Moment of Truth Indicator 1:
A MAJOR TURNING POINT IN THE RELATIONSHIP

When a customer first walks into a BMW dealership after looking at magazine ads for years, or when a couple first arrives at the Caribbean resort they've spent months researching and hours traveling to, these are moments when the customer's eyes are wide open to evaluate the relationship afresh and determine whether the brand is a good fit.

Will Rogers said, "You never get a second chance to make a good first impression." Apple realized years ago that the moment of "unboxing" a new toy was a key moment of truth and put extensive focus on the details of the packaging experience. Today thousands of customers upload "unboxing videos" showcasing their personal experience opening a new iPhone's packaging for the first time.

One of the reasons these moments are important emotionally is that they often reflect a certain risk the customer has taken—a leap of faith that they are doing the right thing in ordering that iPhone or booking that resort. So not only is your brand "on the line" to deliver on expectations, but the customer is evaluating *themselves* to determine if they made the right choice. They will end up either patting themselves on the back for having made a great decision or beating themselves up for having been "duped." This aspect of self-judgment creates an emotional component that further amplifies these points in the journey to "moments of truth."

Moment of Truth Indicator 2:
A CRISIS

When your customer is in trouble, the way you respond is critical. Crises are heightened moments that have a disproportionate impact on the long-term relationship. In a study my team ran on insurance customers, the most remembered moments with the most significant impact on the long-term relationship were almost all during crisis incidents—when your car is totaled or your house is flooded. I recall one customer we spoke with who was a fiercely loyal Allstate customer because of a claim experience *her parents* had 30 years earlier when the customer was a small child.

Not surprisingly, some of the crises that have the greatest impact on the relationship are those that the customer perceives are *caused* by your brand. Canceled flights, data loss from crashed hardware, or salmonella in your sandwich have the potential to be disastrous "moments of truth."

But curiously, these "screw-ups" also have the potential to become some of the most positive moments in the customer journey, if they're handled artfully. This usually involves a sincere apology, fixing the problem, and often a gesture of compensation. Academics term this the "service recovery paradox," and it's why Ritz Carlton empowers their hotel workers to use their judgment and spend up to $2,000 to solve a customer problem without manager approval.

Moment of Truth Indicator 3:
UNEXPECTED DELIGHT

One last category of "moments of truth" are opportunities to create surprising delight. This means delivering something of value that is unexpected and reflects insight into the customer's needs.

I experienced a moment of surprising delight recently when I was flying out of Newark Airport on United Airlines and sat down to have dinner before my flight at one of the nicer full-service restaurants in the airport. The restaurant had an iPad at every seat and encouraged you to scan your boarding pass so that they could keep you updated regarding your flight departure time. I scanned my ticket, and in addition to the flight notices, I received a message from United Airlines letting me know that they would be "picking up the check" for my dinner to thank me for my loyal patronage.

Triggered by this digital interaction, the waiter then brought over a printed card to this same effect. Although I was dining in the United Airlines terminal, this restaurant was a steakhouse, not a United Airlines branded club. Such recognition and willingness to seek me out and buy my dinner even when dining at what at least appears to be an independent establishment was an especially unexpected and appreciated surprise. While I do love getting first class upgrades and free "frequent flyer" flights from United, frankly, I have come to expect these as "part of the deal," so, while perhaps more valuable, they don't necessarily rise to the same level of unexpected delight as this gesture did.

Future State Journey Mapping Step 7:
DRAFT STORIES

Now that you have a prioritized set of new ideas, you are ready to start drafting stories. Each story will feature a different persona as the "hero," as well as lay out a different starting situation. For example, if you are an office supply retailer, one story might be about an office manager who needs to arrange weekly deliveries of copy paper. Another might be about a teenager who needs to get supplies to make a science fair diorama. Yet another might be about an executive who is traveling but has forgotten her laptop cable and needs a replacement. The goal is to define a manageable number of stories that reflect a breadth of customers and interactions and to showcase the prioritized ideas for transforming the experience.

There are several reasons why creating these future state journey stories are so valuable. In theory, we *could* just stop at a bullet-pointed set of "big ideas," but the future state journey stories are much more powerful. First of all, they make for more effective communication because the human mind is far more attentive to stories than to lists.

But there is an even more fundamental reason they are so beneficial: customers *experience* their journey as stories. Have you ever come back home and said to a friend or family, "You won't believe what happened to me at the grocery store today!" then proceeded to describe the reason you went to the store, the challenges you faced, the way people in the store responded, etc. It may be a story of a great deli-counter service experience or one where the lobsters somehow escape from the tank and terrorize the shoppers.

In any case, it's a story.

So, by chaining together your improvement ideas into journey map *stories*, you get to see how they fit together. Do these ideas form a cohesive whole? How do they interact with each other and play off each other? When casting a movie or play, it's not just about getting a great actor or actress in each role, but it is about making sure the combined cast synergizes in the right way. It's the same when stringing ideas together into stories.

Each story should start by introducing the main character and their key characteristics. It should describe the "situation" and then walk through a series of events, describing how the customer interacts with the brand. And, of course, it should have a resolution that is positive, reflecting the vision of success that your new journey is intended to drive.

But although these are aspirational stories of *successful* brand interactions, they should also include complications. It may seem like we are trying to write stories of the "optimal" user experience and therefore nothing should go wrong. But if we take that approach, we will miss many important details of what happens in the real world. After all, no matter how great your brand's experience, things that are beyond your control will go awry, creating the opportunity for moments of truth.

Weather will cause airline delays; some products purchased at a store will turn out to be defective; occasionally diners at a restaurant will not like the food they ordered; investments will lose value; any car will, at some point, break down or get a flat tire. Our goal is not to write an experience story that edits out these inevitable problems, but rather one that shows how the journey anticipates these bumps in the road and creates the best possible experience despite them.

For example, a tow truck is immediately dispatched to deal with the broken-down car and a loaner is provided. Or, during a travel delay, the customer is given great hospitality and a free meal, as well as thorough and accurate communication.

All great experiences are great stories. Of course, terrible experiences can also be interesting stories, unfortunately, which is why customers talk about them so much.

The ones in the middle? Far less so.

As an example, there are over 100 stories in this book. Here is the very worst one: Yesterday, I was driving on the highway and noticed the gas in my car was getting a little low. I looked around for a minute and then saw a gas station, pulled in, put some gas in my car, paid, and drove off.

Is this even a story? Yes, it is. It has a main character (me), a problem (though not a very dramatic one), a conflict (need to find a gas station) and a resolution (I found one easily), but it's not at all engaging. If you asked me how my day was, I'm pretty sure this wouldn't come up.

That's because "good" experiences make boring stories, and boring stories do not create customer love. You might get repeat business when it's convenient, but not passion, not emotional momentum for that customer to seek you out again. You probably also won't get people talking about your business. Few people rave about their daily taxicab rides, but Uber got many people buzzing.

If you look at most products on Amazon, you will see this effect. For many products, there may be 100 ratings of 4 stars or 5 stars, 15 ratings of a 1 or a 2, and almost no 3-star ratings. Is that the actual distribution of people's experience? Probably not. More likely, people's response to any given product is a standard bell curve, a small percentage of people love it or hate it and most people are in the middle, satisfied but not excited. But the *review* distribution is shaped like an *inverted* bell curve because it is only the people at the edges of experiential satisfaction that are motivated to write a review. Those are the people with a compelling story to tell, whether good or bad.

Future State Journey Mapping Step 8:
CREATE PRETTY MATERIALS

I love to read a good novel. But experience has shown me that no matter how well-crafted the story, it's tough to get most people engaged in customer journeys that are limited to *just* written text. It's more effective to create visually rich materials to convey customer journey stories.

One format we have often used, which was described earlier, is a sort of comic strip layout, which includes imagery to illustrate each stage of the story with text underneath to narrate.

Another is a storybook format, in which each page has a couple of lines of text and an illustrating image.

In workshops, we often have groups act out live skits based on the stories they have created. At our Innovation Loft workshop facility in New York, we maintain a closet full of costumes for just this purpose.

Yet another format is to create the video version—use actors or even your colleagues (if they have the chops) to portray the future state story cinematically. We've also used animated "explainer" videos to tell journey stories.

Future State Journey Mapping Step 9:
SELLING THE VISION

It's not enough to have a clear and effective vision. You have to be able to *sell* it to your organization. As discussed, having a visually appealing and engaging way to tell the story is one important tool. Another tactic that can be very helpful is to involve key stakeholders in the journey mapping process itself. That way, by the time you have a crystallized version of the future state vision, they feel ownership over it.

Also, since the work you have done on the journey map is focused on delivering business value, not just a squishy goal of "improving customer experience," be sure to articulate that fact when socializing the vision—explain clearly how this "story" is not just good for the customer but has been *engineered* to drive strategic value-creating behaviors.

Of course, the story represents only a *hypothesis* that if the customer is given those experiences, they actually will engage in the value-creating behaviors described in the journey. But it's not a wild guess; it has been rooted in a rich set of customer research. Be sure to highlight those connections to help reinforce the reasons you believe that this experience will drive results.

Lastly, when socializing, be sure you contrast the future state vision with the current state maps. Remember the CEO who saw the future vision and asked, "Isn't this what we are already doing?" It's helpful to start with an overview of the current experience and create the burning platform of the "need for change" before presenting the proposed solution for transformation.

In addition to using your journey maps in presentations to drive alignment and secure funding, they should serve as constant reminders to teams of what the experiential North Star is. Your journey maps can be printed and hung on walls in public areas of the office, distributed to employees as printed books, or posted on intranet sites as videos or PDFs. The key idea is that these should not be rolled up and left in the corner of someone's office. They should be seen and socialized.

Journey maps should also be considered "living documents." Undoubtedly, the vision will evolve over time and the journey maps should be updated to reflect those changes.

THE BENEFITS OF JOURNEY MAPPING

Journey mapping offers many benefits, and they can be sorted into two categories: mindset benefits and actionable benefits. Mindset benefits are the ways journey maps get the team in a beneficial frame of mind for driving transformation. Actionable benefits are the ways in which the journey maps can be leveraged in specific, practical ways in delivering on the vision. Here are some of the specific benefits from each category:

Mindset Benefits

- **They Increase Customer-Centric Thinking**
  Customer journey maps get teams to think of their work in terms of customer experience and behavior.

- **They Promote a Relationship Focus**

  Journey maps encourage thinking about building loyalty over time rather than only transactional interactions.

- **They Bring Strategy to Life**

  Journey maps help both senior stakeholders and implementers envision the strategy "in action."

- **They Show How Pieces Fit Together**

  Journey maps enable teams working on different pieces of the journey to understand how they interrelate.

- **They Bring Research to Life**

  Journey maps help communicate the insights of customer research in an accessible way.

Actionable Benefits

- **For User Experience**
  Journey maps help drive specific decisions in terms of features and interaction design.
- **For Personalization**
  Journey maps provide a high-level framework for how to tailor experiences for individual segments.
- **For Data**
  Journey maps help define the data elements that need to be captured and utilized.
- **For Content Planning**
  Journey maps help clarify which content and information should be used to engage the customer at which touchpoints.
- **For Marketing**
  Journey maps help shape marketing messages and channel choices.
- **For Metrics**
  Journey maps help define how best to measure progress toward business results.

. . . .

Once you have the overall customer journey defined and have organizational alignment, you are ready to start making that vision a reality, which is the topic of the next section of the book.

BONUS TOOL: *Before you go on to Activity 3 of the Customer Love Digital Transformation Formula, we want to remind you that we have provided summary slides and relevant exercises for each chapter on the book website. If you're looking to use this book's content in meetings with your team, this supplemental content is a great time saver.*

 wdc.ht/SLIDES

ACTIVITY 3:
BUILD THE FUTURE

IMPLEMENTATION CONSIDERATIONS

CH. 12

DEVELOPING BREAKTHROUGH PRODUCTS & SERVICES

CH. 13

PRE-IDEATION ACTIVITIES

CH. 14

IDEATION

CH. 15

AFTER THE IDEATION

CH. 16

DESIGN THINKING 2.0

Now that you have a "North Star" description of the customer experience you want to create, you are ready to start driving the transformation necessary to deliver on that vision—to build the future.

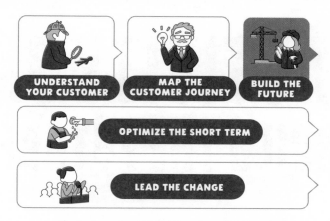

The Customer Love Digital Transformation Formula

Delivering on your bold, ambitious vision will involve many considerations—some technical, some organizational, some operational, some political. In fact, you will probably need to involve every part of your company, from the finance department, to marketing to legal, and maybe some parts you didn't even realize existed.

Also, though your journey maps lay out a high-level vision for the customer experience and they no doubt imply a variety of different, specific touchpoints, such as websites, mobile apps, and chat-bots, they do *not* describe the precise detail of these individual systems, such as their exact features, user interface, and technical architecture in sufficient detail to actually build them. That work must be done now.

In the first chapter of this section, we will give an overview of some of the major themes you will need to consider as part of your overall implementation plan (Chapter 12). Then in Chapters 13 to 16, we will provide a detailed description of how to apply the technique of Design Thinking 2.0 to define and execute your vision in a manner most likely to deliver optimal business results.

CHAPTER TWELVE

BUILD THE FUTURE

IMPLEMENTATION CONSIDERATIONS

CUSTOMER EXPERIENCE IS THE TIP OF THE ICEBERG

N ew York and Singapore are located almost exactly opposite each other on the globe. You can travel east or west around the planet and the flying time is similar. On a recent business trip to a speaking engagement in that part of the world, I was excited to learn that our pilot's planned route was *neither* east nor west. Rather, we were flying north from NYC, over the North Pole, and then south back down to Southeast Asia. Many on the plane chose to sleep through the trip, but I spent much of it taking photos of the Arctic Circle from the airplane window.

If you've ever *been* to the Arctic or even flown over it like I did, you've seen icebergs there that are not only miles wide but also rise hundreds of feet above sea level—truly massive objects. But as big as they appear, 90% of a typical iceberg's mass is *invisible*—it's underwater.

If you are in the "iceberg business"—studying them for science or cutting through them for ships to pass—it's quite important to understand not just the visible component but the full scale and depth of the iceberg—seen and hidden.

And if you are undertaking a digital transformation, driving the realization of your customer journey vision, you *are* in the iceberg business.

As we've discussed throughout the book, creating a seamless, elegant, and differentiated customer experience is essential for success in this increasingly digital world. Getting to an effective vision of that optimal experience, as we have been doing up until now, isn't an easy process. But *delivering* that customer experience vision is often even *harder* because if the user experience is the part of the iceberg that's visible to your customers, in order for that part to work, a great deal has to happen beneath the waterline.

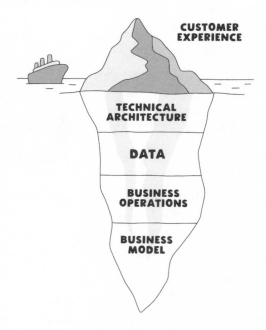

The Customer Experience Iceberg   < wdc.ht/ICEBERG

Four supporting elements must be effectively delivered and very often transformed in order to achieve an excellent customer experience: technology, data, business processes, and the organization's economic business model.

In this chapter, we will discuss these supporting layers and provide some criteria for success. Of course, each of these topics, such as technology or business process, could be a library of books in and of itself. But, this chapter will provide high level insights into each. Recommendations for additional reading will be available on the book website.

Beneath the Iceberg Level 1:
TECHNICAL ARCHITECTURE

Outstanding customer experiences are supported by modern technology stacks that must provide two essential capabilities: secure access from any touchpoint and flexible frameworks that can deliver a broad range of services and capabilities.

SECURE ACCESS FROM ANY TOUCHPOINT

Customers today expect to be able to choose from a diverse set of choices for how to interact with your brand—web, app, kiosk, chat, etc. They also expect those touchpoints to be completely synchronized and operating in a consistent manner.

For example, I placed an order for a washing machine part a couple of years ago from HomeDepot.com and within moments realized that I had made a mistake and ordered the wrong one. Doh! I wanted to "undo" my error, but soon came to learn that once an order was placed, you couldn't cancel it from the website; you could only do that by calling the call center. Sigh.

3: BUILD THE FUTURE

So, I *called* the call center and they told me that they wouldn't be able to "see" my order (and therefore, wouldn't be able to cancel it) until the systems synchronized in about an hour and that I should call back then. I called back in an hour but was told the systems were now *down* and I should try back in 15 to 20 minutes. Grrr. Not a great or accessible customer journey, but also surely not an experience anyone intentionally "architected." Rather, a *symptom* of inflexible technology that is not integrated across touchpoints.

Companies that succeed in delivering elegant digital experiences have modern, unified architectures based on micro-services and common data layers so that these types of situations are impossible. Furthermore, they have systems designed to have near-zero percent downtime. If your company is not there yet, technology transformation needs to be a priority.

FLEXIBLE FRAMEWORKS

Think of any customer experience you love. How did that customer experience get to be so great? It's not by having a genius team that got it right the first time. It was through an iterative process of testing, learning and improvement. To do that, you have to be able to efficiently code, test, then evolve (or kill) failing ideas quickly. Furthermore, the frameworks for presentation, business logic, and transaction processing need to be flexible so that you can experiment with many different ideas to find what works best.

On a recent project, a client asked my team to figure out how to get a higher percentage of their website visitors to sign up for their subscription service plans. Like many e-commerce sites, they had a lot of "lookers" but a small number of buyers. The company spent quite a lot of online advertising dollars to bring those "lookers" to the site, so increasing what is called the "conversion rate" (the percentage of people who buy) had the potential to give them far more bang for their marketing buck.

We conducted user studies and examined data about the behavior of customers on the site. From our analysis, we hypothesized that changing the sequence of the sign up process to be more intuitive could increase conversion. Our team created an offline prototype and tested it with a bunch of users, and eureka, it made a huge difference.

But when we went to the client's IT team that "owned" the commerce platform to have it implemented—major problem. The back-office systems that determined which plans and prices were applicable to any given customer were built on very specific assumptions about the order that information would be gathered. We couldn't just reprogram the website to give the user a different sequence because that would totally break the back-end, and those systems were the only components that "knew" how to price the options that were available to the customer.

There are two ways to get past this type of obstacle. The first is to just replace the core back-end systems with something much more modern and flexible. This is probably the best long-term approach but can be quite challenging because those ancient systems are often full of all kinds of logic created over many years. Typically, they aren't well-documented, and sometimes there are only a few people at a company who really understand them. Often, *those* few people have zero interest in seeing them replaced.

The second approach is to create an API or micro-services layer "on top" of the problematic legacy system. That is what we did for this particular client, but it was not a trivial undertaking. We needed to "fool" the back-end system by creating an order, providing dummy data, and fully submitting it before the customer even started the process. Then each step of the new order process required our code to recall up the dummy order and submit the next bit of information as an "edit" and save the record. We had to implement our own logic to ensure the data would be valid because we were circumventing the way the back-end system normally checked validity. It didn't run quite as fast as we would have liked, and it was a bear to create. But it worked! The client saw big increases in conversion. And because we implemented our technology changes as an API, if there is a need to change the sequence again in the future, it should be straightforward. They now have a "flexible framework" for the ordering process. Of course, that's just *one* of many processes in their business, so the job of transforming this layer of the iceberg at that company is far from done, but this is the type of work that gets you there one step (or one chunk of ice) at a time.

No matter how much pain it entails, companies in this situation need road-maps to upgrade, redesign, or replace these inflexible systems to permit the creative evolution of their customer experience.

Beneath the Iceberg Level 2:
ROBUST & SECURE DATA

Under the iceberg of so many of the digital experiences you love, data is making it possible. Whether it's your Netflix recommendations driven by knowledge of everything you've ever watched, FedEx letting you know exactly where your package is on its delivery route, or Google taking your search query and scouring mountains of information to return the perfect result, behind these magical capabilities are massive repositories of data with sophisticated algorithms running on top of them.

HAVING THE RIGHT DATA

If you are like most enterprises, you have a lot of data—terabytes or even petabytes of data. The key is to be sure you have the *right* data and are leveraging it in the right way.

200

Many companies are swimming in more data than they know what to do with, and yet determining what data you *need* to deliver a world class customer experience can be challenging. While I have no metrics to back up the chart below, I have drawn it on the whiteboards at many enterprise clients' offices and received vigorous nods of agreement.

The Data You Have vs. The Data You Need

◁ wdc.ht/DATAYOUHAVE

In other words, although you may have tons of data, much of which you don't know what to do with, when you do the analysis to determine the data you really *need* to deliver an outstanding experience, some of it *is* usually contained in the vast lake of data you already have. But often, a lot of it is data you don't yet have. My hope for you is that your boxes overlap more than these, but if they don't, know that you are in good company.

201

WHAT DATA DO YOU NEED?

For most enterprises, there are two main categories of data that will be the foundation for great digital experiences:

CUSTOMER DATA   **PRODUCT DATA**

Two Categories of Data

‹ wdc.ht/DATACATEGORIES

 ## CUSTOMER DATA

Knowing your customer's characteristics, history, and preferences is key both to personalizing their experience and to making it as sticky as possible.

Banks, for example, rely on the fact that once you've entered all the details on your bill "payees," you probably won't want to go to a bank that doesn't have this data—where you need to enter it all again.

Customer data is of three primary types:

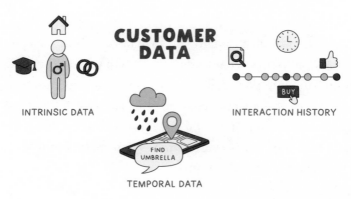

INTRINSIC DATA   INTERACTION HISTORY

TEMPORAL DATA

‹ wdc.ht/DATATYPES

Customer Data Type 1:
INTRINSIC DATA

Intrinsic data are static bits of personal information about the customer, like their name, gender, location, and marital status.

Customer Data Type 2:
TEMPORAL DATA

Temporal data is information about *this moment*—such as where the customer is located right now, what device they are currently using, and what task they are trying to complete. For example, Google uses your search terms and current geographic position to deliver you the most relevant search results. The most sophisticated companies are even using sentiment analysis to figure out what you are *feeling* right now and using that data to optimize their interactions with you. Temporal data changes very quickly so it must be re-gathered on an ongoing basis.

Customer Data Type 3:
INTERACTION HISTORY

Interaction history covers things which have happened in the past and includes purchases the customer has completed and their delivery status, items they have placed in their shopping cart, ratings or reviews they may have contributed, and even browsing patterns.

BONUS VIDEO: *On the book website, we've provided a video about "The Types of Customer Data that Can Make or Break Your Business." As you start thinking about the data you have and the data you need, make sure to give this video a watch.*

▶ wdc.ht/DATA

203

PRODUCT DATA

Very likely, your business activity includes connecting customers with the right product or service. You probably have a lot of *information* about your products, but a great digital experience requires that information to be available as structured data so that it can be effectively searched and used to filter and sort. The data you need will depend somewhat on your industry, of course, but common types of data you want to make available include:

- Product name and description
- Category (e.g. dry goods, apparel)
- Product sizes/colors available and shipping dimensions
- Technical specifications and marketing materials
- Certifications (FCC, LEED, etc.)
- Support materials such as manuals and drivers
- Cost, including any taxes or duties based on destination
- Shipping options and their costs (by destination and speed)
- Any geographic restrictions on shipping
- Ratings and reviews
- Images and videos
- Eligibility for various discounts, coupons, promotions or rebates
- Related products
- Stock available
- Warranty terms

Of course, you might not want to present *all* of this information to the user, at least not all together. But when this data is available in a structured form, it can be incorporated into search tools, product pages, proposals/quotes, checkout processes, and other key moments in the journey.

Another type of product data that is becoming increasingly valuable is 3D models. Furniture companies such as Wayfair are using 3D models to create product "photos" of home furnishings, shown in different fabrics and colors, without needing to incur the expense or time of a photo shoot. This data can also power augmented reality applications where users can visualize new furniture in 3D superimposed on their existing living room. Part manufacturers are providing 3D models of industrial parts for potential customers to import into their engineering software so they can determine if the part will fit properly. And real estate companies are creating 3D virtual walkthroughs of properties for sale or lease.

Sophisticated companies are always looking to expand their product data to create a better customer experience. For example, some clothing retailers are storing data about whether sizes of a given item "run large" or "run small" to help users feel confident about ordering online without trying on the garment. This can also increase post-purchase satisfaction and reduce returns.

The *intersection* of customer data and product data is what creates personalized recommendations. Netflix famously scours through customer interaction history and maps it against product data to suggest the thriller you might like to watch next. Amazon is encouraging customers to add the make and model of vehicles they own to their customer profile so that when a user navigates to an automotive part—such as an oil filter or spark plug—they can be immediately informed whether the product is compatible with one of their vehicles.

MAKING DATA ACCESSIBLE FOR USE

Having the data you need is not enough, however. Many companies have piles of data spread across large numbers of systems and servers, making it difficult to leverage the data in an integrated manner. Digitally effective companies use a combination of techniques to bring data into common repositories, such as data lakes, data warehouses, and digital asset management systems, and then implement integration technologies like Tibco or MuleSoft to permit data sharing between applications.

To make that work, the data not only needs to be visible, it's essential that data be effectively "keyed." Keying data means that you have a unique reference number or code that connects data in different systems. For example, modern data architectures will always have a unique customer ID number for each customer. If one system stores a customer's purchase history and another one stores their email subscriptions, both records store that common customer ID so that systems can connect the data together for analysis and customer interaction. A simple idea, but we see many large enterprises where significant work still needs to be done before all customer data is keyed in a consistent manner.

DATA ACCURACY AND FRESHNESS

Of course, data is only as valuable as it is accurate. Many enterprises have volumes of data with questionable accuracy and inconsistent formats.

And the longer the data sits, the less accurate it gets because things change—people move, get new jobs, get married and take new last names, etc.

To deliver the most critical aspects of a strong digital value proposition, such as personalization and hyperconvenience, it's essential that your enterprise have not only the right data, but also high-quality data.

It's easy to be fooled into thinking you have the data you need for an exciting new feature only to implement it and learn that, actually, what you've just done is expose the fact that the data is wrong.

We once got burned on a project because of this very problem. We were working with a client that served a lot of commercial customers that had multiple facility locations (such as stores or factories). Prior to our involvement, the client's account information portal only allowed their customers to view information about one single location at a time. To view another, they had to log out and log in with *that* location's account number and password. A major point of pain for those customers that had several or even dozens of facilities and who were, of course, our client's best customers.

To improve customer satisfaction, we developed a slick interface that allowed a customer to log in with a single username and password and see data from across *all* their facilities, aggregated and grouped in different ways—graphed, compared, and benchmarked against each other. Our usability testing of a prototype of the system showed that these features would be very much appreciated by customers.

However, once the customers started using the *actual* system with their *real* data, the complaints started pouring in. The system was easy to use, but the information that they were seeing, once they could easily slice and dice it, just didn't make sense. There were massive data problems which had always been there, but it hadn't been easy for customers to see them when they could only look at the data from one facility at a time. Now that they were looking at the data in an integrated way, and with tools that allowed them to compare across locations, they could see that it didn't add up.

What we had inadvertently done was to create a super easy-to-use tool that put a big spotlight on how bad the underlying data was. Whoops! Needless to say, the next step was a giant and urgent data cleanup effort. Eventually, the problem was solved and the customers were happy, but clearly it would have been a lot better to have done that *before* releasing a tool that exposed all that mess.

DATA SECURITY

Sorry to say, but once you have collected all this great data and kept it fresh and accurate, someone will want to steal it.

We live in an era of unprecedented cybercrime. According to *Industry Week,* cyberattacks rose over 250% last year and they are rising even faster this year.[1] *Information Age* estimates that hackers are attempting about 3.9 trillion intrusions a year.[2]

Part of love is trust. If your customers don't trust you to guard their personal data, then it's going to be hard to inspire love no matter what else you do. This means not only ensuring their data *is* safe, but also letting them *know* that it is and giving them a reason to believe.

In contrast, the experience of having a brand allow your data to be stolen can be a truly terrible customer journey, going as far as identity theft, massive headaches and possibly significant financial loss for the customer. Even when these negative consequences do not occur for an individual whose data was exposed in a breach, the knowledge that a breach occurred creates the *fear* that they might, which is nearly as harmful to the customer relationship. No doubt, you've followed the news of how companies like Target and Equifax have suffered significant reputational as well as financial damage as a result of data incursions. The *average* cost to a company when a data breach occurs is over $3.6 million according to IBM,[3] and some cost far more.

One of the reasons the financial impact is so substantial ties back to our strategic customer experience model and how customer behavior is inspired by thoughts and feelings. What thoughts and feelings are triggered by learning that your personal data has been stolen?

We've studied customer mindsets at several companies who have suffered data breaches, and we have observed a common pattern in the "meaning" customers give to data breaches after the fact.

It doesn't matter the reason. It doesn't matter who was to blame or how clever the hackers were or how hard it is to keep data safe. To customers, if it happened, there's only *one* reason: the company didn't care enough about their customers to be sure it didn't.

Beneath the Iceberg Level 3:
BUSINESS OPERATIONS

Let's move on to the third level of the iceberg. Serving the digital customer effectively is not just about creating digital touchpoints but about evolving the *total* experience with digital at the center. That means you will need to change the way you do business in a variety of ways.

Customers who use online chat to ask questions expect answers far faster than those who email, let alone those who use postal mail. Digital customers opening an account at a bank online don't want to have to wait to receive a thick packet of forms in the mail that they have to sign in 17 different places. If you are a retailer, you probably want to offer digital customers the ability to order online and have merchandise held for them at the store.

Figuring out how to deal with all these "real world" operational considerations is about a lot more than programming an app. For example, buy online/pick up in store implementations require training, possibly new roles for the in-store team, and even physical changes to counters and store traffic patterns. Truly optimizing for digital will probably change your approach to merchandising, your return policies, your customer support, your customer communications, and, well, everything.

Service Blueprinting is a technique that takes all the interactions you've mapped out for your customer and connects them to your various back-office processes so that you can clearly see what happens *operationally* when a customer, for example, places an order, requests a refund, or creates an account. Then, when seeking to optimize the customer experience, you can evaluate what about the current service blueprint is *creating* the "before" experience and determine what changes are necessary in the operational processes to achieve the more desired outcome.

Digitally driven companies also seek to automate business operations wherever possible, supporting employees with AI and machine learning tools and sometimes replacing human activity with code or robotic machines.

While there are many critical roles for *people* to play even in the most digital companies, those delivering outstanding experiences and value are generally doing so by leveraging the efficiency of automation to deliver an outstanding experience at the lowest possible cost.

Beneath the Iceberg Level 4:
BUSINESS MODEL

One of the benefits customers receive from digital leaders is a huge improvement in the value they receive for their money. As mentioned earlier, Skype has taken our long-distance phone bill from hundreds of dollars to pennies. Spotify has given us access to practically any song ever recorded for a few dollars a month, while Netflix has done the same for movies. In many markets, Uber has halved the cost of a taxi. This is awesome for consumers but threatening to incumbents whose business models are dependent on the pricing levels of the "legacy world." Jeff Zucker, the former CEO of NBC, echoed this concern over a decade ago when he bemoaned having to trade, "Analog dollars for digital pennies." [4]

How are digitally-centric companies able to offer consumers a "better deal?" Very often, it is either by using digital technology to reduce the cost of the core service, as Skype has done, or by innovating the business model they use. Airbnb's business approach of allowing anyone to list their property on their website is totally different from Marriott, who has to build and staff large hotel facilities. Spotify offers a subscription model and pays record companies on a "per play" basis, which is totally different from an old-fashioned record store that paid up front for inventory shipped to their location that they hoped to sell eventually.

So bear in mind that figuring out how to deliver the experience that will be a winning value proposition in the new digital world may entail shifting how you make money.

Many of the most successful digital properties utilize multiple digital revenue models simultaneously or have found growth as a result of a clever shift or expansion in business models. For example, Amazon created Amazon Prime, a subscription service. They also have sponsored listings, which is an advertising model. And, of course, they took their strength in technology and turned that into a very successful B2B business selling cloud hosting services.

We've worked with several companies who have decided to create new revenue streams by selling data, adding new subscription offerings, creating co-marketing or ad sales platforms, or establishing directories of third-party services to create referral revenue.

BONUS VIDEO: *On the book website, we've provided a video that goes into further detail on the 10 Digital Business Models. Make sure to watch this video, then use the provided group exercise and infographic to brainstorm with your team what new business model opportunities might be appropriate for your business.*

▶ wdc.ht/DIGBIZMODELS

211

· ·

THE ICEBERG ABOVE THE SURFACE

This chapter has provided an overview of some of the key business processes and technology changes that will need to be transformed below the surface of the water in order to deliver the customer journey you have envisioned.

All that is going to be a lot of work, but we're also not done with the *visible* part of the iceberg—the customer experience. When you mapped the customer journey, you defined a flow for how the experience should elegantly move from touchpoint to touchpoint and, no doubt, documented a few key potential features at each touchpoint that would create customer delight. But that's still only a high-level conception of those individual products—whether they are websites, mobile apps, chatbots, or digital capabilities integrated into the products you sell. In seeking to bring that vision to life and actually *build* these experiences, it will be necessary to embark on a more detailed product development process for each touchpoint so that you can document their exact features and interfaces with enough detail to implement them.

· ·

The next few chapters explain how to use Design Thinking 2.0, a powerful methodology that will continue the theme of focusing on the customer to drive business results.

CHAPTER THIRTEEN

BUILD THE FUTURE

DEVELOPING BREAKTHROUGH PRODUCTS & SERVICES

B ack in the early 2000s, I was managing part of the digital practice for Ernst & Young when we moved into a shiny new skyscraper in Times Square right next to where the ball drops on New Year's Eve.

That building was the first I had ever seen with a keypad-controlled elevator. Instead of pushing an up or down button, the elevator is called by a numerical touchscreen. To request an elevator, you type the number of the floor you want to go to, and you then receive a response from a screen with the letter of the alphabet corresponding to the elevator to which you have been assigned. You go to "your" elevator and, when it arrives, you get in and it automatically takes you to your floor.

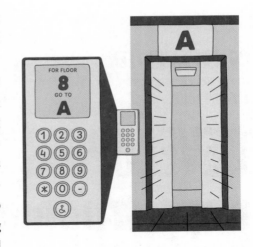

This change enables better optimization of elevators, presumably speeding your journey to your destination. In theory, it also reduces user effort since, in the traditional system, a user has to "call" the elevator by pushing an up or down button, and then once in the elevator, the user has to pick a floor. But instead of two points of interaction, the new system has just one. And as a bonus, there's no worrying about the kid in the elevator who decides to push all the buttons—there aren't any!

But I was fascinated to observe that when clients started arriving for meetings at my office in our new building, their first comment was almost inevitably irritable, "What the heck is up with your crazy elevators?" I had nothing whatsoever to do with these elevators, mind you; I was just a guy who worked there. But I found myself repeatedly apologizing for the confusion that my clients experienced when simply trying to get up to my 25th-floor office.

There were clear downsides to this innovation. For example, if you're already in the elevator, there's no opportunity to change your mind without getting off on the wrong floor and repeating the whole process. *Plus*, even if you don't *actually* change your mind, visitors didn't like feeling that they *couldn't*. They were locked in a metal box that was taking them to one place, and they were powerless.

But the biggest downside of this innovation is simply that it requires users to learn something new.

214

Clear instructions explaining how to use the elevators were printed above the keypad. The problem was that users didn't *want* to read instructions to know how to use an elevator. We were requiring them to relearn a skill they had already fully mastered—even though it only took 30 seconds.

Of course, we all choose to learn new things periodically. Most of us have learned how to use iPhones and Kindles and DVRs. But these devices delivered enough value to us that it justified the investment to learn them. The keypad elevators didn't seem to be delivering enough value to overcome the pain of change. Furthermore, users weren't being *asked* to adopt something new. It was pretty much non-optional for anyone who wanted to get to a meeting in the building. The consequence was some pretty negative reactions.

I've watched with interest over the years to see if these keypad elevators would *eventually* catch on. It turns out, not a lot. *Some* additional buildings installed them, but most didn't. Recently, I was visiting a client in Houston. The building had actually spent a fair amount of money to *remove* the keypad system and replace it with the traditional two-step process. Wow. You know your innovation is not doing well when your customers are willing to invest tens of thousands of dollars to get rid of it and go back to the old way.

Clearly, delivering a product that takes off and is appreciated by users is a bit more complex than having a new idea. Rather, it's an equation of value and "cost" of a variety of types—including "ease of use." If there is too much friction to a new way of doing things, it can be difficult to get consumers interested.

This is an important consideration as we start to implement the future state journey maps we created in the previous section. In them, we have envisioned a potential future based on our understanding of customer points of pain. But in truth, it's just a hypothesis. Just because we have conceived a solution to a point of real customer pain doesn't necessarily mean it's one that customers will appreciate or adopt. After all, waiting a long time for elevators is certainly a point of user pain in office buildings. But despite helping relieve it, the keypad system hasn't been a runaway success.

The bottom line is that a huge percentage of well-intentioned innovations fail, *even when conceived with knowledge of customer needs.* The good news is that there are specific methodologies to massively reduce the likelihood of this outcome, which we will overview in this chapter and go into more detail on in the subsequent three chapters.

The approach we have utilized most successfully to overcome these risks is rooted in a concept called Design Thinking. Among other things, Design Thinking is a process used to incorporate customer research throughout the product development process. It describes not only how to conceive a product based on user needs but also how to validate your solution *hypotheses* throughout the product development process to ensure you are creating a solution that users will respond well to.

Before we get into the details of the Design Thinking product development methodology, let's examine the more fundamental question of what a product *is* and elaborate on some of the other challenges in bringing successful products to market.

WHAT IS A PRODUCT?

There are many ways to use the word "product," which are completely legitimate in different contexts. For the purpose of our discussions, by "product," we mean anything your company offers that creates an "experience" when users interact with it.

A hairdryer is a product. An app is a product. Your website is a product. The CRM tool that your call center reps log in to is a product. If you build it and someone uses it, it's probably a product.

And we aren't trying to make a significant distinction between a product and a service. If you are an accountant, your tax preparation services *are* your product, as we mean it here. And if you have built a process that your customer experiences when they interact with your company *around* tax preparation, that *process* is another example of what we mean by a "product."

So, it's a diverse set of things that we call "products," but the good news is that the same Design Thinking processes can be applied to whatever product we are focused on, no matter the flavor.

The future state customer journey that you envisioned is most likely the story of your customer interacting with a whole string of "products," some of which you may charge the customer for (like a Netflix subscription) and some of which may be more focused on commerce or customer service (like the Delta Airlines or eBay apps).

In order to bring your new customer journey to life, you will most likely need to create or update a large number of different products, and to do it *successfully* you'll need to get the details of these products as "right" as possible so that they resonate with customers.

But, as we said earlier, a huge percentage of new products fail. Let's take a look at why, so we can avoid the same fate.

· ·

WHY DO NEW PRODUCTS FAIL?

The classic Mel Brooks film, *The Producers,* tells the story of Broadway impresario Max Bialystock who has spent years debuting a long string of theatrical flops—failed products in our parlance.

Bialystock then hatches a scheme to actually *try* to produce a Broadway play that is so bad that it is *sure* to fail in order to defraud investors. Ironically, this sabotaged play becomes a smash hit, foiling Bialystock's criminal plot and getting him into hot water.

BONUS VIDEO: *If you haven't seen it, here is a clip of Nathan Lane and Matthew Broderick musically hatching their devious plan from the Broadway musical adaptation of the film.*

▶ wdc.ht/PRODUCERS

But other than in a Max Bialystock scam, no product is *designed* with the intent to be a failure. And yet many *are*. If we can understand the various *reasons* for product failure and remove them from our approach, we set ourselves up with a far higher likelihood of success.

Let's evaluate the different reasons first. Then, when we start to look at the Design Thinking methodology, you will observe how it has been architected to avoid most of these common problems. There are three "root-cause" reasons new products fail:

THE WRONG VALUE PROPOSITION **FAILURE TO EXECUTE** **LACK OF AWARENESS**

Three Reasons Products Fail

◀ wdc.ht/FAIL

The First Reason Products Fail:
THE WRONG VALUE PROPOSITION

For a product to be successful, it has to meet customers' needs and do so in a way that is "worth" more than the cost the customer is asked to bear. Furthermore, it must offer value that is superior to *competitive* options at that price point.

HURDLE 1:
BE WORTH ITS COST
TO CUSTOMERS

HURDLE 2:
BE A BETTER VALUE
THAN COMPETITIVE
PRODUCTS

❮ wdc.ht/HURDLES

This "value proposition" is the core of any product idea—a specific solution to a customer problem delivered at a defined price point and revenue model.

The quality of a Skype call may not be the same as expensive teleconferencing equipment, but it's free. So, for many customers, it's a more compelling value proposition. Of course, other customers prefer to pay more and have more reliable connections. That's fine as well; both are valid propositions and address different markets.

Spotify offers vast amounts of music for a monthly subscription. In contrast, Apple's original iTunes model encouraged customers to buy music one track at a time and own it forever. Both models appeal to certain customers, and now Apple has also added a subscription product to compete with Spotify.

The "right" idea for a successful product is one that will resonate with its intended customers, be worth the cost, and be either better than the competition or cheaper. Ideally, both.

How do you find it? As discussed in previous chapters, understanding your customers' unmet needs, pain, or problems is the starting point. But a given problem can have many solutions. Some solutions may work well for the customer, while others might just not be worth the trouble, like the numerical elevator keypad. Some might be good but not *as* good as a competitor's solution.

The Design Thinking process, which we will describe in detail in this section, is designed to help you ensure that you are factoring these things into your product development calculus.

PRODUCTS AND THEIR VALUE PROPOSITIONS ARE MULTI-TIERED

Product ideas are multi-tiered. There is a "core idea" at the top, but there is a whole hierarchy of ideas that have to go below that core idea to form a full product.

For example, here's a core product idea: create a hybrid between a cell phone and a PC that uses a touchscreen to allow customers to make phone calls and also runs a wide range of applications. This is, of course, the core product concept of the smartphone. Whether you're talking about a coconut-flavored breakfast cereal or a computer vision-enabled shopping app, the core idea behind most products can be described in a sentence.

But core ideas must then have idea *pyramids* developed beneath them to round out the product vision. Once you decide to work on a core idea, it requires many more ideas in order to turn it into a build-able product concept.

- What is the full set of features?
- How will the user interact with it?
- What will it look like? Sound like? Feel like?
- How will we brand it?
- How will we create awareness about it?
- How will we make money from it?
- How will we get it to customers?
- How will we support it?

Consider the fact that the iPhone and Microsoft Zune phones were pursuing the *same core product concept*. Why was one an unprecedented success and one an abysmal failure? Because many of these "next-level" qualities were different.

The Four Key Levels of a Product Concept

‹ wdc.ht/4LEVELS

There are many examples of breakthrough products that copy-catted most of the levels of this pyramid from competing products while innovating on just a single one. The iMac was like many other computers running the Mac operating system but came in five colors. Gmail was like many other mail services, but it was free. The new Sony mirrorless cameras do 90% of the same things as Nikon and Canon DSLR cameras, but they introduce a few key feature innovations, like automatic eye focusing, that set them apart.

COMPETITION COMES IN MANY FORMS

Although you must offer a superior alternative to competitors (at a given price point) to be successful, in many categories, your largest competitor *may* be inaction. When the Apple Newton came out, despite being innovative, sales were poor. Clearly, the product did not meet the needs of most customers. Did they buy a competing tablet product?

221

There actually weren't any. What did they do? Nothing. There was no product that was "worth it" to buy in that category at that time, so consumers kept their money in their pockets.

Also, you may think that if your product is "free," you don't need to worry about beating your competition on price. However, this is not necessarily the case. There are different types of "cost" for a user other than monetary payments. If your product requires more effort, that may be perceived as a cost. If your product interrupts the user with more advertising than a competitor, this can also be perceived as a higher "cost."

Some products even reward customers such that the customer is effectively being *paid* to use the product. Wikibuy, certain credit cards, and airline loyalty programs are examples of this. In these cases, not rewarding your customer *enough* to be competitive may factor into that cost equation, as well.

The Second Reason Products Fail:

FAILURE TO EXECUTE

It's not enough to have an idea with the right value proposition (*even* at *every* level of the idea pyramid) because ideas are not products. You still have to bring them to life. Many products born of great ideas fail in their execution.

In 2017, Samsung unveiled one of its most sought-after new products, the Galaxy Note 7 smartphone. The screen vibrance, battery life, and improved cameras wowed customers. Even though the price was high, pre-orders were record-breaking. The product shipped and received rave reviews in the media—that is, until the batteries started catching on fire. Whoops.

Fortunately, nobody was seriously injured, but Samsung had to recall 2.5 million phones[1]—A massive failure of execution. As a consequence, Samsung's valuation dropped by over $26 billion.

But a product doesn't have to explode to be an execution failure. Some products just don't work quite the way they are supposed to.

My team was brought in a few years ago to try to help "save" a project management software tool that a client had launched. They built what they thought was a "killer" app, but the market was rejecting it.

We conducted some customer research for them. The tool had awesome features that really aligned with what users wanted. It had a beautiful user interface. It just had one problem, really: it was slow. The product concept was so sophisticated and required so much computational power that each change to your project plan took 5-10 seconds to "recalculate." That was all it took for users to reject it. This is one of the challenges of product development: a lot can be *right,* but if one critical thing is off, it can tank the whole thing. It's hard to keep your eye on everything, which is why we have structured methodologies like Design Thinking.

We improved the project management software in part through performance optimization but mostly by removing features that weren't "worth" their impact on speed. After that, the product was more successful.

We've developed a model called the Execution Gap Model to help with these types of diagnoses.

The Execution Gap Model

wdc.ht/EXGAP

BONUS VIDEO: *If you're looking to apply the Execution Gap Model to your new products, visit our website and watch the explanatory video called "Diagnosing Execution Gaps Using a New Model."*

▶ wdc.ht/DIAGNOSE

The Third Reason Products Fail:
LACK OF AWARENESS

Ralph Waldo Emerson is popularly credited with coining the phrase, "If you build a better mousetrap, people will beat a path to your door."[2] Interestingly, historians have uncovered evidence that Emerson was *not*, in fact, the originator of this saying.

But even more importantly, the idea *itself* is false. The U.S. Patent Office has issued well over 4,000 patents for new ideas for mousetraps,[3] and yet the world largely continues to use the classic "snapping" model invented by John Mast in 1899,[4] despite the fact that no doubt millions of people have managed to "snap" their own fingers in it. Despite the fact that it's unsafe around small children. Despite the fact that you have to put cheese or peanut butter on it, and that attracts bugs. Despite the fact that a mouse of even below average intelligence can find a way to get the cheese without getting whacked. Despite the fact that when it *does* work, you then have to look at a pathetic dying mouse with a broken spine wriggling in front of you. This customer journey clearly has many points of pain, and it strains credibility that *none* of these 4,000 new patented designs are a "better" mousetrap. So, clearly there's more to a successful product than the "famous but fake" Emerson quote implies. That's because even if a great idea is well executed, it still can fail if nobody knows about it.

But awareness does not *just* mean knowing that your product *exists.* It actually consists of three critical components:

- The product's existence *and* core value proposition.

- The product's claim of *differentiation.* Why choose this one over all the other options?

- How to take action—where to order the product or how to access it.

If you are a new Chinese restaurant in town, you need to first make sure that people know you exist and that you are a Chinese restaurant.

But there may already be five other Chinese restaurants in town. I live in the New York City area—there are hundreds. So, second, you need to let them know what makes you *different.* Maybe it's crunchier egg rolls, faster service, cheaper prices, or a better view. And third, you need to let people know how to find you—what number to call for reservations, what URL to use to order delivery, etc.

In "old school" product development thinking, solving these problems of awareness would be considered "marketing issues" that were totally separate from product development. But this is not the approach we advocate.

First of all, part of your future state customer journey is focused on how customers find out about the existence of your products or services, how they get more information to evaluate them, and how they make a decision to purchase.

Plus, as we have previously stated, your sales and marketing "touchpoints" such as websites, brochures, stores or sales kiosks are *also* a type of product. Fortunately, the Design Thinking process can be applied to the "products" customers interact with as part of their marketing journey just as effectively as it can be applied to the products for which you collect money.

As we delve into the details of the Design Thinking product development process, consider it a methodology not just for the creation of salable items but for the construction of every experience the customer will have as part of their brand journey, including those that help ensure your product isn't just relying on "being" a better mousetrap.

THE HISTORY OF DESIGN THINKING

Design Thinking evolved from the work of a range of thought leaders and practitioners trying to solve some of the product development challenges described so far in this chapter. It's tough to date the exact beginning of the movement, but the roots have been traced back to Buckminster Fuller at MIT in the 1950s,[5] subsequent work by teams in Scandinavia, and then the design agency IDEO,[6] as well as programs at Stanford University that popularized it in the 1990s and early 2000s.[7] Today, Design Thinking is widely used by many creative firms, consulting companies, and large brands.

The "original flavor" of Design Thinking—the 1.0 version, so to speak, is classically composed of five key steps:

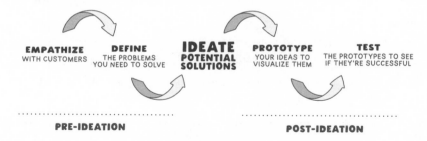

EMPATHIZE WITH CUSTOMERS   **DEFINE** THE PROBLEMS YOU NEED TO SOLVE   **IDEATE POTENTIAL SOLUTIONS**   **PROTOTYPE** YOUR IDEAS TO VISUALIZE THEM   **TEST** THE PROTOTYPES TO SEE IF THEY'RE SUCCESSFUL

PRE-IDEATION   **POST-IDEATION**

Design Thinking 1.0

‹ wdc.ht/DT1

This five-part Design Thinking approach really brought two major *new* ideas to the process of product development. If you look at the five steps above, notice that the middle one is "Ideate." Ideating was certainly *not* a new idea when Design Thinking was invented. People had been coming up with ideas and implementing them for thousands of years.

But the first important concept Design Thinking introduced was that you shouldn't *start* with ideating. Rather, there are several "pre-steps," which, when practiced, make the ideation much better.

The first of these is *Empathize*, which is really just another way of saying "understand your customer," an idea we discussed intensively in an earlier section of this book. The second is *Define*, which is about getting clear about the *problem* that you are actually trying to solve through design. "Define" is similar conceptually to the current state journey maps that we described in the previous section.

The second area in which Design Thinking brought innovation to the design process was the phase *after* teams come up with ideas. Without a Design Thinking approach, product teams might generate what they believed to be a great idea and then start building it with the hope that it would be successful. Design Thinking emphasized creating different types of prototypes and testing them, including with prospective customers, to ensure that the idea was really a winner—in terms of the idea's *desirability* to the market, in terms of its *feasibility* to build and in terms of its *viability* from a commercial perspective. And if tests showed that it wasn't, Design Thinking taught teams to learn from these unsuccessful tests and iterate a solution until it tested well (or until it became clear that the idea just wasn't going to work). While this can take some additional time, it actually *saves* a tremendous amount of time (and money) in the end by massively reducing the likelihood that you will go to the trouble to build and launch a product that will be unsuccessful in the market.

The Customer Love Digital Transformation Formula leverages the heritage of Design Thinking heavily, and I imagine you already see many parallels with steps described up to this point.

In the work my team has done over the past 20 years of implementing Design Thinking, we have added some specific additional steps that we find make it work *even better* for the digital world in which we operate. This updated version—what we like to call Design Thinking 2.0—is the version we will be documenting in this book. It contains *all* the key ideas from 1.0 that we have discussed so far but adds some additional concepts.

THE STEPS OF DESIGN THINKING 2.0

Here are the steps of Design Thinking 2.0, based on work done at my company. You can see that we have moved from five to seven steps and that the original ideas are all contained in the list but with new items added.

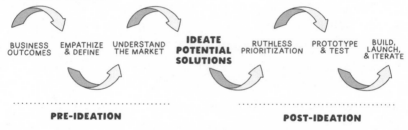

BUSINESS OUTCOMES · EMPATHIZE & DEFINE · UNDERSTAND THE MARKET · **IDEATE POTENTIAL SOLUTIONS** · RUTHLESS PRIORITIZATION · PROTOTYPE & TEST · BUILD, LAUNCH, & ITERATE

PRE-IDEATION · · · · · · · **POST-IDEATION**

The Steps of Design Thinking 2.0

 wdc.ht/DT2

The next chapter, Chapter 14, will describe the "pre-ideation" activities of Design Thinking 2.0. Chapter 15 will provide a number of best-practice techniques for ideation itself, and Chapter 16 will describe the post-ideation activities.

. . . .

Before we dive in, one last thought. Despite being shown as a linear process, real world applications of Design Thinking (1.0 or 2.0) often involve teams working in multiple "steps" simultaneously, as well as moving back and forth between steps. A piece of customer research will spark an idea. The idea will suggest new research questions, more competitive analysis, or even a reassessment of the objectives. That's fine and encouraged. Design Thinking, like any framework, is just a tool to enable you and your team to work more effectively, and you will inevitably adapt it to your own situation as we have done.

CHAPTER FOURTEEN

BUILD THE FUTURE

DESIGN THINKING 2.0: PRE-IDEATION ACTIVITIES

A rchaeologists have found traces of campfire sites dating back to more than one *million* years ago,[1] indicating that very early man discovered the recipe to create fire. As a modern human, you probably already know that fire requires three ingredients in order to ignite: oxygen, fuel, and a spark.

I mention this because the process of ideation is a kind of creative blaze and has an analogous set of necessary ingredients. The *fuel* of ideation is knowledge—the information and insights about the customer, problem, market, technologies, or other factors that come together to inspire an idea.

Fires need a continuous supply of good fuel to keep going, and ideation uses information to keep it going, as well. You probably experienced some of this when you started getting new customer insights as part of the research we talked about in Part Two of this book. The insights almost spontaneously start inspiring ideas.

The *oxygen* that feeds the ideation fire is a mindset—it's the *feeling* that you have the freedom to innovate, that you are empowered, that your ideas will be welcomed. The more oxygen, the hotter a fire burns.

If you've ever had a job where "the boss" doesn't seem interested in ideas for improvement, you are not only less likely to *suggest* ideas, but in fact they become less likely to even consciously *occur* to you after a while. Your mind knows there's no reason to generate them, so it doesn't bother.

But, in an "oxygen-rich" environment *welcoming* of ideas, where the fuel of relevant insight is *also* available, the spark that sets the whole thing ablaze is a specific outcome—the clarity of what you are trying to achieve.

SPARK
GOAL

OXYGEN
EMPOWERMENT

FUEL
KNOWLEDGE

The Ideation Process

 wdc.ht/PROCESS

232

The human mind is a "problem-solving machine." The instant that "spark" of a clear problem is presented, the mind wants to start solving it immediately—*especially if* it has the "fuel" of the information needed to generate a solution and the "oxygen" of the feeling that a new solution is welcome.

If "the boss" finally asks for "ideas to improve things around here," you *might* have some, but your idea-making might not ignite all that well because you really aren't sure what type of ideas she wants. But if she says, "Give me three ideas for how we can get our weekly reports done in half the time without compromising accuracy," now you have sparked a clear goal to ideate towards.

Let's play a quick game to prove that the human mind naturally starts to develop ideas as soon as the three elements are present. That, indeed, when they are, it's nearly impossible to *stop* ideation from occurring.

I am about to provide you an outcome, a situation where ideas are needed, and some information. BUT, I want you to *not* come up with *any* ideas to solve this problem. Not one. Got that? Tell your brain right now, "Brain, once you read the next paragraph, *don't* give me any ideas." Are you ready to *not* come up with any ideas? Let's see what happens. 3-2-1...Go.

"A college student is setting up the food for a party in her dorm room and realizes she has forgotten to buy plates. She looks at the clock and sees that the party starts in 20 minutes. She has no car. The closest store is a mile away. She tries to figure out what to do."

Did ideas to solve her problem immediately start occurring in the back of your mind? Are they still occurring now? Bad reader! But seriously, don't beat yourself up; you can't help it. I described a situation where someone genuinely wanted and needed ideas (oxygen). I gave you a bit of information about the person and her problem (the fuel), and I gave you an outcome (get plates, the spark). Try to prevent a *real* fire from lighting when oxygen, fuel and a spark are all present. It's pretty near impossible, and likewise ideas.

But nevertheless, before we move on, give your brain permission to start giving you ideas again. No sense taking any chances.

. . . .

THE "PRE-IDEATION" STAGE OF DESIGN THINKING

As a reminder, Design Thinking 2.0 is broken into three primary stages—pre-ideation, ideation, and post-ideation.

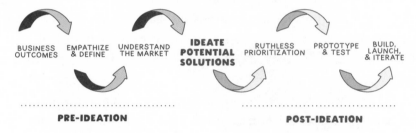

This chapter focuses on the "Pre-ideation" stage, which is about preparing the *ingredients* for the blaze of ideation that we will be setting off in the next chapter. In Design Thinking 2.0, Pre-Ideation consists of three key steps.

- **BUSINESS OUTCOMES:** Being clear on the ultimate measure of victory for the product.

- **EMPATHIZE & DEFINE:** Understanding the customer and the specific customer problems that need to be solved to achieve the business outcomes.

- **UNDERSTAND THE MARKET:** Gaining inspiration from competitors and getting clear on the alternatives that your product will be evaluated against by potential customers.

BUSINESS OUTCOMES

If you want to launch a successful product, it's important to know before you begin what the definition of *success* is. Is it a certain level of sales? A certain impact on customer satisfaction? A specific increase in traffic? A percentage reduction in calls to the call center? It's basic to "good business" to understand what you are trying to achieve so that you can focus on that outcome throughout the process and know whether you've been successful at the end. And, as we mentioned earlier, human creativity works best when given a very clear and precise goal.

Also, you'll get the broadest range of ideas generated when you articulate the most *fundamental* goal possible. An example we used earlier is also applicable here. Henry Ford famously said, "If I'd asked people what they wanted, they'd have said a faster horse." So, avoid defining the problem as "a faster horse" instead of "a better way to get from place to place."

Is your goal to get more people to the website? Or is it *really* just to serve more ads (and *one* way to do that would be to get more people to the site)? Is the goal really to reduce the time call center reps spend on the phone, or is it actually to reduce the *cost* of the time spent for a given amount of sales? If so, maybe you'll realize you should actually *increase* the time spent if it results in more sales and an overall net improvement in the cost per dollar of sales.

Though you may already have a theory about the type of solution you are looking for, you are still better off defining your goals at the most fundamental level and shooting for a broader set of ideas. You might wind up *choosing* ideas that are based on the same general approach you had in mind to begin with. But as long as you are ideating, encourage the unexpected; perhaps you will discover a totally different type of solution which is far superior.

We have observed this in many of our Design Thinking 2.0 workshops, hearing comments like, "If we didn't use a process like this, we never would have even considered *thinking* about a solution like that. But now that we have, it's clearly so much better than the approach we were intending to take."

DEFINING CONSTRAINTS

As much as it's good to encourage broad thinking, it's also valuable to define constraints.

All creativity exists within some kind of structure, whether it's the syllable pattern of a haiku poem or the frame of a painting. If a potential solution has certain characteristics that will definitely take it off the table, it can be very helpful to define those constraints right up front.

For example, say we are looking for ways to reduce the handling time of call center calls *as long as it doesn't reduce customer satisfaction*. That second part, the "as long as," is a constraint.

If we just start brainstorming ways to reduce the call handling time *without* the defined constraint, what's to stop someone from suggesting, "How about just hanging up on all the customers three seconds into every call?" The right constraints can save the wasted energy of generating ideas that are outside of what is really sought. More importantly, it can be demoralizing for teams to later learn that their ideas have been discarded because of constraints that weren't revealed to them up front, and that can diminish the enthusiasm for the next brainstorming request.

But in this example, the *greatest* problem is *not* that someone might suggest hanging up, but rather that most likely *nobody* would. Why not? Because it's "obviously" not a good solution. But why *not*? It *would* reduce the call handling time. It fills the requirements.

For the creative mind to *conclude* that hanging up is *not* a "good" idea, it has to layer on top of the "stated" goal (reduce call center handling time) some *unstated but assumed* constraint (we don't want to annoy the customers). This all happens subconsciously, for the most part, and the subconscious only brings to the conscious mind the ideas that it believes are "appropriate."

The problem with this is the unintended consequence: what *other* unstated constraints is the mind *also* subconsciously using to limit or filter the possible solutions? It might also be making assumptions like, "We have to make this work with our current staff," "It can't be too expensive," "It has to be able to be done this year," "It can't require a change to our CRM system," or "It can't sound too 'crazy.'" Are these all real constraints? Maybe some yes. Maybe some no.

So, while it might *seem* limiting to state constraints—that you'd get the broadest range of ideas with *no* constraints—it doesn't work that way. When the mind is given no constraints it tends to supply its own, and it may do a bad job of it.

What we want instead is to telegraph to the subconscious creative mind, "Here's the problem, and here are *all* the constraints—*all of them.* You don't have to make up or assume any others. Therefore, *any* solution that solves this problem within these constraints is welcome, no matter how wacky or unfamiliar."

The creative mind thrives when given this kind of freedom. But it only "believes" it when it sees that the constraints are provided and it doesn't need to assume them. This is why it's worth focusing on getting those constraints right.

But only add those that are *true* constraints. Remember, this is for *ideation*; you can later reject some or even most of the ideas and keep only the best ones. If you think, "Well I'd *rather* have a solution that can be completed this year, but if someone has an amazing enough idea that takes two years, then I'd definitely want to know about it," then that's not a constraint. Let the ideas flow and sift through them later. However, if you are coming up with ideas for the Christmas sale, and it's already November 1, then ideas that take three months to implement are pretty much off the table. State that up front.

Getting clear on the objectives also helps in preparing the *fuel*. The fuel, you may recall, is the information—the insight—that we need to come up with ideas. Objectives are not, in and of themselves, the insight the team needs, but they can point the team in the direction of that information.

For example, in many industries, there are regulatory constraints. We may decide we want to find ways to tell people how amazing our new mutual fund is, a*s long as* it's permitted under federal banking regulations (a constraint). If the regulatory standards are an important constraint, then we'd better get some *information* about what they are, in addition to learning as much as possible about what makes this new mutual fund so amazing. Or, if we have certain physical constraints on the manufacturing capabilities of our factories, let's go get that information before we ideate products that must be manufactured there.

DEFINING TARGET CUSTOMERS AND BEHAVIOR

Since we know that the end goal we are trying to achieve through our ideas will likely be influencing human behavior, clear objectives should let us know specifically what types of *customers* (or other users) this particular idea is seeking to influence and what types of *behaviors* we are trying to drive in them. This helps us not only focus the ideation, but also to be clear about exactly who we need insights *about* to fuel the creative process.

For example, we recently ran an ideation session as part of a project for Sesame Workshop. We were focused on taking an existing smartphone game and making it more usable by children with certain special needs. Once we were clear on the goals, we knew we needed to provide the team with the "fuel" of insights about the limitations of children with the specific disabilities we were focused on.

LOOKING BACK TO THE JOURNEY MAP

As you work on defining the right objectives for a given product, one place to look is at the outcomes that were identified back in the future state customer journey mapping process (Ch. 11). Those outcomes were for the entire journey, while any given product within the customer journey might only focus on a portion of it, so it's not going to be a perfect match, but they should align.

For example, if you are working on a chatbot to help customers assemble your furniture when they receive it at home, your goals for the product ideation may focus on reducing returns of furniture, increasing the customers' initial satisfaction, and generating more positive online reviews from new purchasers. But since the customer has already *bought* the furniture at the point the chatbot is used, it's probably not an objective to try to get new users to buy the product. That may be one goal of the *journey* but not of the chatbot.

EMPATHIZE AND DEFINE

Let's move on to the *second* step of the pre-ideation portion of Design Thinking 2.0, which is "Empathize and Define."

"Empathize" is really just another way of saying "understand your customer"—what they want to accomplish, what they see and hear, what they think and feel, and what they do.

Frankly, I don't love the term "empathize" because it can seem like it focuses primarily on feelings, so we use the term "understand your customer" as part of our broader digital transformation methodology. But the term "empathy" is so ingrained in the history of Design Thinking that we keep it there on our DT2.0 model as a nod to tradition. Nevertheless, what we mean by empathy in *this* context is to understand both the logical and emotional sides of the customer.

So, what is the difference between the "understanding" of the customer we need to do here versus what we did in Step 1 of our Customer Love Digital Transformation Formula? Just like with objectives, it's about the level of granularity. DT2.0 is meant to be applied to individual products. For example, if you are working on a virtual reality tour of a new car you are bringing to market, you may have some very specific things you need to understand about your customer's needs that are uniquely applicable to a VR tour—the kinds of angles they might want to see it from, the kind of information they want, etc. This level of detailed customer research specific to the VR product may not have come out of your broader research to understand the customer at an overall car buying and ownership journey level.

Of course, you should be *leveraging* your prior research, and if it gives you *all* the insights you need for any given product, then great—there is no need to do it twice, as long as it's reasonably recent. But if there are gaps where your higher level of research didn't look at the nuances specific to an individual product, then you can supplement that research by using the same types of direct and indirect research methods that we talked about in Chapters 7 and 8. You just need to have a more localized set of research questions governing the additional inquiries.

In DT2.0, we group "Define" *with* "Empathize" in one step because we see them as very much intertwined. "Define" in Design Thinking parlance means to synthesize all the empathy data gathered and to write the "problem statements" that we are going to try to solve for the user through the products we create.

Here's an example of a Design Thinking problem statement:

*"It takes a long time for employees to wait for elevators,
and that frustrates them. How can we get the
employees to their desks more quickly?"*

A problem statement is really just a structured way of stating a customer point of pain and identifying a solution objective.

Problem statements, when solved, become a *means* to achieving business objectives. For example, a business objective might be to improve morale so as to reduce attrition. As part of the "empathize" process, we might conduct a study of employee morale that identifies 30 points of pain for employees, *one* of which is how long they have to wait for the elevator. This can then lead us to a "define" problem statement, such as the one above, designed to frame the need to solve that point of pain. Define statements are just a way of clearly documenting the detailed objectives of the ideation—stated as specific problems to solve—and, therefore, they are part of the "spark" that ignites creative ideation in our fire metaphor.

Take a moment to notice the wording of the example problem statement about the elevators. We try to get to the *underlying* issue, not just the problem with the current situation. The problem statement proposed does not say, "How can we speed up the elevators?" Because employees don't really *want* faster elevators—they want to get to their desks faster. It *may* be that a faster elevator is the way to do it, but who knows? Maybe jetpacks that let them fly up the side of the building is the right way, or moving all the offices to the first floor, or getting employees excited about taking the stairs. In fact, the problem statement doesn't even say that they have to go to a floor of a building. Maybe one solution is letting them work from home. When problem statements are articulated more broadly, there's a much richer set of possibilities. Of course, you may wind up back at "the obvious" solution of speeding up elevators. But it's valuable to take the broader ideation journey because that's how you find the innovative approaches that may solve an old problem in a new or better way.

UNDERSTAND THE MARKET

Classic Design Thinking does not explicitly direct practitioners to focus on the competitive market. However, we have found doing so to be essential, and thus, it's a defined step of Design Thinking 2.0. As discussed in the previous chapter, successful products must not only effectively solve problems for customers but also offer a value proposition that's *superior* to competitive alternatives. That is true whether you charge for the product or not. The Google and Bing search engines are both free, but one is far more successful because it's perceived as superior.

So, once we have defined the problems we are looking to solve for customers, we should start to look at what competitors are doing, both to understand where the competitive "bar" is and because some competitors may have *already* solved those same problems in different ways, and there is no sense in reinventing the wheel.

But the first step in competitive research is to be clear on who your competitors *are*. It's natural to think first of your company's obvious direct competitors, but ultimately you'll want to focus more broadly. For this purpose, we define a competitor as anyone who is selling a product or service whose success will reduce your business *or* whose business is analogous to yours. Consider the four tiers of "competitors" shown below.

DIRECT COMPETITORS

DISRUPTIVE COMPETITORS

NEED OBLITERATORS

COMPARATIVE COMPANIES

Four Tiers of "Competitors"

Competitor Tier 1:
DIRECT COMPETITORS

Direct competitors are the most obvious. They are the companies who are battling to fill the same customer need as you are, and they are doing so in more or less the same way. Domino's versus Pizza Hut. Coke versus Pepsi. Chase versus Citibank. Of course, most companies have more than one major direct competitor. Chase also has Wells Fargo, American Express, PNC, and so on. Since your direct competitors are often selling something mighty similar to what you are selling, they are probably working right now to figure out how to differentiate themselves from you. They want to better serve their customers (and, if possible, yours) via digital and other channels.

Thoroughly understanding your major direct competitors' products and experiences is essential to engineering yours for differentiation. You need a structured program in place to maintain *constant* awareness of their competitive moves—new features in their apps, usability changes to their websites, new social strategies, etc.

In addition, at any given time, there may be smaller direct competitors who, while not substantially impacting your sales due to their size, may be *utilizing* that smaller size to be nimbler and to implement innovative ideas faster. Pay more attention to these companies than their size might seemingly justify. They may be the incubator of the next great idea, and you want to jump on that before your larger competitors do.

Competitor Tier 2:
DISRUPTIVE COMPETITORS

Disruptive competitors are focused on solving the same problem for customers that you are, but in a very different way. Airbnb is competing with Marriott, but not in the same way that Hyatt is. When email started to become prominent, it was major competition for both delivery services and companies making fax machines. Digital cameras decimated the film camera market, and subsequently, *phones* with cameras diminished the consumer digital camera market. DVDs disrupted the movie theater business, and now streaming media has disrupted the DVD business.

Competitor Tier 3:
NEED OBLITERATORS

Tier 1 competitors solve the same problem that you do in more or less the same way. Tier 2 competitors solve the same problem that you do but in a very different (often innovative) way. But *tier 3* competitors, the need obliterators, make the problem you are solving irrelevant or less necessary, at least to a segment of customers. For example, the Kindle is not solving the same problem as a bookcase, but bookcase sales have decreased since e-book sales skyrocketed, just as the growth of digital recordkeeping has reduced the sale of file cabinets.

Competitor Tier 4:
COMPARATIVE COMPANIES

Another important group of companies to keep in mind are comparative companies. These organizations are not competing for the same dollars as you, but they may be solving some of the same "problem statements" within their own industries, and therefore we can learn from them just like we would from "true" competitors. This is why we include them in our "competitive analysis." For example, a bank looking to improve customer service might study a high-end retailer such as Nordstrom.

BONUS TRAINING VIDEO: *Review our video "A Detailed Look at Competitive Analysis," which provides examples of each of these four categories and tactics to gather competitive insight.*

▶ wdc.ht/COMPETITIVE

As you develop your product and its value proposition, it's beneficial to keep the four tiers of competitors in mind. A strong understanding of the market will help ensure that your Design Thinking 2.0 process generates not just promising ideas but superior value propositions.

. . . .

Once you are clear on the business objectives of your product, have gathered the relevant customer insights, defined the problem statements, and taken a look at the competitive market, you are ready to begin the actual ideation, which we will do in the next chapter.

CHAPTER FIFTEEN

BUILD THE FUTURE

DESIGN THINKING 2.0: IDEATION

A s an avid SCUBA diver, I've logged more than 500 dives over the last 20 years. If you add them all together, that's more than one week of my life "living" underwater. But when I *first* learned to SCUBA dive, it freaked me out, and I'm not the only one.

When you were taught to swim as a child, what was the first and most important thing you learned? *Don't breathe underwater.* In fact, you probably got that wrong once or twice and had a pretty unpleasant experience.

But after multiple lessons and practice, you learned *not* to breathe underwater and stopped thinking about it because you *conditioned yourself* not to breathe underwater. It became ingrained in your subconscious— like driving a car or brushing your teeth.

But here's the *problem*. One day, you decide to take a SCUBA diving class. You are standing in the shallow end of a training pool. An instructor hands you a regulator to put in your mouth. You suck in through the regulator, and the tank on your back supplies you with air. Nifty. Breathing air with your head above the water—no problem. The instructor then tells you to go down a few feet below the surface of the pool and practice *breathing underwater.*

You dunk down and prepare to take that first breath, and it's quite weird. Your conscious mind understands that it's ok to breathe underwater *now. Y*ou have an air supply. *However,* that conditioned part of your subconscious—the one that you worked so hard to habituate through practice so you don't have to think about it anymore—doesn't adjust that fast. Even though you rationally know it's fine to breathe underwater with a regulator in your mouth, there is a part of your brain screaming, "STOP! DANGER! DO NOT DO THIS!"

Once you manage to relax a bit and take a few breaths, you may feel like you are doing ok, but for many people, the panic comes and goes in waves. You're fine for a few minutes, and then your subconscious mind sort of wakes back up and says, "WAIT! What have you been doing while I wasn't paying attention? Get out of there! YOU HAVE TO STOP BREATHING UNDERWATER!" For many people, it takes a few dives before the voice is quiet enough not to be a problem. *Eventually,* you condition yourself in a new way. You train your subconscious with a new rule: it's ok to breathe underwater *if* you have SCUBA gear on.

· ·

THE UNFAMILIARITY OF IDEATION

What does learning SCUBA diving have to do with ideation? Oxygen.

Corporations are generally built around process standardization. That is how they scale, protect against risk, and ensure that they provide the customer with a consistent experience.

If you got a job in high school working at McDonald's, you might have shown up on the first day with some new menu ideas or, after working there for a few weeks, come up with an idea for a faster way to make the burgers. Did they *want* those ideas? No. They trained you in how to do it "their way" and measured whether you were "doing it right." If you did it in a more creative way (which equals "wrong") too many times, you got fired or assigned to clean out the grease traps.

This isn't just true in fast food. Get a job as a bank teller or an auditor. Go to medical or nursing school. Get a job as a teacher under "No Child Left Behind," or start working as a software developer or on a manufacturing floor. At junior levels, where we bring people into the workforce, we train them to do their job the "right" way, and companies have processes to seek out and discourage variance.

This is done for all kinds of good reasons. You don't want every bank teller to get creative with how they document your deposited check, just like we don't want kids trying to breathe underwater in the town pool. However, when the day comes that, after years of training you to "do as you are told," we invite you to a brainstorming session and tell you to "be innovative," we've basically put a regulator in your mouth and told you to breathe underwater.

The first reaction is often somewhere between mild anxiety and panic. Or put in the context of our combustion metaphor, we are trying to make fire without the "oxygen" of the feeling that new ideas are *truly* welcome and encouraged. Even if we tell people that they *are*, their subconscious programming still warns them that they aren't—just like even though you have a regulator supplying air when SCUBA diving, your subconscious is not immediately convinced.

To deal with this conundrum, the compromise behavior most employees settle on is to either:

1) To just sit quietly and hope someone else will fulfill this "dangerous" request for new ideas; or 2) to generate "ideas," which are either the "same old" ideas (hence not new and rule breaking) or which are only very small iterations on what already exists; or 3) focus on ideas from direct competitors because these at least feel like they are "tried and true" and therefore also not really new.

When unimpressive results come back from these brainstorming sessions, executives often draw the conclusion that they simply don't have creative people on their teams. But that's generally not true. Creativity is a natural and common gift, and most people have massive creative potential. Your existing team's knowledge of your business, customer, and industry usually puts them in a far better position to generate great ideas than any "more creative" people you'd run out and hire. The solution instead is to recondition your team to release their ideation potential. We'll talk about *how* to do that in this chapter.

· ·

THE CORE OF DESIGN THINKING 2.0: IDEATION

As we've said, Design Thinking 2.0 is made up of three primary stages. The first stage is Pre-Ideation, which we covered in the previous chapter. In this current chapter, we will focus on the second stage of Design Thinking 2.0: Ideation. Then in the next and final chapter of this section, we will complete the overview of Design Thinking 2.0 with a description of key activities to conduct *after* ideation to ensure those ideas will really be successful.

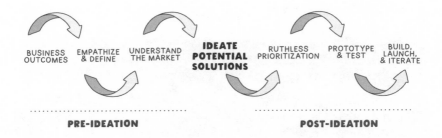

BUSINESS OUTCOMES EMPATHIZE & DEFINE UNDERSTAND THE MARKET **IDEATE POTENTIAL SOLUTIONS** RUTHLESS PRIORITIZATION PROTOTYPE & TEST BUILD, LAUNCH, & ITERATE

PRE-IDEATION   **POST-IDEATION**

Design Thinking 2.0 – Ideation

The goal of *Ideation* is to generate concepts for possible features, capabilities, or other characteristics of the product on which you are working. You may already have had many ideas occur to you while you were focusing on gathering objectives, customer insights, and competitive data in the pre-ideation stage, since the human mind naturally starts to develop ideas as soon as the right elements are present.

But our goal is not just to *have* ideas but to optimize the quantity and quality so that we can ultimately land on those that have the very highest possibility of success. That is why we worked so hard to prepare before formally starting Ideation.

Now, there are a wide range of different formats and structures you can use to generate ideas: assembling groups of executives in facilitated workshops, using cloud-based collaborative innovation tools such as BrightIdea, or waiting for spontaneous "eureka!" moments in the shower. *All* of these can work. In this chapter, we will focus on eight key success practices for maximizing the effectiveness of product ideation, whether it's in the boardroom or the bathroom.

Specifically, we will cover:

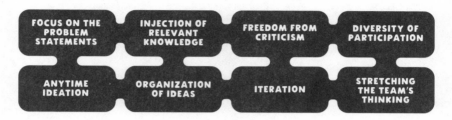

| FOCUS ON THE PROBLEM STATEMENTS | INJECTION OF RELEVANT KNOWLEDGE | FREEDOM FROM CRITICISM | DIVERSITY OF PARTICIPATION |
| ANYTIME IDEATION | ORGANIZATION OF IDEAS | ITERATION | STRETCHING THE TEAM'S THINKING |

Eight Ideation Practices

 wdc.ht/IDEATE

Ideation Practice 1:
FOCUS ON THE PROBLEM STATEMENTS

The spark of innovation is *always* a clear, focused objective. In Design Thinking, this is provided by the problem statements you defined in the previous chapter. Teams can work on one at a time, or you can bucket them into related problems to be brainstormed together.

That list of problem statements is your ideation "North Star." Any time ideation processes seem to be spinning or stuck, return to the list of problem statements to direct the effort.

You may find, as you start to work on these problem statements, that they have ambiguity or points of confusion that are sub-optimizing the ideation process. Don't be shy about editing the problem statements if improving them at this point will yield better ideas.

Depending on how many problem statements you defined, you may be tempted to prioritize them according to their importance, so you know where to focus first. Just be careful about prioritizing them *too* rigorously. After Ideation, DT2.0 has a step we call "Ruthless Prioritization," which we will discuss in the next chapter. During Ideation, it can be fruitful to brainstorm on *all* of the problem statements. This is because some ideas can be very complex to implement, while some may be very simple. You may have a "problem" that is only a three out of ten in terms of its importance, but if you brainstorm a way to fix it that only takes one day's work, that's probably worth doing. At the same time, you may have a problem that is a ten out of ten in importance but for which you continue to struggle to find a workable idea that can be achieved at all. By ideating across the full range of problem statements of varying levels of "importance," you will create a larger set of ideas, and in a future step, we will get very rigorous about how to prioritize *them*. Bottom line, we'll put most of our energy into prioritizing *ideas* rather than the problem statements.

Ideation Practice 2:
INJECTION OF RELEVANT KNOWLEDGE

As we said in the previous chapter, insight is the *fuel* for ideation. Insights might include competitive data gathered from the market review or customer research from the empathy phase or other types of information. Once the team has been oriented to the objectives of the ideation, immerse them in relevant knowledge.

Since our ultimate goal in ideation is to come up with optimal solutions for the *problem* statements we defined in the previous chapter, one way to think about the relevant domains of knowledge is along the two dimensions of the problem/solution continuum:

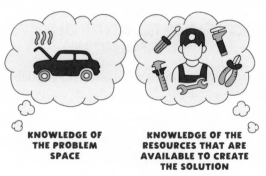

KNOWLEDGE OF THE PROBLEM SPACE   **KNOWLEDGE OF THE RESOURCES THAT ARE AVAILABLE TO CREATE THE SOLUTION**

The Two Dimensions of Relevant Knowledge < wdc.ht/KNOWLEDGE

Knowledge Domain 1:
KNOWLEDGE OF THE PROBLEM SPACE

There are many types of knowledge that can help teams understand "the problem." Here are some categories of "problem space" knowledge and where you will have already documented them if you have been following the processes outlined throughout the book:

PROBLEM SPACE KNOWLEDGE	POSSIBLE SOURCES
Who are the users for whom we are creating the product?	User personas and insights gathered from customer research in Chapters 7-8
What are the problems we are trying to solve?	Problem statements, defined in Chapter 14, as well as the customer pain map and related customer research from Chapter 10
What will the product need to compete with?	Market analysis, covered in Chapter 14
What are we ultimately trying to achieve?	Business goals, defined in Chapter 14
What else does this solution need to "connect" to in order to be part of an overall effective customer journey?	Future state customer journey map, discussed in Chapter 11
What other attempts have been made to solve this problem (within your organization or outside)? What were the results?	Information from business stakeholders, ideation team members, competitive analyses, or internal documents gathered as part of research in Chapters 7, 8, and 10

Knowledge Domain 2:
KNOWLEDGE OF THE RESOURCES THAT ARE AVAILABLE TO CREATE THE SOLUTION

You may have a specific set of resources available for whatever solutions your process yields. For example, you might only have a certain amount of time, a certain budget, certain technology, equipment, teams, etc. Also, you may have additional assets that could be optionally leveraged to bring an idea to market more rapidly, less expensively or in a way that has better competitive positioning. These might involve anything from brand awareness to technology patents to specialized expertise. Be sure the ideation team clearly understands what they have at their disposal to work with, as that will help them focus their thinking.

In the Academy-Award-winning movie *Apollo 13*, the astronauts' spaceship experiences technical difficulties with the filter system that removes carbon dioxide from the air and their lives are put in danger. The team at NASA Mission Control has to come up with a method for the astronauts to repair it so that they can survive the return to earth. Of course, there's no way to run to Home Depot for some supplies—the astronauts have to fix the problem with the tools and materials they have on board.

The leader of the Mission Control team in Houston tasked with solving this problem dumps replicas of all the "stuff" that the astronauts have in the capsule onto a table. He tells the team, "We have to figure out how to [fix the filtration system] using nothing but *this*," as he points to the pile of miscellaneous parts on the table. These are the resources that the team has to work with to come up with a solution. Watch this one-minute clip at ▶ wdc.ht/APOLLO. It's a great example of a clear, focused objective with precise knowledge provided about the *resources* available to solve the problem.

Your teams hopefully have a less constrained set of resources than the astronauts on Apollo 13 did, but they still have *some* resources that are easier to leverage, others that are more problematic and possibly still others that are out of reach. Give them a full understanding of these factors—which may mean providing them with software demos, factory tours, access to HR files, detailed budget numbers, or all of the above.

Ideation Practice 3:
FREEDOM FROM CRITICISM

We said that the "oxygen" of the fire of ideation is the freedom to generate new and unexpected ideas. It's important to create a culture within the team where all ideas are welcome and appreciated, no matter how wacky, unlikely, undeveloped, or just plain wrong.

Here are some helpful directions someone once offered me on how *not* to grow a tree.

1. Plant a seed and give it plenty of water and sunshine.

2. Eventually, a small shoot will push its way through the soil and unfurl one or two tiny leaves.

3. As soon as you see that little shoot, put on a big pair of combat boots and stomp all over it, shouting, "That doesn't look like a tree!"

It doesn't work with trees and it doesn't work with ideas. Nobel Prize winner Linus Pauling said of ideation:

"The best way to get a good idea is to have a lot of ideas. " [1]

< wdc.ht/PAULING

Pauling is one of only four people in history that won *two* Nobel prizes, so in addition to clearly being a show-off, he knew a thing or two about coming up with great ideas.

Instead of combat boots, utilize the concept of "divergent and convergent thinking," originally described by the psychologist J.P. Guilford.[2] First, define a phase where *all* ideas are welcome with no criticism (called divergence); *later,* you can prioritize and filter them to focus on the best ones (convergence).

It's far better to separate these activities because the human brain isn't good at coming up with ideas *and* critiquing them at the same time. The mind is very sensitive to the threat of a negative response. Have you ever been in a meeting and had an idea but didn't say it because you thought it wasn't the "right" idea—it was too bold, or impractical, or too obvious, too silly, too politically incorrect, too expensive, too big, or too small? Perhaps it would require resources you don't have. Perhaps it would take longer than you think is available. Turns out there are a million reasons to "not share" an idea. Your mind is constantly judging the things you *might* say and filtering out most of them to save you from the negative judgments of others. This is terrible for effective ideation.

You need to create an ideation culture that recognizes that it's good to have a large number of ideas, and it's fine if many or even most of those ideas turn out to be dead ends. Because more often than you'd think, something that starts as a "crazy idea" turns out to be the seed of the right solution. Certainly, not every crazy idea turns out to be useful—in fact, most *don't*. But we have an expression on the wall at our Innovation Loft in Manhattan:

"IT DOESN'T MATTER HOW MUCH SAND THERE IS IN THE PAN, ONLY HOW MANY FLECKS OF GOLD."

< wdc.ht/GOLD

During the California gold rush of the 1800s, prospectors would "pan for gold"[3] in rivers and lakes by filling receptacles up with silt and sifting through it looking for the bits of precious metal. The gauge of success wasn't how much sediment was discarded, but how much of the shiny stuff was found.

So, endeavor to get "all" the ideas "out there," even if many of them never go anywhere. A few of them *may* be gold, and even if a given idea *is* just river mud, once we get that idea "out" of its creator's brain and added to the idea list, then their mind can stop thinking about that one and start working on generating the next one—maybe one that's better. When we demonstrate to our delicate idea-generating subconscious that we are "listening to it" by documenting its ideas, it encourages further ideation. The creative mind can be a bit like a child; we have to praise it and show it appreciation to get its best behavior.

Ideation Practice 4:
DIVERSITY OF PARTICIPATION

It's extremely helpful to have a diverse group of people partic-ipate in the ideation process, for several reasons.

First, ideas often come from experience, and a more diverse group will have a more varied pool of experiences from which to draw. For example, someone who has lived in Australia might be aware of solutions only sold there that could contain the seed for a relevant idea. Someone who is a single parent will understand the particular needs of that segment. Someone who majored in art history may bring a perspective that is quite different from that of your engineers and which turns out to be very valuable.

Second, once you create an environment free from criticism as described in practice two, many ideas will be shared that are "half-baked"—they may have interesting characteristics but also problems. These ideas can often be a point of inspiration for *additional* ideas that fix the problems in the original ideas or are variations that effectively remove the problematic components. Teams with diversity will see more ways to improve half-baked ideas into solutions that can work.

Third, when the ideation process transitions into prioritiza-tion, which we will focus on in the next chapter, a diverse team will be in a better position to evaluate a given idea's likelihood of success because they will see a broader range of potential implementation opportunities, as well as more of the potential challenges. For example, someone with IT knowledge may have insights from that domain, while someone with finance or legal knowledge would bring a dif-ferent understanding.

Here are some of the types of diversity that you should try to include on the team:

Key Types of Diversity

TYPE	BENEFIT
Geographic Diversity	A more geographically diverse team can reflect a broader cultural awareness, as well as bring knowledge of specific practices, products, or competitors from different regions.
Functional Diversity	Having team members from technology, marketing, manufacturing, or even legal or finance can help to bring different perspectives, ensure different organizational entities are "bought in," and identify factors which will impact the "salability" of the idea to stakeholders from different parts of the company.
Gender Diversity	While recent research has debunked the idea that men's and women's brains are fundamentally wired differently, they still do often *work* differently from each other, and different genders experience the world somewhat distinctly. Take advantage of this.
Age Diversity	Having years of experience is valuable, but so is a first-person perspective on the next generation of consumers. Bring in a mix of the "seasoned" and the "wet behind the ears."
Level Diversity	It's good to have both the perspective of senior executives who have the full business view and the less senior "implementers" who understand the reality "on the ground."
Company Diversity	You may want to include partners, vendors, suppliers, distributors or other participants who are not employees of your company. They may see opportunities and adoption or implementation considerations from other angles. Also, if your organization is made up of multiple corporate entities, or you have had recent mergers or acquisitions, individuals from these different teams may have very different cultures, perspectives or priorities. This diversity can bring valuable insight to the process.
Personality Diversity	It's helpful to have some wide-eyed optimists as well as some hard-nosed realists; some extroverts and some introverts; some who are emotionally oriented and others who are rationally oriented. Consider using personality inventories such as the DISC or Myers-Briggs assessment to test for this type of diversity on a team.

Of course, this is not a comprehensive list of the types of diversity that can bring value. Your ideation can benefit from diversity of religion, sexual orientation, politics, education, affluence, interests, disability, physical characteristics, marital status, age of children, and so on.

Be sure to explicitly *tell* the team you have sought them out *for* their diverse experiences and backgrounds. This will further encourage each of them to bring forth their unique perspectives.

Ideation Practice Number 5:
ANYTIME IDEATION

Once the ingredients for ideation have been put in place, the fire should keep burning for quite a while. The subconscious "idea generation" machine works 24/7—even while we are sleeping. So, while some ideas are likely to start appearing as soon as the right ingredients are supplied, other ideas may pop up later.

You may wake up with a eureka moment or have one while driving, while in the shower, while working out or while engaged in another totally unrelated activity.

You will also find that you are more attuned to external inspiration. Once your brain is "on the lookout" for solutions to a particular problem, you may notice things in your day-to-day life that spark new ideas—the behavior of shoppers in a store, a magazine ad, a new product a friend shows you.

When these ideas occur to you, even if they are only *partial* ideas, WRITE THEM DOWN. This both ensures you don't forget them and demonstrates to your subconscious that you value the ideas it is generating, encouraging it to generate more. Of course, not everything you jot down will be a brilliant solution, but it might be difficult to know initially which are which, and your other colleagues on the team may also be inspired by some of your "first draft" ideas and further improve them—perhaps turning one of your initial vague notions into an ideation masterpiece.

To be certain that you are always ready to write things down, either carry a small journal and pen on you at all times and keep it by the side of your bed or have an app set up on your phone with a place to store ideas. Popular apps for this purpose include Evernote and Microsoft OneNote, which is the one that I use. I like the ability to dictate ideas rather than having to type or write them, which most smartphone note-taking apps support.

Ideation Practice Number 6:
ORGANIZATION OF IDEAS

Successful ideation processes often yield hundreds of discrete ideas, which will later need to be narrowed down. These ideas may be generated by a variety of people through a number of different mechanisms, including meetings/workshops, calls, and non-real-time collaboration tools such as Google Docs. It's important to have a structured method to capture and organize these ideas. This can be done with an Excel spreadsheet, a database, or a special-purpose idea management platform tool such as Hype Innovation or Spigot. Some things you will want to capture about each idea include:

- The core concept of the idea.
- What problem is it seeking to solve?
- Who generated the idea, and when?
- What benefits are expected?
- Are there other examples of this idea (such as competitive implementations)?
- Are there variations on the idea?
- Who is aligned with this idea? Who opposes it? Why?

- What challenges are anticipated?

- What budget might be needed?

- Does this idea depend on or otherwise connect to another idea?

- Has a decision been made on this idea (kill it, develop it, prototype it, implement it, etc.)?

Of course, ideas often start as a scrawl on a whiteboard or index card. You won't necessarily have this data for *all* the ideas you are tracking, but it's good to have a system that is set up to document a fairly large number of ideas and their associated metadata. This way, as your ideation process goes on, the information stays organized and easy to view, sort, filter, and edit.

BONUS TOOL: *On the book website, we've provided a sample Excel spreadsheet idea log, as well as recommendations of various cloud-based software products designed to organize ideas. These tools are essential for ensuring that your collection of ideas remains manageable and useful as it grows.*

wdc.ht/IDEALOG

Ideation Practice Number 7:
ITERATION

As we have alluded to already, great ideas are rarely born perfect but rather evolve, usually through group collaboration. Incorporate methods by which ideas are reviewed and re-reviewed to consider how they can be made better. This can be accomplished within a workshop setting by handing one break-out group's first draft ideas off to a second group for their improvements, or in a non-real-time manner through posting ideas in a collaboration tool and allowing other team members to review and comment on them at their leisure. Iteration is also at the heart of the "Prototype and Test" phase of Design Thinking that we will discuss in the next chapter.

Ideation Practice Number 8:
STRETCHING THE TEAM'S THINKING

Given our goal of ideating the broadest set of possibilities, we want to be sure we aren't limiting our thinking. We sometimes hear clients say that they feel like their teams just keep, "Coming up with the same ideas over and over," rather than exploring new territory. To overcome this common pattern, we have collected and developed a variety of techniques to drive ideation in ways that deliberately stretch thinking.

To use a popular phrase, these techniques help teams think "outside the box." But what *is* this box that everyone talks about that constrains thinking? Like any obstacle we want to overcome, the better we understand what holds back creative ideation, the easier it will be to overcome barriers.

At my company, we use our custom-built workshop space, The Innovation Loft, to help teams from some of the largest brands in the world move beyond that metaphorical "box," and this enables them to create breakthrough products, processes, or entire businesses. So, we've spent quite a lot of time studying the barriers that *limit* individual or team thinking and testing methods to break free of them.

It turns out, there really isn't just a single "box." Instead, there are five main nested barriers that limit ideation, as seen in the next diagram.

You can use facilitation techniques and exercises to help get past each box, but they differ depending on which box you're stuck on.

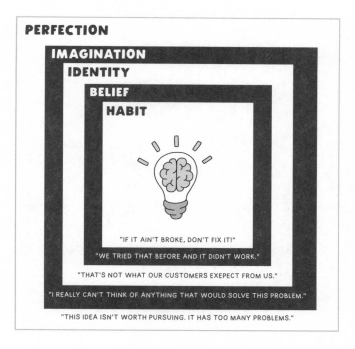

The "Boxes" That Limit Ideation   < wdc.ht/BOXES

The 1st Box that Limits Ideation:
HABIT

People constrained by habit are best described by the phrase, "If it ain't broke, don't fix it!" It's our comfort zone—where we know what works. But uncharted territory is where much of the treasure lies.

How do you move teams beyond habit? One way is to explore "stretch" or "moonshot" goals that are well beyond what's possible using your current methods of doing business.

For example, if your manufacturing process takes 90 minutes to produce a carton of ice cream and you'd like ideas to speed it up, conduct an exercise to brainstorm how you could produce that same carton in only 5 minutes. This type of exercise requires completely different thinking about the entire manufacturing process. It might not actually be practical or cost-effective to make the cartons in five minutes, but the process of thinking about how it *could* be done is one way to explore what lies beyond the box of habit.

Another technique to get beyond habit is to ideate in a different type of workspace. At the Innovation Loft, we use music, toys, physical activity/games, and mixing teams in unexpected ways to get people to *think* in new ways. You can also take teams to the park, or on retreats in the desert, or to a museum in the middle of a city to shake up their habits and inspire new thinking.

The 2nd Box that Limits Ideation:
BELIEF

Even when we're ready to move past habit and try something new, there's another box that constrains what we *believe* will work or believe we are capable of accomplishing. The box of "belief" is epitomized by statements like, "We tried that before and it didn't work," or "We can't compete in that space."

Even when these beliefs have some truth to them, they're often overgeneralized. Take, "We can't compete in that space." It may not be *wise* to compete in "that space," but is it really impossible? If you hired the right people? Launched a new product? Put sufficient marketing behind it? By staying in the box of belief, you could be dismissing possible opportunities. The goal of ideation is to explore the *possible*; so, you *want* to be thinking about ideas that *might* not be "wise," but are at least worth evaluating. Get the ideas down first and then assess them later using the converge/diverge model described earlier.

One way to tackle the barrier of belief is to use exercises that highlight the differences between beliefs and facts. Accurate facts are helpful, whereas beliefs can be limiting when masquerading as facts. It's critical to know which are which.

An exercise we use to address this "box" is to have teams make lists of the *reasons* why something can't be done or document the barriers they face. Then we ask them to figure out which of the statements they documented are actual facts and which are beliefs.

Often, many of the "reasons" something cannot be done turn out to be beliefs. The way we coach teams to figure out the difference is by asking them to look at each statement and inquire, "Is that *really* true? Is *every part* of that statement true? Is it based in fact or is it just an opinion we keep repeating?" It's ok if it's an opinion, by the way. Opinions can be insightful—they're just dangerous when viewed as facts. At this stage we just want to determine the difference.

For example, take the statement, "Our customers won't buy insurance products from us." It may be that there are genuine reasons to be skeptical of whether they would, but is every part of that statement 100% true? Are there *no* customer segments who will buy *any* type of insurance product from us?

This exact phrase was the subject of an exercise in a workshop we did with a client recently. Initially, the participants were fairly unanimous in agreeing that it was *true* that their customers wouldn't buy insurance products from them due to their brand and certain trust issues.

When we did this exercise, what did we find? Well, one breakout team came back and pointed out that in one division of the company, they sell extended warranties, which are really a *type* of insurance product. So, they actually *already* have *some* customers buying insurance products from them. Wow. Not only is it *not* true that nobody ever *would*; it's happening already. This is the power of re-examining your beliefs.

Of course, just because they realized the statement isn't 100% true doesn't mean they wouldn't face challenges launching a major new insurance product in a different market. But if your brain holds a false belief about what's possible, it's a box holding you back from coming up with a rich set of ideas for further analysis.

Sometimes a statement like the insurance one above *will* pass the "is it true" exercise, and everyone will still agree that, "Yes, we looked at it, and this statement *is* 100% true." There's one more question that we use that can sometimes break down a more persistent belief. It's a simple one. "How do we know?" If it's a fact, there should be some validation. If there isn't, then maybe it's really just a belief or opinion.

In another workshop, the client teams brought up their belief that their company was "incapable of delivering cutting-edge technology." This belief was holding them back from generating ideas that required AI or other advanced computer science. The teams went through the first exercise and validated that it was really 100% true.

Then we asked, "How do we know?" And we got a *slew* of examples of problems with various IT projects. IT, apparently, had messed up a lot. But after discussion, the teams agreed that all those stories didn't really prove it was *impossible*. They decided to change the statement to, "Our company has a very low likelihood of being able to deliver cutting-edge tech." This is actually more progress than it initially appears because it acknowledges that success is *possible*, but it still meant they were going to stay away from generating ideas that required ambitious technology, so clearly there was more work to do.

We then went into a final round of the exercise, which is powered by one last question: "How could we change that?" The teams came back with a wide range of ideas about how it could be changed, mostly by getting external teams to work on the advanced technology. They wound up finalizing the statement, which is the last step of the exercise, to say, "Our *existing* IT teams are weak when implementing cutting edge technology," a far more accurate and *solvable* problem.

Because getting past the box of what Tony Robbins calls "limiting beliefs" is so important, I want to describe for you a second exercise construct that we use—an alternative to the approach described above. In this second approach, rather than addressing the *individual* reasons that may be holding back thinking, we address it holistically.

We call the exercise, "How Will We Get Here?" and it is adapted from the work of Matt and Gail Taylor, pioneers in group collaboration and innovation.

It starts by providing teams with a written scenario "from the future," which describes massive success. For example, we might provide a fictional *Wall Street Journal* article that we have drafted and which is dated five years *after* the date of the workshop—an article "from the future."

In this future article we declare that the company has achieved its goal at a level beyond what the workshop participants believe is even possible—perhaps it's launching a blockbuster new product that takes over the market, doubling their revenue, or transforming their customer journey to become "best in class"—whatever long-term goal the workshop is focused on. We make sure the "article" is rich with descriptions of this aspirational level of success, but is intentionally vague about *how* it was accomplished.

We then ask teams to put themselves into that fictional future and work together to answer and document, "How did we do it?" The exercise gets the teams to jump totally past the question of whether we *can* do it and instead simply asks them to reverse engineer how it was done. The groups then share with each other what they "figured out," and often have breakthrough ideas around how their goals can be achieved.

BONUS TOOL: *On the book website, we provide several Word documents with example scenarios for the "How Will We Get Here?" exercise that you can tailor for your own use.*

 wdc.ht/SCENARIOS

A fantastic example of why this psychological trickery works is a decade-plus-old story from the consumer electronics industry. As the story goes, at the time, there was a war between various giant electronics manufacturers to see who could make the thinnest flat-screen TV. The slimmest units back then were about 2-3 inches thick. Consumers wanted flatter screens, and the marketing departments of all the electronics companies were pushing engineers to figure out how to make them thinner.

At one of the larger companies, there was a summit on the topic. The engineering team came back to the marketing department with a three-hour presentation they had spent weeks preparing, explaining, in detail, why two inches was pretty much as thin as these displays could possibly get. There were reasons, like the thickness of certain circuits and space needed for heat dispersion. They explained that in their professional view, the maximum potential "thinness" had been reached, and the industry would have to find new ways to dif-ferentiate "flat screen" TVs because they just weren't going to get any thinner. The presentation was very scientific and persuasive, filled with detailed diagrams and advanced math. Laser pointers were used.

Then, about a week after that presentation, the "competitive intelligence" group at this same company got some hot insider informa-tion. Apparently, their largest competitor was getting ready to release a ONE-inch-thick flat-screen TV. *Half* the thickness of what the first company had on the market.

They pulled the technical department together. The engineers scratched their heads. How was this *possible?* They broke into teams; they brainstormed; they drew hundreds of diagrams on whiteboards considering the different possible ways their competitor could have achieved this incredible feat. They re-examined their math. They worked round the clock for a week surviving on coffee, cigarettes, and pizza. *Then* they reported back to management. They had figured it out!

Exhausted but exhilarated, they outlined an alternative approach to engineering a display that they had conceived of in the middle of the night, saying this was surely the *only* way that their competitor could have achieved such a breakthrough. It was extremely unconventional, but they believed that they could make it work—just like their competitor had.

They started building some rapid prototypes. It was critical to get it to market quickly. After all, their competitor was already ahead of them.

The prototypes were successful, and the product was fast-tracked for manufacturing. Each day, the teams watched the trade announcements with anticipation, waiting for the day their competitor would announce the availability of *their* one-inch TV.

The weeks went by, then months. No announcement. The company was now only four weeks away from launching its *own* one-inch-thick TV. Still, no announcement from their competitor. They were excited, but super confused. What was going on?

Then, they got some updated information.

The original competitive intelligence, it turned out, was totally wrong. Entirely mistaken. Their competitor was *nowhere near* figuring out how to make a thinner TV. That company's engineers were still using laser pointers to "educate" their management about why there's a two-inch limit to how thin flat screens can be. But because the first company's engineers *believed* it had been done already, they figured out how to do it.

And that is the power of beliefs.

And to that point, I *believe* this story is true, but I can't say for sure. But does it matter? LG this year announced TVs that are less than one-sixth of an inch thick.[4] No doubt many product teams never thought we'd get to that point.

Henry Ford famously said,

"WHETHER YOU THINK YOU CAN OR THINK YOU CAN'T, YOU'RE RIGHT." [5]

Of course, not everything that you *believe* to be true will turn out that way, but beliefs can be powerful tools and also powerful barriers to innovation, depending on how they are used.

The 3rd Box that Limits Ideation:
IDENTITY

Even when we're willing to change and we believe that ambitious goals are possible, we can remain stuck inside a box of our own *identity.* This box is best characterized by statements like, "We don't do that at this company," or "We could never get that approved," or "That's not what our customers expect from us."

It's *valuable* to have an identity and a brand that stands for something. However, getting past the identity barrier doesn't necessarily mean *acting* outside the box, but just *thinking* outside the box. Identities need to grow and change over time, and they can't do that if you never even *consider* possibilities beyond your current identity.

For example, we mentioned earlier how Apple used to be called "Apple Computer," but now it makes more money from smartphones and is known as simply "Apple." When Steve Jobs proposed the iPhone, some people at Apple Computer may well have thought, "That doesn't make sense for us. We are a *computer* company." Looking at Apple's current trillion-dollar valuation, it's a good thing they moved beyond *that* box.

One way to spur teams to temporarily think outside their current identity is to play the "What Would Company X Do?" game. We give separate brainstorming teams different companies to use as models

271

and have them look at their *own* company's problem statements the way another organization would.

Some good companies to use include GE, Walmart, Starbucks, Amazon, Netflix, Zappos, Ritz Carlton, Tesla and Disney, as they're all successful entities with very different identities and ways of solving problems.

Another good company to model is Google. We might tell one team, "Google just bought your company, and they put their top people on the problem. How would *they* solve it?" This mindset pulls groups out of their normal assumptions about what is possible within the scope of their company's identity and, strangely enough, even frees them from limiting beliefs about their own *individual* imaginations. You're not solving the problem as "you" anymore—you are solving it as someone else. We've had teams come back and say things like, "Well, the folks at Google would do this wild innovative thing," and go on to describe it, "But that's the sort of thing we'd never even come up with here at Acme Corporation." Uh oh, tricked you! You just did.

And you don't have to limit your modeling to companies. Some other entities we have used successfully include the U.S. Marine Corps, the Catholic Church, and the Freemasons. You can also pick individuals. How would Albert Einstein solve this problem? Or Napoleon? Pick models based on the type of thinking you want to inspire. It can be quite fun to see teams working in parallel on the same problem but from the perspective of wildly divergent identities.

In fact, the whole process should be fun. One of our operating principles in ideation is that people are at their most resourceful when they are having fun.

It's helpful to orient teams to their assigned identity by giving them some information about the entity they are to "think like." For example, when a team is given the U.S. Marine Corps as their assigned model, we provide them copies of a few articles about Marine culture, a Marine basic training manual and show them a short video clip used to welcome new recruits to their first day of basic training. This helps the teams "get into character."

The 4th Box that Limits Ideation:
IMAGINATION

Ideas beyond the box of imagination aren't even a blip on the radar of our conscious or subconscious mind. We don't consider them outside our beliefs. We don't consider them inconsistent with our identity. We just don't consider them at all.

You see, what a person can *imagine* comes from essentially two things: their past experiences and their ability to *take* those experiences and combine them in novel ways.

As mentioned earlier, a team with diverse experiences is a good starting point for the broadest possible "imagination potential." But you can also find ways to provide the ideation team with potentially relevant *new* experiences that can help them get beyond the box of their own imagination.

We worked with one client that was looking to take a very manually intensive legal process and speed it up. We took the team to different factories where products like candy and kitchen appliances were manufactured to observe many interesting methods used to move production along quickly. We also brought in an improv trainer to teach them how comic troupes create entertaining sketches with just a few seconds of preparation. It wasn't clear in advance precisely *how* these experiences would seed their thinking about speeding up the legal process, but in fact, both gave them multiple insights that wound up in the final solution.

The second component of thinking "outside the box" of imagination is combining things in novel ways. To use another Steve Jobs example, when the iPhone was being developed, it was the first phone to use a touchscreen for all interactions (no physical keypad). Jobs and the team realized that the screen would get banged around a lot as it was being handled and stuck in pockets and purses. It had to be highly durable, much more so than the screens of laptops or iMacs, which were plastic and scratched easily. They approached Corning, a leader in making very "tough" glass used in cookware and laboratories. It was a new idea to use glass in the screen of a mobile computing device, but by combining the idea of durable glass used in other domains with the smartphone, they solved a problem, and today nearly all smartphones use glass screens.[6]

So how do you *find* those points of connection? The brain naturally goes to *familiar* solutions to problems and, by default, only searches the larger universe when prompted in specific ways.

For example, I once attended a class led by the famous Hollywood acting teacher Stephen Book. Book asked a room full of college theater students to make a list of different relationships that can exist between people. They came up with: mother/father, sister/brother, wife/husband, boyfriend/girlfriend, aunt/uncle, grandmother/grandfather, grandson/granddaughter, and a few others, but then ran out of steam. Book prompted them, "Think of more relationships." Besides variations of what was already on the board, like "great" aunt, "second" cousin, "ex-" wife, or "step" brother, the room was stumped.

This is the type of situation where some type of stimulation is needed to help people combine knowledge in novel ways. Students were then given magazines and asked to look through the photos to find other relationships. Finally, someone held up a picture and asked, "Is being someone's barista a relationship?" Of course, it is, and then, naturally, 100 other professional relationships started emerging: teacher, doorman, masseuse. Somehow, nobody's brain was thinking in that corner of the universe. What's cool about this sort of thing is that once one person finds a new domain, very often, others can build on it quite effectively.

We often do similar exercises in workshops. We give participants different photos and tell them that the answer to the problem
is something in the photo, then let them brainstorm on that. The
secret is that the photos are fairly random. We really have no idea how
they relate to the problem at hand; we just try to pick photos with
a decent amount going on in them. It's astounding how many great
ideas come out of this exercise. Why? Because the brain is prompted
with new domains to scan.

For example, we were working on a branding campaign for a
client and one person participating in this exercise came up with a
great tagline that compared the brand to angels. The larger group
loved it. When the person showed the photo that had prompted the
idea, it was a picture of a woman at a park. The room was perplexed.
How had this picture given her the idea of angels? She explained
that the person in the photo looked like she might be thinking about
someone she loves, which made her think of Valentine's Day, which
made her think of angels. The answers *aren't* in the photos, we just
need to provoke the brain to look in new spaces.

In addition to these types of exercises generating ideas in and of
themselves, they also train the mind to look for new connections. Steve
Jobs wasn't doing an exercise at our Innovation Loft when it occurred to
him to reach out to glass companies, but he'd trained his mind to look
for novel approaches outside the realm of most people's imaginations.

The 5th Box that Limits Ideation:
THE BOX OF PERFECTION

This box is the voice in your head that is looking for the *perfect*
idea and thus rejects anything that doesn't conform to your precon-
ception of what that might be—or rejects any idea that might have
problems associated with it.

All great ideas have problems. Let's return to Steve Jobs and the iPhone origin. Back then, no carrier wanted to give cell phone manufacturers the freedom to control the user interface of a device, which was essential to the concept of the iPhone.[7] And no doubt that was just the beginning of a long list of challenges. Apple pursued and found solutions to those challenges rather than using them as an excuse. Naturally, there will come a time when it's appropriate to review ideas and determine which ones are worth pursuing and which are more trouble than they are worth, but in the process of *ideation*, you need to get out of the "box" of perfection and get those ideas documented.

One exercise we use to battle this "box" is to challenge teams to come up with the *worst* solution to the problem that they possibly can. We tell them that there will be voting and a prize awarded to whichever team comes up with the most truly awful idea. We aren't looking for garden-variety misses here; we want ideas that will be colossal failures, like what Max Bialystock was looking for in *The Producers*.

This mindset is highly beneficial for a few reasons. First, it creates a culture that says it's ok to come up with bad ideas—in fact, it's encouraged, and it's fun. In our workshops, the "badness" of each presented idea is measured by how raucous the audience's "boos" are. When teams are having fun, they generate their highest quality work. But equally important, it gets teams thinking down avenues they otherwise wouldn't even consider because they assume that down those avenues, it's only bad ideas. Maybe it's the avenue of open source, or outsourcing, or the avenue of letting go of some sacred cow. But they are now willing to look down those alleys *because they are looking for bad ideas.*

And it's probably true that there *are* a lot of bad ideas down those paths. But once you start taking a mental stroll through those neighborhoods, it's not uncommon to find that there are also some really interesting possibilities. Like finding an awesome restaurant in an otherwise sketchy part of town. For example, does it *sound* like a good idea to explore making a screen that has to be highly durable out of glass? With most glass, no. But with a very particular kind of unusual glass, apparently yes.

Above all else, get your teams to stop trying to brainstorm only the *one* best idea. There is no "best" idea. We like to say that for any given problem or opportunity:

THERE MAY OF COURSE BE TRULY **WRONG** IDEAS, BUT THERE ARE ALSO THOUSANDS OF **RIGHT** IDEAS. ALL WE NEED IS TO FIND **SOME** OF THEM AND THEN PICK **ONE.**

< wdc.ht/PICK

That feels like a much more solvable problem than scouring the universe for the single best idea. Because...

When the mind feels it's been asked to tackle a "solvable" problem, it exerts far more energy than if it believes it's been given a puzzle that can only lead to frustration.

< wdc.ht/SOLVE

It's fantastic to have a high quality standard, a strong identity, and defined beliefs and habits. All these aspects of our personality serve us in various situations. But it's also valuable to be able to temporarily turn these psychological limits off in the context of exploratory ideation. You never know what's out there, and you can enrich your value proposition, your brand, and even yourself by embracing the freedom to explore what lies beyond. Then, afterwards, you can decide whether or not to *use* what you find "outside the box."

. . . .

Utilizing the practices in this chapter, you should be able to generate a robust set of ideas that can then be prioritized and tested in the final steps of DT2.0, which we will look at next.

CHAPTER SIXTEEN

BUILD THE FUTURE

DESIGN THINKING 2.0: AFTER THE IDEATION

I remember my first childhood visit to the horse races at Arlington Park, near Chicago (where I grew up). My Uncle Ed gave me $2 to bet on a horse, and I agonized over the decision. At nine, I was not an experienced gambler, but I understood that if I picked the right horse, my $2 could become $4, or even $20, and then I would be able to keep betting all day, and maybe even wind up with enough to get an Atari. But if I picked the *wrong* horse, my $2 would be gone forever, and I would sit the rest of the day unable to participate. I looked at the names of the horses. Would "Lettuce Entertain You" run faster than

"Bob's Your Uncle?" "Al's Favorite" had a boring *name*, but a supposedly lucky number: 7.

We went down to the dress circle to inspect the horses. One was taller; one was livelier; one looked friendlier; one was cuter. But who would be *faster*? The grown-ups were looking at their racing forms to study the horses' past histories as well as the opinions of various handicappers. Would that information enable them to bet successfully? I gathered advice from several people and got conflicting recommendations. Ugh. Twelve horses, and I didn't know who to pick.

It could be said that the only problem greater than having no ideas is to have a hundred ideas. Indeed, while some clients come to us *looking* for ideas, others come to us because their organization has *so many* ideas that they just don't know where to start and aren't confident they have the right method to prioritize.

If you have applied the prior steps of Design Thinking 2.0, your number of ideas is potentially quite large. In this chapter, we will focus on the activities that occur *after* ideation. These activities help you identify the best ideas and then ensure they will work effectively.

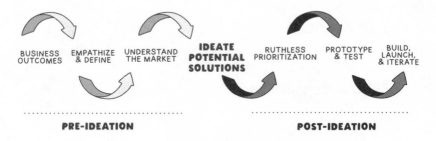

Design Thinking 2.0 — Post-Ideation

RUTHLESS PRIORITIZATION

There are elements of prioritization present in *every* stage of Design Thinking 2.0.

① The first step of "Defining Outcomes" requires prioritization to finalize the objectives the effort will focus on.

② The Empathy process requires prioritizing which types of customers you will study and what methods of research you will use.

③ As we mentioned in the previous chapter, during Define, you may wish to prioritize which problem statements are the most "painful."

④ And when you do your market research, you need to determine which competitors you will focus on.

In this step, however, our focus is on prioritizing the *ideas* generated during the Ideate stage. Repeating Linus Pauling's insight, the best way to have a great idea is to have a lot of ideas. So hopefully, that's what you have. And that's a great thing *as long as you have a way to prioritize them so you can take action.*

In DT2.0, we separate the prioritization process into this discrete step for reasons discussed in the previous chapter—we want to first give teams the freedom to ideate without simultaneously imposing critical judgment.

With that level of freedom from being "wrong," you will probably finish the ideation activities with many more ideas than you could even prototype, let alone launch, so there is a need for a structured process to filter and score what could be dozens or even hundreds of ideas to find the few that you want to carry forward. This is the "converge" portion of the diverge/converge process we discussed in the previous chapter.

Figuring out how best to prioritize is often not obvious. Just like the horses, different ideas are of different sizes, have different owners, and have different characteristics that make them potentially appealing, as well as challenging.

And, prioritizing ideas effectively is *just* as critical as *generating* the ideas. If prioritization is done poorly, several major problems can develop.

1 If you fail to prioritize rigorously enough, you may take on too much all at once, and a product or effort can fail under its own weight.

2 If you select the wrong ideas—ideas that won't be successful—you waste effort and money and potentially create even larger issues, like reduced credibility or increased liability.

3 If you reject the ideas that were the optimal solution, you risk depriving your customers and the company of the potential benefits.

But don't let that stress you out. No process is perfect. In order to be sure that *only* the ideas that will be successful are picked, you'd have to have a crystal ball. We don't have one, and yet we've had a stellar track record. The trick is to not *need* to be perfect up front and instead let the process optimize your efforts, as we will explain.

Classic Design Thinking (1.0) incorporates prioritization into the ideation phase, where ideas are ranked based on:

- *Desirability* (to the customer),
- Business *Viability* (does it make business sense?), and
- Implementation *Feasibility* (can it be accomplished?)

DT2.0 expands the model of prioritization to be more comprehensive than in classic Design Thinking, incorporating the concepts of Desirability, Viability, and Feasibility, and also adding additional considerations such as Risk and Confidence Level, which will be described later in this chapter. The goal is to provide you a clear process to follow to decide which ideas to focus on.

I wish I had had a clear process to follow at the track when I was nine. My only real option was to go with my gut and face the fact that if I didn't make a decision before the bell, I'd lose the opportunity to participate at all. I put my $2 on Barnaby's Bunch. He was the one who looked liveliest during the inspection. Somewhat arbitrarily, I decided that *that* was the most important factor.

282

Because I didn't really have confidence in my pick, I kept it safe and bet "to show" (which means you win *something* if the horse comes in first, second, *or* third, but not much). I was screaming with excitement when my horse came in second place. It was around 3-to-2 odds, so my $2 bet yielded me back something like $2.80. No massive victory, but disaster averted.

Let's take a look at a series of prioritization steps that will enable you to base your decisions on something more methodical than I had back then and hopefully give you the confidence to bet to win.

RUTHLESS PRIORITIZATION

CONSOLIDATE IDEAS   DEFINE VALUE FOR EACH IDEA   DEFINE COST & EFFORT FOR EACH IDEA   ASSESS RISK FOR EACH IDEA   DEFINE MINIMUM VIABLE PRODUCT & ROADMAP

< wdc.ht/PRIORITIZE

Prioritization Step 1:
CONSOLIDATE IDEAS

Once you have finished the ideation phase, you will most likely have a large number of ideas from different sources and with different levels of detail. Some of these ideas may be duplicates, variations, or cousins of each other. Combine these related ideas into "master ideas." This will make it easier to prioritize by *groups* of ideas. Then, for those groups you choose to prioritize for further evaluation, the team can dive into the different variations to prioritize among those.

Prioritization Step 2:
DEFINE VALUE FOR EACH IDEA

The whole reason you would implement an idea is to drive *value*, so the next step is to take each master idea and seek to quantify its potential value. We generally measure potential value along four dimensions:

1. Desirability, as measured by the degree and type of value to the *customer* (what pain does it solve and how valuable is it to solve that pain?)

2. The breadth of customers impacted (not all ideas benefit everybody).

3. The frequency of benefit to the user. How often does the "problem" this idea solves occur?

4. The amount of business impact (as might be measured in dollars Net Promoter Score increases or other metrics as appropriate to the category).

Of course, it may not be possible to be *precise* at this stage about the value that could result from implementing the idea, but for the purpose of prioritization, it's important to at least approximate it so that ideas can be weighed against each other. It may also make sense to do some additional research to more accurately quantify the value of high potential ideas.

For example, if an idea is targeted at increasing sales and you have data on the average value of a sale, how many sales you are making today, and the profit margin, it becomes possible to estimate the bottom-line dollar impact of, for instance, a 0.5% increase in sales.

As you try to measure the value that you believe an idea could generate, you should also take the opportunity to look at all the possible *categories* of value. Consider whether this idea could be further evolved or improved to generate *even more* value. It's totally permissible for the ideas to keep getting better as you go through the prioritization process.

Here are some examples of ways a given idea might generate value:

- Cause existing customers to buy more or more often
- Lower marketing costs
- Lower costs to deliver your product or service
- Lower customer support costs
- Increase customer satisfaction or referrals
- Improve the reputation of the company/brand
- Generate intellectual property that could be resold or licensed
- Create opportunities for sponsorship or advertising
- Bring in outside publicity, funding, grants or tax benefits

It's not uncommon to discover that an idea initially conceived to address one of these categories can be expanded to deliver in multiple categories. If you can devise an idea that you only have to pay to execute once but that simultaneously delivers value in multiple categories, that's going to increase the odds of that idea being a winner.

Prioritization Step 3:
DEFINE COST & EFFORT

Next, we want to identify the level of *cost and effort* it will take to implement the idea. Businesses are usually looking for ideas with a strong "return on investment," which means that the cost will be paid back many times over. In order to calculate that, we need to know not only the value, which we defined in the last step, but also the investment necessary to realize that value.

Furthermore, we need to understand the *effort*. In some cases, effort and cost are synonymous because if the budget is available, the necessary resources can be procured. However, sometimes there are other constraints on resources. For example, if you only have ten people who understand how to make changes to your mainframe system, and a given project is going to take that whole team four months to develop, then no amount of money is going to make that possible if those resources are not available.

When gauging likely cost, here are some example categories of activities or investments you may need to estimate:

- Requirements definition and creative design
- Software purchase, configuration and development
- Hardware purchase and hosting
- Physical construction
- Installation/deployment
- Training/change management
- Marketing
- Customer support
- Other ongoing costs such as operations or consumables

As you attempt to estimate the costs, this is also a good opportunity to ask the creative question, "How can we keep the costs as low as possible?" What is the "minimum viable version" of this idea? The less it costs to get the value associated with an idea, the more likely it is to be a winner.

Prioritization Step 4:
ASSESS RISK FOR EACH IDEA

Let's say you have an idea that has a really strong value proposition, if successful. That's great, but how *likely* is it to be successful? Most new ideas come with some level of *risk*. It certainly makes sense to *take* risks and be willing to fail—in fact, it's the only way to be innovative and improve. Nevertheless, if an idea has a high level of risk, and it's being weighed against another idea with similar cost and benefit but far lower risk, then that is an important and possibly decisive consideration.

So, what types of risks should you consider? Here is a list that you can tailor depending on the types of ideas you are prioritizing. Some ideas will have nearly zero risk in some of these categories, while others may have unacceptably high risks in one or more.

8 Common Types of Risk

TYPE	DESCRIPTION
Technical Risk	Does the idea require new technologies to be created? Might they not work as anticipated, cost more than originally planned, or take longer to build than forecast? Technologies can include software, manufacturing or construction techniques, or whatever applies to your industry.
Implementation Risk	Can your company effectively execute this idea? Do you have the skills, bandwidth, and training to get it done?
Operational Risk	Once the idea is "built," do you have the processes, team members, or other assets needed to continue running it as long as is necessary to realize the value?
Alignment Risk	Are all the key people on board with this idea? Or will there be internal parties trying to sabotage it or unwilling to support it?
Adoption Risk	If this idea is realized, will customers want to use it? Will they behave the way you expect?
Regulatory/ Legal Risk	Is there an aspect of this idea that might run afoul of laws or regulations in any of your markets or violate protected intellectual property or existing contractual commitments?
Partner Risk	Are you relying on parties external to your company to make the idea work? If so, will they deliver reliably? What if they don't?
Competitive Risk	If you were to implement this idea, what would your competitors do? Copy it? Counter it? Sue you? Would these actions undermine the idea in a significant way?

Looking at this list of possible risks may be daunting, but remember that your outcome is not to "sell" an idea—your outcome is to pick ideas that will be successful. So, it's positive if you identify key risks to an idea that could cause it to be unsuccessful. This is true for three reasons.

First, if the risks are too great, it may make sense to pick another idea. Hopefully, you have plenty.

Second, seeing the potential risks gives you the opportunity to devise strategies to avoid these risks. While you won't be able to eliminate risk entirely, by looking at an idea through the lens of these defined categories, you may be inspired to further improve the idea and adjust specific details of its scope, approach, or features in such a way as to make it less risky and hence more likely to succeed. For example, you may be able to reduce competitive risk by filing a patent. You may be able to reduce partner risk by defining new service level agreements or having backup vendors. And you may be able to reduce adoption risk through the prototyping and testing activities we will talk about a little later in this chapter.

Third, some risks pertain to the *unknown*. For example, you may have identified a risk that the technology build could turn out to be more time-consuming and expensive than defined in the cost model. That may be an unknown, but not *unknowable*. Perhaps additional analyses could increase the accuracy of the technical estimates and decrease this risk.

In DT2.0, we call this the "Confidence Factor." For example, one idea may be rated as low effort, and we're pretty sure that's true, while another idea may be rated as low effort, but there's more uncertainty about whether that's accurate. The difference between these is the Confidence Factor, and you may want to use this as a consideration in your prioritization.

Prioritization Step 5:
Prioritization Step 5:
DEFINE MINIMUM VIABLE PRODUCT AND ROAD-MAP

The last step of the prioritization process is to make some decisions about what is "in" and what is "out" for the actual product. This can be made much less gut-wrenching through the concept of the Minimum Viable Product, or MVP.

The idea of a "Minimum Viable Product" was popularized in the book *The Lean Startup* by Eric Ries and is now used widely in digital product development. It describes a philosophy whereby the initial release of a new product should be kept as "stripped down" and simple as possible—the *minimum* product that will still provide at least a basic, usable experience.[1]

The primary benefit of limiting your initial product to the "minimum viable" version is that it gets it to market sooner and at a lower cost. It's based on the proven belief that the best way to evolve and enrich a product's feature set is with continual customer feedback *after* the product is in the market.

At the time when Design Thinking was first formulated, the largely physical products being created may have required expensive tool and die setups for manufacturing and may have taken years to change once launched. This necessitated a high degree of polish before the product was released. But today's digital products can be rapidly tweaked and improved on a nearly continuous basis.

From a prioritization perspective, this alleviates some of the pressure. You may have 100 ideas for product features, but at this stage, you don't need to decide definitively which ones you will include in the *ultimate* version of the product. You only need to decide which ones are so essential that the product cannot be effectively used without them. When creating the MVP, you can choose to leave out some features that you know users will "want" or "ask for" but which are not truly essential to the core value proposition. Once the product is launched, you will learn via customer feedback whether users really *do* want those features. If so, then those can be the next capabilities that you add. If your launch has tons of customers using your product but clamoring for more features, that's a great start.

It's still valuable to create a multi-release product road-map at this stage to define what features you *believe* you will add to the product in the months following launch. Just know that this vision should be flexible and adjusted based on feedback *after* launch.

And, in fact, even *before* launching, you will validate your MVP hypothesis in the next step of the Design Thinking 2.0 process, "Prototype and Test."

BONUS TOOL: *The process of weighing each idea in terms of its combined profile of benefits, costs, risks, and confidence factor can become somewhat complex to think about all at once, and it becomes essential to use some kind of tool to store and analyze all these data elements for an entire portfolio of ideas. We have provided a detailed guide on the book website, as well as an Excel spreadsheet that we use for scoring ideas across these various dimensions.*

 wdc.ht/IDEASCORING

PROTOTYPE AND TEST

If there are two concepts that are fundamental to both the original conception of Design Thinking as well as our updated 2.0 version, they're (1) driving product development based on customer insights and (2) prototyping products before they are built and launched. This next step, Prototype and Test, incorporates both of these key concepts.

A prototype is a model of something you intend to potentially build later on a larger scale. Da Vinci made miniature, working replicas of his inventions to tinker with before constructing them at full size.[2] Michelangelo created small clay models of his sculptures before starting to chisel the giant slabs of marble.[3] Airbus spins up virtual reality simulations of their new aircraft before they start riveting steel panels together.[4] The idea of prototyping has a pretty good pedigree.

It makes sense. If you're going to make a mistake or change your mind, you'll want to do it in a medium where the cost is low to rework and improve.

But what kind of prototype should *you* create? A clay model like Michelangelo? A virtual walkthrough like Airbus? Here are three dimensions to think about when planning your prototype.

MISSION **SCOPE** **FIDELITY**

Three Dimensions of Prototyping

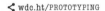 wdc.ht/PROTOTYPING

 Dimension 1:
MISSION

The first dimension of prototype planning is defining the mission—the objectives or goals of your prototype. There are many possible reasons to create prototypes, such as technical proof of concept, collaborative visioning, pitching a product, developer communication, or user testing. Each of these reasons provides value in and of itself, and it could be beneficial to create a prototype for any one of these reasons.

However, prototypes can often help achieve multiple objectives, so when planning, it's good to consider where the prototype could provide additional value beyond its primary benefit. If you wish to gain those additional benefits, there may be certain things you want to do in planning that prototype to make sure that it works well for multiple purposes.

If you are struggling to figure out the mission of the prototype, consider this. Prototypes primarily exist for three reasons:

① To increase the certainty that a given concept will "work" when implemented at full scale

② To help "work out" aspects of a concept in a low-risk environment

③ To help communicate the "concept" of a product to others

So, ask yourself:

① What do I need to become more certain of?

② What do I still need to "figure out" about this concept?

③ Who do I need to understand the concept better and what do they need to know?

The answers to these questions should help you clarify your prototype mission.

Dimension 2:
SCOPE

The second dimension, *scope*, determines how *much* of the total experience is included in the prototype. For example, are all of the screens in your application needed in the prototype, or only a subset? In general, the broader the scope, the more expensive and time-consuming the prototyping process will be. You may not need to prototype every feature in order to drive key decisions. In some cases, the prototype may be used just to prove out the most difficult areas of a solution or to give a "general idea" of a product. So look to your mission and keep the scope as narrow as will accomplish it.

Dimension 3:
FIDELITY

As we said earlier, a prototype is a model of something we intend to potentially build on a broader scale in the future. In theory, this "model" could range from a napkin sketch to a functioning application.

We typically think of five primary levels of fidelity for digital prototypes. Each level down this list increases the realism of the prototype, but also increases the level of time and effort, so use the mission of the prototype to guide you in finding the right balance.

The Five Primary Levels of Prototype Fidelity

LEVEL	DESCRIPTION
Paper Prototype	Hand drawings or computer-graphic sketches that can be used to illustrate how the product will work.
Clickable Image Prototype	Sketches or mock-ups similar to paper prototypes, but linked together using a tool like PowerPoint or Adobe Acrobat. This way, a user can click or tap through a digital product and get a sense of how the flow works.
Video Prototype	An animation that illustrates various scenarios of use. This provides a richer sense of the full flow of how the application works, but it's a "canned" story that does not permit spontaneous interactivity the way a real product would. Video prototypes are often created in animation tools like Adobe Animate or After Effects.

Interactive Prototype	A partly coded version of the intended screens that may show certain elements of interactivity, such as rollovers or animations. These types of prototypes are often built in tools like InVision or Balsamiq.
Simulation	A functioning mini application that allows a user to "play" with the prototype in a manner that is similar to how the real product will work. For example, a shopping prototype might actually allow a user to arbitrarily pick products, add them to their cart, and then see the items they picked go through the checkout process with prices, sales tax and shipping calculated correctly. Such prototypes typically need to be database-driven and are often built in specialized simulation software such as Axure or iRise.

There are gradients of realism within each level, and sometimes it makes sense to plan a *series* of prototypes that increase in fidelity. As Michelangelo prepared to create his now famous sculpture of David, he first created sketches, followed by small clay models, followed by small-scale marble carvings, and only then did he move on to carve the final, full-scale marble sculpture that stands today at the Galleria dell'Accademia in Florence, Italy. (Tip: visit in the early morning or after five to avoid the crowds.)

. . . .

TEST

This step of DT2.0 is called "Prototype *and Test*," so once the prototype is created, how should it be tested? The *Mission* of the prototype should help determine the type of testing that is appropriate. For example, if the goal of the prototype is to determine the "feasibility" of whether an app can pull a customer's account information from the back-end and display it in less than a second, then the testing should clearly involve running the prototype to assess whether this benchmark is being hit.

Often, prototypes exist to gauge product "desirability" by measuring user response. As we continue to discuss, most business value comes from driving human behavior, and products are built in order to create experiences that drive the thoughts, feelings, and actions of customers (or prospects). A prototype is an opportunity to test whether users, when given the opportunity to interact with the prototype, are, in fact, exhibiting those target behaviors.

The exact format of user testing can vary based on the type of prototype, as well as the type of user. Very commonly, however, we build clickable prototypes and then ask users to interact with them in 45- to 60-minute one-on-one research sessions. We may provide the user a task, such as purchasing a product or booking a trip, and let them loose on the prototype so that we can observe their experience. The approach to structuring these research sessions is similar to structuring the observational research activities discussed in Chapter 8.

We find that taking a prototype and testing it with 12-24 users across a range of different user types—which can often be done in just a couple of days—can help avoid the potentially sizable amount of time and money it would take to rework and relaunch a product with undiscovered problems.

BUILD, LAUNCH, AND ITERATE

Once the results of prototyping and testing have been used to iterate the product vision, it's time to build and launch the MVP, or minimum viable product.

Most modern digital products are built using micro-services and Agile development. The actual details of doing this will vary widely depending on the type of product, so we won't attempt to cover those details in this book.

RECOMMENDED READING: *Some suggested reading on leading software development practices is included on the book website.*

wdc.ht/DEVPRACTICES

What's most important from a Design Thinking 2.0 perspective is that there is an effective plan and approach for measurement and iteration.

The idea of an MVP is not only to launch "lean" products but also to evolve them iteratively so that the launch is not the end but really only the beginning. Therefore, as the product is being developed, it's critical to consider how you will start learning immediately following the launch to support the continued improvement of the product.

There are a variety of specific methods and data sources you can use to evaluate products post-launch:

- For digital products, embedded metrics such as Google Analytics are a gold mine because, if properly set up, they can tell us who is using it, how often they're using it, and which features they're using. But typically to get this benefit, you need to go beyond the basic setup and customize the implementation using features like "events" and "goals."

- Sales, returns, subscriptions, and cancellations (depending on the type of product), give us a sense of whether customers view the product as valuable.

- Reviewing customer support calls, emails, texts, or other interactions can let us know about problems users may be experiencing with the product.

- Customer surveys, interviews or focus groups are helpful tools to proactively get feedback from users.

- Observational research (described in detail in Chapter 8) where we watch users interacting with the product and gain insight into what's working and what can be improved, can be wildly helpful.

. . . .

When a product is launched using a Design-Thinking-based, customer-centric process, and its initial MVP is measured carefully and then iterated further based on market feedback, the likelihood of success is many times greater than that of any other method we have seen.

Carrying out the whole process we have outlined so far—fully understanding the customer, crafting the current and the future state customer journeys, and then implementing Design Thinking 2.0 for the range of different customer-facing products that make up the journeys—will not happen overnight, to say the least. Massive transformation usually requires at least a year, often several, but executives, investors, and customers aren't always that patient.

In the next section, we will dive into the short-term tactics you can use in parallel to rapidly improve the customer experiences you have today while you build your more ideal long-term future vision.

CUSTOMER LOVE DIGITAL TRANSFORMATION FORMULA

ACTIVITY 4:
OPTIMIZE THE SHORT TERM

AREAS OF OPTIMIZATION

CH. 17

THE OPTIMIZATION PROCESS

CH. 18

Building the future can take quite a while. While you are working on it, you can generate more immediate value by focusing on "low-hanging fruit"—areas where you are "letting the customer down" that you can fix quickly. This section will dive into how to get quick results within your current reality, no matter how far along you are in your overall transformation.

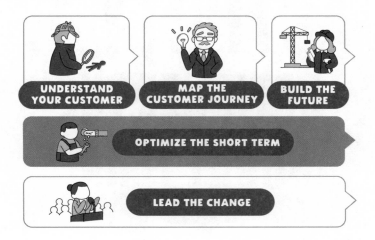

The optimization process should start in parallel with other transformation activities and continue on an ongoing basis. It should deliver quarterly or even more frequent improvements to the customer experience, as well as to the bottom line, while more long-term efforts are brewing. Frankly, even once your transformation is "complete" (if that is even possible), optimization is a process that should continue indefinitely. No matter how great your customer experience is, there is always an opportunity to improve.

The first chapter in this section, Chapter 17, will provide some insights into the optimization process and a structure for identifying the various *areas* of possible optimization. Then Chapter 18 will provide a robust, step-by-step methodology for approaching, finding, and fixing the "quick hits."

CHAPTER SEVENTEEN

OPTIMIZE THE SHORT TERM

AREAS OF OPTIMIZATION

S earch YouTube for the iconic comedian Bob Newhart, and the first result will likely be his classic comedy sketch called "Stop It!"

In the famous scene, a patient comes to Newhart's therapy office for her first visit. Newhart explains that as a psychologist, he charges $5 for the first 5 minutes and then absolutely nothing after that. When the patient smiles and says that sounds, "Too good to be true," Newhart nods and says nonchalantly, "Well, I can almost guarantee you that our session won't last the full five minutes," and he asks her what the problem is.

The patient explains that she has a fear of being buried alive in a box. She elaborates that this fear is ruining her life because she is afraid of elevators, tunnels, even houses. "Anything 'boxy.'"

Newhart nods with compassion and responds, "Ok. I think we can take care of this." He pauses then begins the therapy, gently explaining, "I am going to say two words to you now...Then I want you to take them out of the office with you and incorporate them into your life...Are you ready?"

She nods, "yes," with great anticipation, and Newhart leans forward in his chair, breaks from his calm tone, and shouts harshly at her, "STOP IT!"

She seems confused. He asks her impatiently, "You don't want to go through life being afraid of being buried alive, do you?" She whimpers "N-n-no," and he responds with even more force, "So then stop it! Just STOP IT! That's all you have to do. *JUST STOP IT!*"

Newhart then declares the therapy complete. Confused but wanting to get the most out of the remainder of her five minutes, the patient sheepishly mentions a few of her other problems.

"I also have destructive relationships with men."

"STOP IT!" shouts Newhart.

"I'm afraid to drive."

"STOP IT!" Newhart bellows. And so on. Eventually, she pays the $5 and leaves.

Now, as it happens, my wife, Lana, is a professor in the PhD Clinical Psychology program at Fairleigh Dickinson University. I consulted with her to get a professional opinion about this approach. She was quite adamant that Newhart's technique would *not* be an effective treatment for actual mental illness. BUT, based on *my* areas of expertise I am happy to report that it *can* be a good strategy to find some quick wins as you begin down the road of digital transformation. Before you do that, however, take a break and check out Newhart's hysterical video at ▶ wdc.ht/NEWHART.

STOP WHAT?

Up until now, we've focused on how to "go big" to earn the love of your customers through the dramatic reinvention of your brand experience. But the road there will be long and winding. It will probably take transformations in the areas of technology, business processes, organizational structure, your business model, and more. A bit like *real* psychotherapy, it can take years and years and be quite expensive, though very beneficial.

But while you are engaged in those types of long-term transformations, there may be some much quicker ways to at least *improve* your customers' experiences. These shorter-term fixes may not get you all the way to customer love, but if you can identify some things that you are doing that confuse, frustrate, anger, or disappoint your customers that you can just STOP, that's a step in the right direction. Some problems *are* tough to fix, but some aren't. So, start with those.

Here's a nice, small example:

FROM: UNITED AIRLINES

TO: HOWARD TIERSKY

TELL US ABOUT YOUR FLIGHT FROM CHICAGO, IL TO NEWARK, NJ
SEPTEMBER 30, 2013, 4:47 PM

*** REPLIES TO SURVEY@UNITED.COM ARE NOT MONITORED ***

DEAR HOWARD,

This is an email from United Airlines asking me for my feedback on a flight from a number of years ago. Nice idea. But do you see anything wrong with this customer experience? The first thing the email tells me in ALL CAPS and bold type is that any replies I send are not monitored. Will my feedback just be sent to email limbo? When I kept reading, I found that lower in the message, it provided a link for me to take a survey. Clearly, they *wanted* my feedback; they just didn't want the feedback via email. But it doesn't require a psychology degree to decipher the subtext the customer is likely to interpret from this message: "Tell us about your recent flight. But we aren't actually listening to your response!"

Really, United? STOP it!

It's not about United. Almost every company has these types of seemingly small glitches in user experience that add up over time to form an impression. This becomes even more problematic when a digital disruptor offers your customer a modern, elegant digital journey that has avoided these types of flaws.

Actually, United has "sort of" stopped it. Since I received that email, they've removed the giant, "We aren't listening to you" message shown. But as recently as this past week, their survey messages to solicit my feedback still come from an email "sender" named no-reply@united.com.

This problem is an epidemic, actually. Walgreens recently sent me a similar request for feedback from a mailbox named "donotreply@photo.walgreens.com."

Walgreens! STOP it!

There are many reasons why most companies' digital experiences are full of little flaws like this just waiting to be "stopped." Whether it be a rush to get things done, a lack of customer insight, a disconnect between departments, a lack of ownership, or a focus on new, bright, shiny objects, many companies do not take advantage of the quick routes to improvement lying in front of them.

. . . .

WHOSE CARES ABOUT THE "LITTLE" STUFF?

I worked with one giant retailer where all the executives involved with e-commerce acknowledged that, yeah, the navigation menus on their $1 billion+ e-commerce site were very confusing. They all agreed they should be fixed. Yet nothing was being done about it. Why not? Nobody really considered it their job. One executive focused on merchandising, one on pricing and promotions, and one on the checkout process, but there wasn't a clear owner of cross-site navigation. No one wanted to step on toes or go outside of their mandate. So, it stagnated, despite the fact that everybody's bonus was tied to total sales, and the menus were clearly turning off some customers.

Whoever's job it is, fixing one small thing like the "Do-Not-Reply" messages in emails or even some confusing navigation is not going to be transformational for Walgreens or United or the retailer with whom I worked. But they are relatively quick and easy fixes. No big icebergs here. And if you fix 100 things like that this quarter, and then 100 more next quarter, over time, you can have a substantial impact.

And sometimes you get a little lucky and deliver some substantial impact right out of the gate. Doing this type of work with dozens of companies, I have seen *many* situations where customer research led us to identify single issues that were having a big negative impact *and* were easy to fix. In one example, we changed a few simple but critical sections of the *content* of an e-commerce site and improved sales by many millions of dollars a year. It's fun when it's that easy.

HubSpot did a study of over 40,000 "call to action" buttons for email signups. They found that if the text of a button said "Click Here," site visitors were *three times* more likely to click than if it said "Register." [1] Of course, that doesn't mean that every button on your site should be labeled "Click Here," but merely points to the potential opportunity of simply tweaking some wording.

At my company, we worked with one client selling very expensive "six figure" B2B solutions that had a website that was good in many ways, but which had a variety of small glitches, formatting irregularities, inconsistent capitalization and other seemingly minor anomalies.

The potential customers we interviewed in research sessions regularly zeroed in on these small defects as details that made them question the quality of the company's products and services. While, in truth, there was probably no direct connection between those two things, there *was* in the customer's mind. Imagine losing a $100,000 or even $500,000 sale because of lost confidence resulting from a typo on your website.

While not all problems are as easy to fix as a typo or some wording, this section is about techniques to *find* the low-hanging fruit so you can at least *improve* the customer interactions you have today *while simultaneously* working on the bigger picture of higher-value transformation.

You can think of each of these customer experience flaws as a small leak in a pipe. One little leak may not seem like much, but over time, it can do a lot of damage. And if you have a bunch of little leaks, the impact over time can be enormous.

Doing this type of work gives you several benefits. First, it should deliver quick, measurable, sustainable financial improvements. These can help fund larger transformation and demonstrate to key executives that they have a "reason to believe" that your overall transformation program is capable of driving tangible business impact.

Second, you improve your customer's experience, which enhances brand perception and demonstrates progress. Now, I won't kid you; customers today have very high expectations. If you currently have a weak user experience, continually giving customers small improvements isn't guaranteed to cement their loyalty or substantially increase their patience, but it's better than nothing.

NEGATIVITY BIAS

One reason fixing these small problems is so worthwhile is a psychological factor called negativity bias. What negativity bias says is basically that our negative emotions are more powerful than our positive emotions.[2] We might be excited about going on a beach vacation, but if we are worried that it might rain, those negative feelings can outweigh the positive ones.

In the context of digital customer experiences, this means that no matter how promising or worthwhile a digital experience is, when it starts to trigger negative reactions in users, they usually abandon it quickly, no matter how interested they may have been initially. This trigger can be something as simple as not being able to find the button to go to the "next" step or confusing search results.

There is just one exception to this phenomenon, and we call it the "Bruce Springsteen Rule." For many years, the Ticketmaster site was quite terrible, and yet, the moment that a new Bruce Springsteen concert opened up for sale, tens of thousands of people would flock to the site and, frankly, *suffer* through the purchase experience to get those tickets. So, if you're confident that the payoff from your site or app is the digital equivalent of a Bruce Springsteen ticket (millennials, please substitute Beyoncé), then you may have found a way to neutralize negativity bias. Otherwise, you need to focus on optimization.

. . . .

CONFUSION AND FRUSTRATION

There are two primary emotional reactions that drive a lot of undesirable customer behavior: confusion and frustration.

Confusion is usually the first emotion we see when there are problems with a user experience. Perhaps a user begins to search for a product on your site or research a topic in your app, and they don't fully understand the interface or instructions. They start to feel confused and uncertain if they are "doing it right." Confusion is a very harmful emotion because it tends to make people feel that *they* are at fault—that they're perhaps "too stupid" to figure out how to use your site or app. You might think, "Well, that's better than blaming us!" But in fact, it's not.

They say the best thing you can do on a first date with someone is to leave them feeling great about *themselves*, and so it goes with digital experiences. If a user feels they aren't smart enough to figure out your site or app, they may not actively blame you, but, nevertheless, they leave. They develop the belief that your brand is not for "someone like me." And they may, subconsciously, blame you for *making* them feel dumb anyway.

So how do we avoid confusion? We compulsively study users' paths through a digital experience via the type of "task analysis" approach described in the rental car reservation example of observational research—studying users while they are attempting to complete defined tasks to find their points of difficulty. Any time we test a site, app or other type of experience, even a very successful one, we always find many points of confusion. It's a matter of basic hygiene. Most digital experiences are constantly changing, and it's hard to make sure that any given change doesn't have some unintended confusing consequence. Doing quarterly or at least annual user tests to make sure you are aware of any confusion "bombs" that may have been planted on your site is just a matter of digital professionalism. Furthermore, confusion-related problems are often inexpensive to fix. Sometimes it's simply about rewording a button or repositioning a call to action. Sometimes it's about removing a feature that's causing more confusion than benefit.

The second emotion that creates a lot of undesirable customer behavior is frustration. When you are frustrated, you aren't feeling confused at all. Generally, you know—or at least believe you know— *exactly* what the product you are using is supposed to do; it just isn't doing it! Frustration can be triggered by site defects, slow performance, checkout processes that have more steps than the user feels there "should be," policies that don't give the user the outcome they want, or missing features that the user perceives "everybody else has" (which may actually just mean that Uber and Amazon have them). It's quite easy to frustrate users today since their expectations are so incredibly high.

Triggering frustration in digital users is super damaging to your brand because many users create a *meaning* around the frustration that the brand just "doesn't care." Customers believe that brands *know* what they expect. If they aren't providing it, there can only be one reason: they just aren't bothering.

Of course, this may be a completely erroneous conclusion. In our experience, companies very often don't *realize* the points in their customer experience that are creating frustration. It may seem unreasonable that customers assume you already know what it is that they want and expect. But at the same time, effective research can *reveal* this information and make it actionable, so it's not an unsolvable problem by any means. Your competitors are doing it, so you must do so, as well.

Frustration problems are sometimes easy to fix, but other times, they can be very challenging, as they may stem from underlying technology issues that are expensive to remediate. Nevertheless, it's essential to understand where these problems exist and to gauge the impact they are having on your business results. This will allow you to make an informed decision about whether or when to invest in addressing them and to quickly fix those that *are* easy.

FEAR

Before we leave the important topic of emotion, let's talk about one more feeling that is perhaps more powerful at influencing people's behavior than any other: fear. In *Star Wars*, Yoda tells Luke, "Fear is the path to the Dark Side." FDR famously said during the Great Depression, "The only thing we have to fear, is fear itself," which, while perhaps a bit of an overstatement (what about bears? global warming? the zombie apocalypse?), nevertheless highlights how negative a force fear can be. It keeps people from living the lives they desire, from pursuing their ambitions and romantic relationships, and it keeps people from doing *business* with you.

Unlike confusion and frustration, it's not likely that your brand *creates* fear in your customers (unless perhaps you are a school of skydiving or public speaking). However, customers come to their consideration of doing business with you with *preexisting fears*. Furthermore, as they move toward increasing their commitment to your brand, their fears can increase. As a customer starts to seriously consider buying that new car, he worries about whether he can afford it, if it will break down, and what his friends might think. As a new client thinks about hiring your firm, she starts to worry that you won't deliver the way you promised, or that she'll come to rely on you, only for you to go out of business. Fear creeps in at every step of the customer journey, and in order to achieve our goals of moving the customer to the next level, we must neutralize it, or at least minimize it.

Exactly how you do that will depend somewhat on the specific fear, so the first step is using research to understand what those fears *are*, and they may vary somewhat by customer segment. It's a cliché that the word FEAR is an acronym for "False Evidence Appearing Real," but very often customers' fears *are* unfounded. When this is

310

the case, it may simply be a matter of communications. I mentioned previously our client whose customers feared that if they signed up for a competitive electricity plan, their power would be restored more slowly in the event of an outage. That's just not how it works, and by addressing that fear and explaining why it's not a problem, we largely dissolved it.

In other cases, you may want to adjust your product or your offer to address fear. Zappos addressed customers' fears that shoes ordered on-line might not fit them by offering free shipping for returns. Money-back guarantees are a similar method to combat certain fears. In most cases, identifying the fear is the hardest part. Once it's clear what it is, the solution is often straightforward.

And you are doing your customer a great service when you help them overcome that horrible feeling of fear. Dale Carnegie says,

"Inaction breeds doubt and fear.
Action breeds confidence and courage."

So help your customers overcome their fears so they can take action, and you create a virtuous cycle that can radiate well beyond that single purchase. The customer who finally decides he has enough faith in himself to purchase that new home or car or suit may then approach other areas of their life with more confidence.

PERSUASION AND TRANSACTION

Digital experiences usually focus on two key outcomes: persuasion and transaction.

Persuasion is that part of your experience that tries to convince customers, whether in an obvious or subtle way, to do what you want them to do. It may be buying something, applying for a credit card, filling out a petition, submitting movie reviews, uploading a funny video or inviting their friends to the latest social media site. The *transaction* is the part of the experience that *enables* the user to take the action you want them to take.

If your site is confusing, frustrating, or filled with other "issues," it may prevent you from successfully *persuading* the customer to take the action you want them to. It may fail to present the user with the right information to convince them, or it may provide an experience which, by the nature of its design or implementation, leads the customer to the conclusion that you are not a brand they want to engage with.

But even if you *do* persuade them, you still have the opportunity to screw it up. Have you ever had the experience of *deciding* to order something from a website and adding it to your cart, but somewhere between that point and the point that the retailer had your money in their bank account, you got frustrated, said "forget it," and decided not to proceed? Whether it's a broken checkout process, the company not taking PayPal, confusing terms and conditions, mistakes in sales tax calculation, or errors when submitting promo codes, when things go wrong while you're trying to do business, you may very well bail out and, if necessary, go to a competitor.

. . . .

12 AREAS OF USER EXPERIENCE

We've talked about avoiding negative emotions like frustration and confusion and how any digital property needs to remove barriers to persuasion and transaction, but let's be more specific. What exactly *are* these barriers and problems that create negative emotions? When I go to Jiffy Lube, they do a 15-point inspection on my vehicle and look at the suspension, transmission, drive-train, and so on. Perhaps it would be helpful to have something like that for your digital properties.

In fact, we have exactly that. While digital experiences are more diverse than cars, at my firm we developed a list of "issues" that we have seen across digital properties over the years, and we use this as a diagnostic tool with our clients. Our list of things to "look for" has over 800 unique standards, many specific to certain types of sites, such as check-out processes, account maintenance, or content sharing. A set of rules such as this is called a heuristic in the user experience biz. Going through our complete set would require an entire book even longer than this one. However, here are the twelve "top-level" categories that we evaluate, which will give you a sense of how to get started.

12 Areas of User Experience   ◁ wdc.ht/12AREAS

SO MANY THINGS TO FOCUS ON!

A number of years ago, my mother was in intensive care with a life-threatening condition. Thankfully, she's fine now, but I spent many evenings at the hospital where she was kept sedated and under constant monitoring via various machines and frequent blood tests.

One evening, a doctor came in and started reviewing the clipboard attached to her bed. It contained many different stats that measured her circulation, respiration, the function of her lymphatic system, kidneys, pancreas, liver, enzymes, hormones, blood sugar, and more. Many of her "numbers" didn't look so good.

He slowly flipped through the clipboard's pages, frowned a bit and shook his head as he said to me, "You know, if you think of all the things that have to go *right* in the human body, it's amazing that *any* of us stay alive for even five minutes."

While that might not have been the most reassuring thing to say to a concerned son, it's a profound point. And digital experiences can feel like that too. You can have it 99% right, but that *one* thing that's not right can sink the ship. It's critical that you have a way to find and address those problems wherever they may pop up, and quickly.

THE DANGER OF NOT HAVING THE RIGHT PROCESS

If you apply the full set of categories provided above, you could wind up with quite an unwieldy list of problems to solve. So how do you go about prioritizing the specific problems that are negatively impacting your current digital properties?

One common tactic is asking your business stakeholders to identify the most important "fixes" that will help their business and make their customers happier. That sounds logical, but really, it just kicks the can to someone else. How are *they* supposed to determine that? Senior executives usually have a lot of self-confidence, so if you ask them to prioritize things, they may very well do it for you. But are they giving you high-quality answers based on knowledge of what will really make the most impact or are they just guessing?

In the next chapter, we will lay out a structured process for prioritizing and managing an ongoing optimization effort to maximize its speed and impact.

CHAPTER EIGHTEEN

OPTIMIZE THE SHORT TERM

THE OPTIMIZATION PROCESS

The CEO of one of our clients received an angry complaint from a very important customer that the "hold times" in the call center were unacceptably long. The CEO became insistent that reducing contact center delays was a number one priority, and he wanted a plan to expand call center capacity immediately.

We were asked to consult on this urgent request and began by conducting some rapid research activities such as data analysis and call center observations. The data showed that the average wait time to speak to someone in the call center was forty seconds—a little above the industry average, but not terrible.

But we also found that, yes, there were occasional "peak periods" where the call centers became overloaded. High-value customers never waited more than five minutes, but infrequent or unidentified customers could sometimes wait 20 minutes or more during those peaks.

But before we started working on a plan to add call center capacity, we wanted to be sure we understood what *caused* those massive peaks in call center volume. Unfortunately, the incomplete call center records did not give us good data on the *reasons* for the calls. But some conversations with customer service reps gave us a few clues. The clues led us to do some analysis of a few additional data sources. These analyses ultimately revealed that nearly all of the occasions when the call centers developed unacceptable wait times matched up with instances when some critical aspect of the infrastructure driving the company's smartphone app had either gone down entirely or was malfunctioning.

It was fairly clear that the primary cause of the call center overload was the app. We recommended shifting the CEO's initial vision of the "solution" away from increasing call center capacity to addressing the root cause of technology stability problems. This shift helped the client ultimately resolve the issue successfully and at a much lower cost.

This is why it's critical to have a structured and logical process for evaluating and prioritizing "quick fixes" rather than using the "squeaky wheel" principle. We want *quick* fixes, but not *so* quick that we fix the wrong thing.

THE SIX-STEP OPTIMIZATION PROCESS

In this chapter, we will review a process for finding and optimizing small-to-medium scale customer experience problems in digital properties.

You will see parallels to the processes we discussed earlier for understanding customers and mapping their current experience. These ideas are conceptually connected, but here we are specifically looking for issues that can be remediated in the short term. Thus, many of the details of the analysis differ. In optimization, we are looking over the system like a plumber with a wrench hunting for leaks rather than as a visionary looking to create something new. The steps of the approach are outlined below:

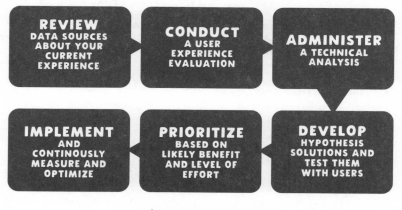

The Optimization Process

< wdc.ht/OPTIMIZE

Let's break these down one step at a time.

Optimization Step 1:
REVIEW DATA SOURCES ABOUT YOUR CURRENT EXPERIENCE

You most likely have a variety of data sources that can help you locate the problems within a given digital property. Seek out items such as those listed below. If you don't have them, put processes in place to acquire most if not all of these.

1. Site traffic reports

2. Conversion metrics, including returns/refunds

3. Digital monitoring and performance measures including downtime, page load speeds and error logs

4. Competitive metrics, such as ComScore, showing how your traffic compares to others in your industry

5. Customer feedback such as emails to the "webmaster," CEO, or anyone in between, as well as more structured tools you may use to collect feedback from customers such as Foresee, NPS, etc.

6. Third-party benchmarks such as from JD Power

7. Social media posts, forums, and online reviews

8. Contact center records, which may reveal specific experiential complaints from users

Example Data Source:
CONVERSION FUNNELS

"Conversion" is a term that refers to the *ratio* of the number of people that complete a transaction to the total number of people who come to your digital experience. In other words, for every 100 visitors, how many actually buy? 5%? 25%? For e-commerce, this is a critical metric. One tool that is helpful for visualizing conversion effectiveness is a funnel diagram. Funnel diagrams are appropriate when you have a series of steps that customers go through with anticipated falloff from step to step. Shopping processes are a classic example.

A certain number of customers will come to your online store each day. That is the top layer of your funnel. Not all of these customers will even look at a product page. For example, some might just want to know store hours, suggesting they probably didn't come to the site to buy something.

Of the customers who *do* look at a product page, some of them, but surely not all, will put an item in their cart. Of the customers who put items in their cart, *some* of them will begin the checkout process, and of those that begin, some of *them* will complete it.

If we visualize the number of customers at each of these steps, it looks a bit like a funnel since they are getting smaller each step of the way.

SALES FUNNEL

VISIT SITE

LOOK AT PRODUCT PAGE

ADD ITEM TO SHOPPING CART

GO TO CHECKOUT

BEGIN CHECKOUT PROCESS

COMPLETE PURCHASE

Sample Conversion Funnel

 < wdc.ht/FUNNEL

Of course, if we could somehow turn our funnel into a cylinder, to have *everyone* who comes to the site turn into a buyer, that would be amazing, but it's not realistic to think we can eliminate all of the fall-offs at every step. For example, some people look at product pages for fun, even if they don't have the money to buy anything. Some people put items in their cart not because they intend to purchase them, but rather to keep a list of items they may be interested in for some other purpose. And of course, some people come looking for something you just don't have.

But optimizing a funnel is about *improving* the ratios at each step. If you can get just 10% more of the visitors to look at a product, and 10% more of those who look at a product to add it to their cart, and 10% more of the cart adders to *complete* their purchases, do you know how much you improve overall sales? The math of compounding reveals it's actually nearly a 47% total sales increase! This is the power of optimization.

Reviewing site traffic in the form of a funnel diagram is a great way to understand what's happening in those critical transaction flows. You can then use that knowledge to sleuth for ways to improve at each level of the funnel. In the coming steps of the optimization process, we'll go over a bunch of approaches to do just that.

Example Data Source:
SERVER ERROR LOGS

Let's delve into another one of the data types listed above that is often overlooked: server error logs. These contain a treasure trove of information that can be enormously useful for site optimization.

Web servers will typically write an entry to a log file if something "goes wrong," such as if a page doesn't load properly, an error is presented to a user, a transaction fails to complete, etc.

Needless to say, if your customers are receiving errors because your e-commerce system is not functioning properly, the customer experience is probably significantly hampered for those users. It's *common* for us to find 4% of users or more generating some sort of error during a given visit. Is that a lot? Well, imagine if you could increase sales by even a quarter of that.

One common analysis technique is filtering error logs by the user's browser and device since it's typical to find that a new version of Chrome or Edge or an iOS or Android update is causing errors that didn't exist previously. This is something that warrants regular attention, and it's often an easy fix.

Another common cause of errors is that many systems rely on external cloud services whose API's can get updated unexpectedly or develop problems. By carefully monitoring the connections to these services, you can ensure that you are immediately alerted when your digital touchpoints "break" because of a change by a third party.

USER ERRORS

Not all errors are the result of technical failures. Many errors are errors of user validation. Examples include when a user enters an invalid email or phone number, tries to complete a transaction without checking the "terms and conditions" acceptance box, or does something else illogical or impermissible.

Now, on the one hand, you might say "That's not my fault! My digital experience worked. It was the user who made a mistake." True, but *wrong*, especially if there are a lot of these types of errors or the number suddenly spikes.

If we want our customers to love us, or even just like us, it's our job to design an experience that makes it *unlikely* that they will make mistakes. If users are frequently overlooking something or misunderstanding what they are meant to do, it's a sign we need to look at that part of the experience and consider how to redesign it so that errors are uncommon. It might be as simple as rewriting the instructions, moving a button or making a field bigger.

Our analyses have shown that customers who encounter an error message *as a result of their own mistake* are 30% less likely to complete their transaction than those who do not. So, we should take great interest in preventing users from making errors.

Another category of errors not necessarily created by technical problems are what we call "user disappointment errors." These occur when a user receives a "nothing found" message on site search results or an "out-of-stock" message.

A traveler wants to rent a car with a pickup at 2 a.m., but the location is closed at that time. Or a shopper wants pants in a 46-inch waist, but they top out at 44 inches. Or a visitor is searching your site for information on bedwetting, but no articles match that term. These types of errors indicate a missed opportunity to meet a customer need, and you should scour error and search logs to consider what steps you can take to fill the gaps and remove frequently recurring disappointments.

GOOD LOGS ARE CRITICAL

All of this is based on the assumption that your site's "back end" is logging errors properly. This is a standard coding practice, but just because it's standard doesn't mean that it can't get omitted or that certain errors might not be getting recorded. It's important to check with your technical team. If your site is *not* logging all errors or not logging them with sufficient detail, this can generally be fixed easily. However, there are certain data fields, such as credit card numbers, that cannot be logged to maintain PCI compliance (which is critical if you take payments). So be sure to consult with PCI professionals when adding logging code relating to payment or personally identifiable information.

Additionally, you probably have logging occurring in multiple systems that run your digital infrastructure and, therefore, have multiple log files. For example, the web server may have one log file, the commerce layer may have a separate log file, and your security/

authentication layer may have its own log files. That's fine. There are tools that can combine them and make them easier to analyze, filter, and sort. Some recommended products are listed for you on the book website at wdc.ht/LOGS.

Data Sources:
BASELINE METRICS

Before leaving the topic of data sources, I'd like to touch on the issue of baseline metrics. Since our focus in the process of optimization will be to make relatively small improvements throughout existing digital touchpoints, it's valuable to keep returning to the same measurements to see whether you have "moved the needle."

As you begin focusing on this area, it's an opportune time to ensure that you do, in fact, have the right metrics reporting on your customer experiences and that those measurement tools are working correctly and consistently. This way, you will have a reliable gauge of progress over time.

BONUS TRAINING VIDEO: *On the book website, you can find a bonus video that presents the 10 most important metrics for any digital experience and how to be sure they are calibrated correctly.*

▶ wdc.ht/METRICS

Optimization Step 2:
CONDUCT A USER EXPERIENCE EVALUATION

I was awakened in the middle of the night by my teenage son, Foster. There was liquid dripping through the ceiling onto his bed. When I checked the attic above his room, I discovered that water was pooling around the air conditioning evaporator and draining down to the level below. I put a bucket on his bed, and he slept in the guest room for the rest of the night. The next morning, the HVAC repairman told me it was going to cost $500 to find the leak and then more to fix it. Feeling as though maybe I was getting ripped off, I pointed out, perhaps a tad condescendingly "We *know* where the leak is! It's leaking on my son's bed."

The repairman narrowed his eyes, scratched his stubble thoughtfully, and then said something I will never forget. He explained slowly, emphatically, "No sir. That's *not* the leak. That's the *drip...*

...JUST BECAUSE WE KNOW WHERE THE DRIP IS DOESN'T MEAN WE KNOW WHERE THE LEAK IS."

That was some real Yoda-level wisdom first thing in the morning. I signed his work order to go through each and every pipe, part, and component of the AC system and find out where it was *leaking*. The final bill to get the ceiling to stop dripping on Foster: $575.

$500 to find the leak. $75 to fix it.

The data sources we reviewed earlier in this chapter are like the water dripping on my teenager, Foster—it's the end result and it shows you there *is* a problem and, perhaps, vaguely where. But what *exactly* is the problem? You need to know that in order to fix it.

For example, your site metrics might reveal that a surprisingly large number of customers get to the shopping cart checkout page and then don't complete their purchase. These are customers who found a product, added it to their cart, actually clicked "check out," and then just bailed.

Why would they be doing that? It could be that they got cold feet upon seeing the total price. It could be that there is a problem with the way you calculate sales tax or shipping charges that confuses your customers. It could be that some people can't locate the "finalize order" button. These are all possible hypotheses, but you may not be able to tell from the site metrics whether it is one of these issues or something else. This is where the user experience evaluation comes in. The metrics guide you to the page itself. The *analysis* is what enables you to figure out what the actual cause is: the leak.

User Experience Evaluation Example:
CIRCULAR ERRORS

As an example, here's an error pattern that often points to "juicy" opportunities. It's one we have named "circular errors." What's a circular error? It's when a user sends identical or very similar input multiple times and receives the same error repeatedly. For example, a customer submits an email address when creating an account and receives a message that the email is invalid. Then the user submits it again and receives the same error, and perhaps again and again with the same error. This data pattern almost certainly points to a user experiencing either confusion or frustration.

Circular errors can occur for several reasons. One is that the user isn't *seeing* the error message. Perhaps, it appears in grey text at the top of the screen, and the user simply doesn't notice it so he just keeps re-submitting the page and not understanding why it "isn't working." The user might then conclude that the site is "broken" and leave.

Another possibility is that the validation formula is wrong. For example, at my company, our email addresses end in "@from.digital," a less common but perfectly legitimate domain name. About 25% of websites, including some major ones, tell me that my completely real email address is "invalid," and I have to then enter a different email in order to proceed.

(I suppose it would make me sound overly sensitive if I admitted that this rejection of my email address makes me feel unwanted and reminds me of what it was like at junior high school dances, but suffice to say that "rejection" is another emotion you want to try to avoid evoking in your prospective customers). And forcing me to provide an alternate email address is bad for the company I am providing it to because I am basically then giving them a rarely checked account rather than my primary mailbox. But the worst-case scenario associated with this "glitch" is that some users may not understand why their valid email is being rejected and keep trying, perhaps abandoning their task entirely, concluding the site is "broken."

FIELD MISIDENTIFICATION

Yet another cause of circular errors is field misidentification. On one e-commerce site we analyzed, we ran a script to comb log files looking for circular errors and found a shockingly high number of them, mostly focused on invalid credit card expiration dates.

We thought, "Well this is strange, why would the shoppers on this *one* site be over ten times more likely to mis-enter their credit card expiration date? And then, why do they do it repeatedly?" A good old-fashioned mystery.

One of my analysts said she wanted to review the *actual* data and examine the date values that had been entered by users. The entered date *values* were not in the log files, only the error codes. She had to monitor the payment gateway itself to see that data—extra work.

Not wanting to waste time, I pointed out to her that she wouldn't actually be able to determine from the data whether the dates were really invalid or not because, for example, if she saw that a given customer submitted an expiration of January 2024, she'd have no way of determining if that date *was* the correct expiration date of that customer's credit card. She didn't disagree, but said she liked to see real data and wanted to monitor the gateway anyway. Sometimes when running a team, you need to "pick your battles," so I said, "Fine, but don't spend too much time on it."

Two days later she came by my office victorious, brandishing a printout of over 100 transactions from the prior day which had triggered the "failed expiration date circular error script." She dramatically dropped them on my desk. I looked over the values the 100 users had entered into the credit card expiration field. They made no sense.

In each case, it was a three- or four-digit number. That part made sense, as a credit card expiration is month + year. For example, August 2024 might be "0824." But this list had mostly illogical numbers like "1216" (December 2016 was several years earlier) and "0139" (a credit card expiring January 1939? Did they even have credit cards back then?) A bunch of the values weren't even valid dates at all. They were numbers like 0023. What were these customers thinking? A couple of oddball transactions you could dismiss, but a hundred in a single day? And when each of these users got an error message, they kept submitting the bad values over and over; that's what got them on this report.

Well, one thing we knew: the validation software code wasn't the problem (as it had been in my email address example earlier). Those entries were definitely *not* valid expiration dates, and I didn't need to see anyone's credit card to know that.

But even though we knew we were onto *something*, we were stumped about why so many users were doing this crazy thing. We brainstormed, and the team's best theory was that the animated ads on the site were somehow blinding users so that they were unable to read the dates on their credit cards. I said it was our *best* theory; I didn't say it was a *good* theory.

Thank goodness we weren't limited only to data analysis to try to solve the problem. The next thing we did was to conduct a user experience evaluation, which is step two of the optimization process.

Eventually, as part of that process, we watched actual users engage with the screens, but we were able to develop a strong hypothesis about the expiration date issue even before that—once we started inspecting the screens in detail. This inspection was part of our heuristic review, typically the first activity of a user experience analysis.

And of course, we inspected the credit card screen *extra closely* because we knew from the data analysis there was something wacky going on there. What we saw in our heuristic review was that the website asked for the credit card number, then the next field asked for the CCV (that extra set of numbers on the back of a card), and *then* the following field was for the expiration date. This sequence went against our documented "best practice" heuristic for the order of fields on a credit card screen (one of the 800 rules we evaluate a website for which we discussed in the last chapter).

While there is no inherent reason why this sequence is "wrong," users are accustomed from other sites to entering the credit card number, then the date, *then* the CCV. After seeing this discrepancy with best practices, our new theory became that, although the fields were clearly labeled, some users were on "mental autopilot" and were just entering the date in the CCV field and the CCV in the date field because it was the sequence they were expecting, and they didn't bother to look closely at the labels.

The site's visually attractive design actually exacerbated this problem because the designers

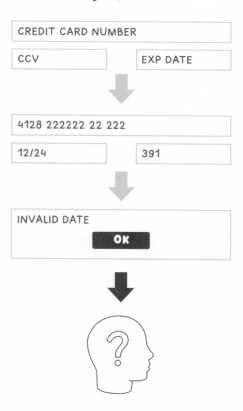

had put the field labels *inside* the fields; so, once you entered a value, the label was gone, replaced by your entry.

Following our heuristic review, we conducted site usability tests with customers. Although the test looked at a broad range of issues, we were especially curious to see whether the user sessions confirmed our expiration date hypothesis.

Our usability tests followed a "task analysis" protocol as described earlier in the book, where customers were asked to use the site to achieve a specific shopping goal while verbalizing their thoughts aloud, so we could observe how well the e-commerce site was working for them and hear what they were thinking and feeling. While not every user had a problem with the expiration date field, about 15% made the mistake more or less exactly as we had hypothesized—transposing the CCV and Date fields.

The customers that did this would hit submit and receive the message "Invalid Date." They would then look at their credit card, look at the screen (sometimes back and forth several times), and then say something like, "The date is correct. I don't understand what's wrong." It *was* correct—it was just in the wrong field. Some users figured it out as soon as they got the first error, but others didn't. They'd hit submit a few times, sometimes tweaking the data they had entered into the CCV field, such as changing 5-19 to *05*-19, then to 05-*2019*. But of course, because they were fixing the wrong field, it didn't help. Most users *eventually* figured it out, but one just declared that the site was broken. Another one even tried two other credit cards, made the same error on both, and then got *really* frustrated.

Again, not *every* user made this mistake. Most *didn't*, but *enough* did that it was clear to us that it was having an impact on sales. Our live data from *one day* included over 100 customers that did, and that only counted the ones that had *repeatedly* hit this error such that it got flagged as a "circular error"; no doubt many more encountered it only once or twice.

Before our analysis, the client was unaware of this issue. The site was doing many thousands of transactions a day, so any impact from this one problem may not have caused a noticeable dip in revenue. However, these errors were occurring *right as customers were trying to pay*, and if there's one place where you don't want to frustrate and confuse customers, it's when they are trying to give you money!

The "circular error" users represented only about .25% of total customers, but first of all, that ain't nothing if you are losing those sales. If the average transaction on a site is $80 and you lose 100 sales every day for a year, that's $2 million a year.

And second of all, this was just *one* of the issues discovered as part of the project.

I've taken this long on this story to help you understand what this process is like, how data analysis and user experience analysis can interrelate and how following the clues of something as simple as a string of error messages may lead you to real money on the other end of the process.

As you can imagine, fixing the expiration date problem was super simple—we swapped the order of the fields to match what people were expecting. Just like my air conditioner problem, the effort to *find* the problem was far greater than the effort to *fix* the problem. We also recommended adjusting the error message presentation and language so that instead of using a dialog box, the error would be placed right below the field along with the *name* of the field, making it absolutely clear *which* field was the problem and what data was supposed to go there.

User Experience Evaluations find the leaks. They diagnose precisely what the problems are so that we know what to fix. If the data shows that the frequency of customers adding products to shopping

330

carts is beginning to decline, that's a drip. We need to find the leak. If the percentage of users on the home page who search for products starts to go down, that's another drip. But what's the leak?

Also, not all leaks *create* a discernible "drip" in the data. Water could be pooling around your malfunctioning AC unit right now but not dripping down someplace you'd notice (better check). And user experience evaluations often find issues in areas where the data does not make it *obvious* that there is a problem.

They also often identify opportunities even where there is no "problem" *per se*, but where some aspect of the experience could be adjusted to take it from good to great and further contribute to business results.

As demonstrated in our epic drama about the expiration date fields, we have two primary tools for finding leaks: heuristic analysis and usability testing. Let's dive more into the methodology for each.

User Experience Evaluation Type 1:
HEURISTIC ANALYSIS

"Heuristic" means rules based. Heuristic analysis involves looking at the attributes of your current experience and measuring them against known "best practice rules," such as the rule about the sequence of fields for credit card data entry that we discussed earlier.

There are known "best" ways to present error messages or search results to a user. There are rules about how big buttons need to be so that they're "tappable" on mobile phones, as well as rules about the best way to format phone numbers so that they are easy to enter in a field. And there are hundreds more, at least.

Of course, there's never only *one* right way to do anything and there's no user experience police enforcing the "rules." But unless you have a compelling reason to do otherwise, it is smart to follow the "best practices" that have been proven through trial and error on thousands of websites, apps, and other types of experiences. A heuristic exam involves a user experience expert carefully stepping through each page and feature of a site, app, or other touchpoint and documenting where the "best practice" rules are being broken.

Imagine it's Christmastime, and you're setting up the tree in your office lobby. To get power for the lights, you run a heavy electrical cord across the hallway to the nearest outlet. Then you duct-tape that cord to the carpet for safety.

One person walks over the taped cord just fine, and the second person does, as well. In fact, the first 50 people have no problem. But then, imagine the 51st person trips on the bump from the taped cord. *Most* people have no problem with the duct-taped cord, but *someone* did. You help them to their feet. Instead of doing your work that day, you keep watching.

The next person is fine. The next 10 people are fine. Then we're almost at the 100th person, and whoops! A second person trips. What have we learned?

Well, we learned that it's really boring to spend all day waiting for someone to trip on a duct-taped electrical cord. But more importantly, we learned that this setup works for *most* people but fails for about 2% of people. Is that a problem?

It *is* if those two people hurt themselves. This is one reason why running cords across hallways in commercial office buildings, even when taped down, is against building codes. If an inspector came by and saw that, you could get a fine, even though it doesn't create a problem for *most* people.

Similarly, let's consider if you have a heuristic "rules violation" on your website that only trips up 2% of people. Is *that* a problem? Nobody is likely to get injured, but how do you feel about potentially suppressing your revenue by 2%? For most businesses operating on a profit margin of 10-15%, that 2% of revenue might represent 20% of their profit. This is the game of optimization—finding the crumbs, the little problems, then patching them up, fixing the leaks, and seeing the results slowly add up to real money.

So, don't run your own wiring—bring in an electrician. Engage professionals who know the rules and can find where you are skirting them and can help you rewire to comply.

User Experience Evaluation Type 2:
USABILITY TESTING

The second technique we use to evaluate user experiences is usability testing, as we described in the expiration date story. For usability tests of websites or apps, we typically bring 12-25 subjects from each customer segment into our facility, one at a time, for about 45 minutes each. We give them specific tasks to achieve as they utilize the digital experience we are testing—such as buying a gift for a 9-year-old or booking a vacation to Iceland. We then observe where or if they hit problems. We ask them questions as they progress so we can understand exactly what they are thinking and feeling and how that's leading them to the actions they are taking. Why did they abandon the search and start clicking on the navigation categories? Why did they look at a product and then decide not to put it in their cart? If they make a "mistake," like entering their expiration date in the CCV field, we seek to understand what caused them to think that was the right place to enter that data.

Very often, we see many of the same issues during a usability test that our experts identified during a heuristic evaluation. However, the usability test is still very valuable for several reasons.

First, just as not everything that is "unsafe" violates a specific law or regulation, not every "problem" in a digital experience relates directly to a general heuristic rule; we almost always find many problems that were *not* flagged during the heuristic review.

333

Second, we know there will be a need to prioritize any issues identified since there are almost always many more problems than can be addressed immediately. The heuristic analysis tells us about the *existence* of variations from best practice, but it's not always completely clear how significantly an individual "violation of the rules" impacts the actual business results.

The usability test can give us a clearer sense of whether a given "rules violation" is tripping up a lot of users in a significant manner or whether it's an issue that, while "nice to fix," is perhaps not causing that much pain.

So, it's valuable to do both. The heuristic review is much less expensive and time-consuming and can actually be more comprehensive because most users won't wind up touching every part of your site in a usability test. The heuristic analysis can also help pinpoint potential flaws that we'll then target in the tasks we give to users *in* the usability test. If the heuristic review shows that your customer service area has a lot of variations from standard best practices, we may spend a disproportionate amount of time there in the usability test, as we hypothesize it's a "problem area."

Optimization Step 3:
ADMINISTER A TECHNICAL ANALYSIS

It's not uncommon for *some* of the sub-optimized aspects of a given digital experience to be rooted in technology platform limitations, so technical analysis is appropriate as part of the optimization effort. Furthermore, when we go to hypothesize potential *solutions* to the highest priority problems, it's helpful to get a sense of what types of improvements are going to be straightforward to implement in the existing technical environment and which are likely to require more effort or systems changes. Similar to the prioritization we discussed in the chapter on product development, we will want to evaluate the cost versus the impact of individual potential fixes.

To support that goal, do a high-level review of the technology supporting the current experience. This review should assess to what degree the technology is creating a barrier to success and potentially identify areas where it can be made to work more effectively.

One simple example: we mentioned previously that for digital experiences, speed has been repeatedly correlated to business results. People often abandon sites or apps that are slow. So, if a site *is* slow, how hard will it be to speed it up? Perhaps adding more servers is all that is needed.

Or perhaps there is a critical bottleneck that cannot be solved without a major re-architecture that's beyond the scope of the optimization effort. It may be difficult to know the difference until the technical analysis is done.

It can be helpful to have this analysis done by a party independent of the team that built and maintains the existing technical systems. Sometimes internal teams develop beliefs about what is or isn't possible (remember the flat-screen TV story from Chapter 15). Bringing in an outside party, assuming they are qualified, gives you another perspective from someone who has seen a broad range of systems because they consult with many companies.

And, of course, if the technical analysis reveals that the current systems are too inflexible to support the *majority* of needed optimizations, and those optimizations appear to have the potential to drive significant business improvements, then this can help build a case for a more transformational approach.

Optimization Step 4:
DEVELOP HYPOTHESIS SOLUTIONS AND TEST THEM WITH USERS

Once you have a good sense of the key problems and understand their likely level of impact and technical effort, you are ready to start fixing those user experience "leaks" that are practical to address as part of an optimization effort.

Of course, understanding a problem is not the same as developing an effective solution. Just as finding the drip is not the same as finding the leak, finding the leak is not the same as knowing how to *fix* the leak.

For example, we worked with a large utility company trying to improve sales on their website. Ultimately, we were able to actually *double the conversion* of the site, which was a huge victory, but it took months of trial and error to get to that level.

We knew from our usability testing that subjects were confused by the "plan" screen—the step of the purchase process where the customer had to choose between a range of different offers. There were 12-month plans, 24-month plans, plans that gave you cash back, plans that gave you a lower price, and plans that included insurance on your home appliances.

When customers got to the "plan" screen, it was somewhat confusing so they often had great difficulty deciding what to pick. They didn't want to make the *wrong* choice, so they frequently went away to mull over their decision. Many never returned.

We designed a new, less cluttered layout for the plans that we believed was easier to comprehend. This was our *hypothesis* solution which we theorized would be better for users. It aligned with what we knew the problem to be.

We could have simply built the new layout and put it into the signup process. However, we prefer to do some prototyping and user testing to validate our hypotheses, especially for critical screens. In this case, the first round of user testing (which took one day) revealed that we had definitely made it less intimidating, but the way the sections collapsed and expanded in our new design created some *new* points of confusion and frustration. The net result would most likely not have been much of an improvement in sales.

Armed with insights from the day of testing, we were able to go back and leverage what *did* work about our new designs while tweaking what was causing problems. It took a few more day-long rounds like that, but eventually, we arrived at a solution that worked well in user testing.

In fact, we actually created four different layouts. After testing them with about 20 users, it became clear that two of them were far better than the others, as well as far, far better than the current "live" site.

We could have simply selected one of the winners and put it into production, but we weren't absolutely certain which one to pick. Both had tested similarly, but that round of testing was only 20 subjects or so. The numbers were directional but not statistically determinative.

HARNESSING MULTIVARIATE TESTING

We decided to use another tool in our hypothesis testing arsenal: AB testing, also called "split testing" and now usually referred to by the fancier term "Multivariate Testing," or MVT. With MVT, a special software layer, such as the package Optimost, is added to the "real" production website. The software allows the site owner to implement several different versions of a key screen or feature and control what percentage of the users receive each variation.

We set up both new screens and randomly sent 10% of the traffic to one, 10% to another, and left, at least initially, the remaining 80% going to the preexisting screens.

After all, even though the new screens had both tested well in the lab, user testing is a somewhat contrived situation. The results are valuable but not 100% predictive of what will happen in the "real world." Therefore, it was worth using a small percentage of the traffic to prove that the new screens would perform better on the live site before sending all the traffic to them. In addition to demonstrating the new screens' superiority, we wanted to learn which of our two most successful page variations was the best.

After gathering data for a week, it was clear that *both* of the new versions of the screens were performing far better than the preexisting screens. Between the two new screens, one performed marginally better than the other.

We always like to slice this kind of data by different segments to see if we find any meaning patterns. In this case, when we looked at the results geographically, we saw that one of the new screens performed much better than the other in *certain* US states, while in other states, the results were reversed. The difference was as much as 20%.

We took a closer look at the individual states that performed well with each screen and found a meaningful pattern. For various legal and business reasons, some states had a broader array of plans to choose from than others. In cases where the number of plans was over seven or eight, then the first layout performed better, whereas when the number of plans was smaller, the second layout performed better.

Our goal had been to pick *one* layout based on the MVT test, but ultimately, we used both and coded simple logic that used the optimal layout depending on how many plans were being presented.

This is the type of analysis and decision-making that can be driven by multivariate testing, and we use it constantly with a wide range of clients to test different text, colors, layouts, or even different discounts, promotions, or site features.

Optimization Step 5:
IMPLEMENT AND CONTINUOUSLY MEASURE & OPTIMIZE

From your initial analysis, you will probably have more "to-dos" than you can get to in a single pass. Therefore, you will want to maintain a backlog of optimizations that have already been identified so that, as resources and funding become available, you can keep chipping away at the improvements, studying the impact you are having, and repeating the cycle.

Optimization should not be a one-time process but rather a continuous hygiene effort to ensure you get the maximum business benefit from your customer experiences. Very often, the return on investment of optimization efforts is higher than almost any other activity in the Customer Love Digital Transformation Formula. This is not because the impact is bigger than more ambitious transformations but because the costs are much, much lower, so the ratio of cost-to-impact can be astonishingly good.

At least monthly, or, more optimally, weekly, someone within your organization should be reviewing analytics reports looking for new patterns that suggest areas for new optimization. Furthermore, I recommend conducting fresh heuristics and usability testing at least annually, or more often if the digital properties are changing frequently.

. . . .

Of course, you don't want to get so focused on short-term optimization that you lose your longer-term vision. Ideally, maintain a balance. In fact, in addition to giving users a better experience and driving better business results, optimization can be very beneficial when done in parallel with larger, more ambitious transformation efforts. This is because optimization can show some quick wins and help to increase confidence in the broader transformation. Validation like this is very useful, as digital transformation almost always faces substantial headwinds within an organization.

In the next and final section of the book, we will take a look at the process of actually leading these multifaceted transformation efforts: how to overcome resistance to change, how to assemble the teams needed for success, and how to get your organization sold and aligned on an ongoing transformation.

ACTIVITY 5:
LEAD THE CHANGE

OVERCOMING
ENTERPRISE
RESISTANCE
TO CHANGE

CH. 19

THE ROAD AHEAD:
YOUR 90-DAY
ACTION PLAN

CH. 21

TRANSFORMATIONAL
LEADERS
& TEAMS

CH. 20

The final activity we'll cover in our 5-step digital transformation formula is to *"Lead the Change."* Of course, leadership doesn't start at the end—it's something that needs to be present from the very beginning. In structuring this book, we felt it would be best to first talk about all the *work* that needs to be done and then conclude by discussing the approach to leadership. Thus, positioning this step as the final one is not about sequence of execution *or* priority but only sequence of explanation.

In fact, it's probably not only the *first* step chronologically but also the *most* important. Digital transformations will face all kinds of challenges and resistance, and without outstanding leadership, the chances are slim indeed.

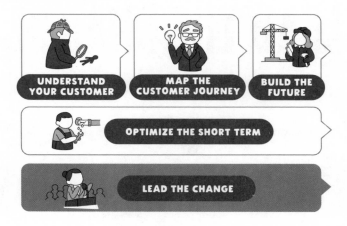

In this section, we will cover key topics essential to successful leadership:

Chapter 19 will focus on the challenge of organizational resistance to change—why it occurs and how to overcome it. Chapter 20 will focus on the types of leaders you need to assemble for the transformation and provide guidance on how to structure the multidisciplinary teams needed. And Chapter 21 will close out the book by teeing up some important ideas for your plan going forward.

LEAD THE CHANGE

OVERCOMING ENTERPRISE RESISTANCE TO CHANGE

t's too late for Blockbuster. Along with brands like Kodak and Western Union, Blockbuster symbolizes the ultimate corporate failure: a company that owned an entire industry and then threw it away because it couldn't or wouldn't change with the times.

But there's a big difference between Blockbuster and those other companies, at least to me.

Because I was *there* at Blockbuster headquarters. I was there *before* it was too late. I was there as a high-priced consultant with a prestigious firm hired to help Blockbuster develop its future digital vision—the one to compete with Netflix. The one to save the company. It was an awesome assignment, but I blew it.

I'm very fortunate to have had the incredible opportunity to consult for dozens of Fortune 1000 companies, including some of the most powerful brands in the world. I'm happy to be able to say that my team and I have played a major role in some fantastic successes, applying principles described throughout this book. But it is the failures that gnaw at you. And at Blockbuster, we failed big time.

At its peak in 2004, Blockbuster had 84,300 employees worldwide and a total of 9,094 stores. How did Blockbuster fall from that scale to oblivion?[1]

They certainly weren't clueless. I can tell you that there were *many* super smart people there. We collaborated with them on a vision that, in many ways, looks a lot like Netflix today: streaming services, episodic television with great navigation, multiscreen devices. In those days, Netflix was exclusively in the DVD-by-mail business. Blockbuster was much larger, with more money, more customers, more Hollywood relationships, and just about every advantage but one: they loved who they *already* were.

As an example of this, let's drill into one of the more profound barriers that kept them from *committing* to the bold digital vision that they paid us to develop. What was it?

Candy.

At its peak, when Blockbuster had its 9,000+ stores, those stores rented a lot of videos. But they also sold a lot of M&Ms, Skittles, and giant Kit Kats. It was becoming harder to make a significant profit renting DVDs, especially after they stopped charging late fees, because the studios negotiated a fair chunk of the rental price

for themselves. But the margin on candy, as well as microwavable popcorn buckets, was *huge*.

Our proposed digital vision faced significant resistance from executives who were perfectly willing to believe that customers would stream video to their homes, but repeatedly pointed out, "You can't stream candy."

How could the company be successful without candy? It seemed to be core to their business model. And that mindset *made* it insurmountable.

Side note: I reviewed Netflix's most recent annual report, and still, to this date, zero dollars from the sale of candy. So, I guess it *was* surmountable after all.

I don't mean to sound like I'm blaming anyone else, though. I consider it my own failure that we were unsuccessful at persuading Blockbuster to take sufficient action. We failed to overcome the politics, resistance, and limiting beliefs. Part of the reason for that failure is that back then we didn't foresee the level of opposition that the transformational initiatives would face. To me, the direction we were recommending was a "no-brainer." Sure, one could legitimately have debates about the details, but the *general idea* of moving from physical to digital delivery seemed an inevitability that everyone would easily see.

And candy is just one *illustration* of Blockbuster's larger problem, which was their "box of identity" as we termed it in Chapter 15.

Blockbuster was in the "stores" business. The most influential executives in the company were "retail store people." They believed in the power of a huge retail presence and had complete confidence that *if* there was a problem in the business, and it became increasingly clear that there *was*, well, the solution had to be a better retail in-store experience: new store layouts, different bundles, the elimination of late fees, and entertaining commercials starring animated guinea pigs (▶ wdc.ht/PIGS) to drive more people *to* the stores. Sure, make it better, but keep the store at the center.

The forces resisting wholesale transformation at Blockbuster weren't opposed to R&D projects like ours. We got a lot of interest— even pats on the back—just not a lot of action. It was "cool" to have teams think up new ideas about the future—as long as they *stayed* in the future. But if those ideas started to threaten the physical store fiefdom and identity, the resistance became powerful. Of the months-long work we did—the prototypes we created, the business models we drafted and refined—none of it really went anywhere. I won't say this was the only reason, but it's easy to follow the downward graph from that point in time to the day the last Blockbuster closed.

IT'S HARD TO CHANGE WHO YOU ARE

And that's one of the core challenges with digital—it creates the potential for truly transformational change in how a given industry operates. But many companies just aren't built to transform—in terms of mindset, culture, or even structure. When you have long-term leases on real estate, it's hard to think about a world where that's unnecessary. When you have certain revenue streams, like candy, that are tied to a legacy way of doing business, it's scary to think about losing those dollars.

Kodak famously invented the digital camera[2] and even brought the first digital camera to market. But, as we talked about in Chapter 5, Kodak's psychology was that they were a *film* company and they just couldn't stomach wholeheartedly pushing a product that eliminated the need for film. As a result, Kodak went from accounting for 85% of all cameras and 90% of all film sold in the US in 1976 to bankruptcy in 2012.[3] Like Blockbuster, Kodak *wanted* to innovate. They wanted to move from *strips* of film to *disks*. Remember the Kodak Disc-man? But the Disc-man "disks" weren't digital storage; they were circular holders of little pieces of, of course, film. Both companies rode their strategies to irrelevance.

. . . .

PEOPLE RESIST EVEN IF YOUR CHANGE IS "THE BEST THING SINCE SLICED BREAD"

Don't make the mistake I did at Blockbuster and assume that the change *you* want to drive is so obvious and necessary that nobody "in their right mind" would resist it. They will.

Archaeologists tell us man has been baking loaves of bread for over 30,000 years. In 1917, an inventor named Otto Rohwedder created a working prototype of the *first* machine to mechanically slice bread. Prior to that, there was no way to slice an entire loaf simultaneously and evenly. All bread was sold "unsliced." Clearly it was a barbaric time.

Of course, today, not only is almost all bread commercially sliced, but the *highest praise* we can give something new is to say it is, "The best thing since sliced bread," the preeminence of the mechanical bread slicer is so unquestioned.

If you are not a student of bread history, it would be reasonable for you to assume that once Rohwedder's revolutionary invention was demonstrated that it was immediately and widely heralded as genius. Not at all.[4]

In that era, most bread purchased in the US was from local bakeries. But local bakers were very skeptical and wary about sliced bread and Rohwedder's invention, insisting that the pre-sliced loaves would go stale more quickly and would be less durable when transported. They shunned the device.

As a result, it took more than a decade and the growth of a new business model that *bypassed* the change-resistant local bakers before "sliced bread" took off. In the early 1930s, the new "Wonder Bread" brand started selling sliced bread in supermarkets and found

great success. By the end of the 1930s *most* of the bread consumed in the U.S. was manufactured at large commercial factories, was sliced, and was primarily purchased at supermarkets, to the dismay, nay the *disgust* of local bakeries.

But it's not just crusty bakers who dislike change. *Most* people actively resist it, often to their detriment. They create rationalizations that it isn't needed and try to focus everyone on its dangers, even when those dangers pale in comparison to the risks of *not* changing. And, if a change still gets adopted, they will go so far as to sabotage it.

For example, smarting from their massively diminished "slice" of the bread market, in the early 1940s certain well-connected "local bakery interests," including the powerful New York City Bakers Advisory Committee, were successful at using their political clout, and lord knows what other kind of backroom leverage, to get sliced bread *banned* by the U.S. Federal Government, until consumers revolted.[5]

Similarly, I've been fascinated over the years to observe the extremes of energy and ingenuity that can go into resisting change: shady politics designed to tank a project, presentations that imply new directions are not consistent with the current brand, competing projects that "pop up" to create internal conflict, sudden budget cuts that require innovative efforts to be defunded.

The "justification" behind the federal ban on sliced bread in the '40s was that it used too much wax paper, which apparently could not be spared due to the war effort in Europe.

What caused the allied soldiers to need all that wax paper I don't really know, but when the ban was lifted as a result of popular pressure, not only was the government elusive about exactly who had *authorized* the ridiculous regulation in the first place, but even its original advocates had to admit that it hadn't had much impact on wax paper consumption.

Such twisted logic, but looked at another way, it's quite inspiring to see the creative thinking and strategic politicking that go into maintaining the status quo.

It's also profoundly counterproductive, as change is often essential for a business to grow or, in some cases, just to maintain its position in a changing market.

. . . .

NINE REASONS PEOPLE RESIST CHANGE

Leaders of transformation need to become *experts* at the various flavors of "resistance to change" and the tactics to overcome them. In this chapter we'll analyze nine discrete reasons that organizations resist change, and then we'll talk about eleven specific tactics you can use to overcome these factors.

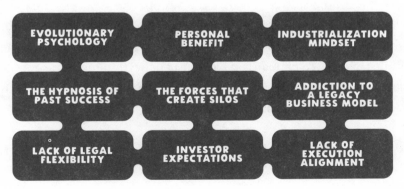

Nine Reasons Organizations Resist Change ‹ wdc.ht/REASONS

Reason Number 1:
EVOLUTIONARY PSYCHOLOGY

Perhaps 10-15% of people in the world naturally seek out and enjoy change—excited by the constant new challenges it brings. Because you are reading this book and have even made it to the last section of the book, it's quite possible that *you* are one of those people. Me too. But for the *majority*, change equals pain. In fact, scientists tell us that most people are actually wired in their DNA to resist change.

Evolutionary psychology examines patterns in our brains that were created to give us an "edge" during the era in which our brains evolved.

Before modern society, we lived in a far more dangerous time of zero technology and no civilization to speak of. In that world, you either learned to survive or you died. In that world, if you found a field where you could reliably kill antelope or a cave that protected you from wild boars, you didn't give it up. Once you figured out how to survive in that world, you did whatever you could to avoid messing with your "recipe for success." In that world, change equaled risk—not the risks we face in business today, but more drastic risks, like death by starvation or being eaten by some prehistoric beast.

When trying to inspire change, it's useful to recognize you are often swimming upstream against the way our brains have evolved. And just like other innate fears, such as loud noises and high places, this preprogrammed fear of change exists for historical survival reasons. While this degree of fear is no longer beneficial in modern times (in fact it's *counter* to survival) because it's hardwired into our DNA, most people can't easily choose to switch it off.

Reason Number 2:
PERSONAL BENEFIT

Irrational evolutionary programming aside, even in our *modern* world, change is not necessarily good for everyone.

Imagine that you have spent a 30-year career thriving because of your expertise in COBOL programming (an ancient, outdated language), and your company's proposed digital transformation is going to replace all the COBOL tech in your company with new modern systems built on platforms that you don't know.

Imagine further that all the "kids" coming out of engineering school are already trained in that new technology that's being implemented, and they are happy to work for half your salary.

It's understandably hard to get fully on board. Similarly, it's hard to expect factory workers to get excited about robotic manufacturing or call center workers to embrace AI-driven chatbots.

And this goes all the way up to the senior executives who *also* tend to view potential transformation in terms of their own careers and security. For those who have built mini empires within the current structure, a significant shift, even if it's clearly in the best interest of the company, might not wind up being in their *personal* best interest, so they naturally resist it.

If a new product or project is truly going to be transformational for your company, expect it to have enemies. These enemies' very survival may be at stake or at least seem to be.

What will they do? If they can't stop the transformation from beginning, they undermine it along the way. Many innovative products that were on the path to "saving the company" were killed through internal sabotage. It's easy. As soon as there is any misstep in a transformation initiative—as there always is—be ready to pounce and convince the powers-that-be that it's time to "put it out of its misery."

Can you imagine Apple killing the iPhone over "Antenna-gate" [6] or the Apple Maps debacle?[7] Neither of these things happened, but I've seen that *sort* of thing happen often at "legacy" companies. I saw it at Blockbuster. And as discussed earlier, forces within Kodak killed or massively hampered any effort there to launch or promote digital cameras.

And when a proposed change *doesn't* threaten a given person's job in an existential way, it *may* not drive them to schemes and subterfuge, but the change can still sound messy and chaotic and therefore unappealing. If you've ever remodeled your kitchen, you know that the noise, dust, and inconvenience it creates can be truly awful, even if it's leading you someplace better eventually. The bottom line is that change is disruptive. So, it's also logical—harmful, but logical—that many people fail to support it simply to avoid personal discomfort, and even convince themselves that it's bad for the company in order to justify their position.

People will often look for data that supports the reality they would prefer rather than face the necessity of change and its associated pain.

❮ wdc.ht/FACE

Reason Number 3:
INDUSTRIALIZATION MINDSET

To a large degree, enterprises today are built on the principle of industrialization, where "experts" figure out how best to produce a product or service, and employees are trained in these methods and expected to comply with them.

Large organizations have extensively documented workflow processes, tons of policies and procedures, detailed performance measurements, and very often, a largely ignored suggestion box in the corner of the break room. That is the culture and psychology of most enterprises today—they are built to keep doing the same thing over and over, not to transform.

So if you have teams who have been steeped in that mindset for years or even decades and you then ask them to engage in rapid change, it can be bewildering and unnatural at best, just like the SCUBA metaphor that we discussed in Chapter 15.

Reason Number 4:
THE HYPNOSIS OF PAST SUCCESS

Bill Gates famously said, "Success is a lousy teacher." [8]

‹ wdc.ht/GATES

Many great legacy brands have a history of success during periods of time when change was not so essential. When faced with the pain of change, it can cause both management and the rank-and-file to question whether such a degree of transformation is *truly* necessary— "After all, we've been successful doing it this way for many years." This mindset tends to encourage denial of the real urgency of change.

Reason Number 5:
THE FORCES THAT CREATE SILOS

The digital experiences that customers love almost always require seamless interaction between many different touchpoints and business areas of a brand. However, large organizations are designed in silos— departments, divisions, product teams, even different corporations.

Each silo often has its own leadership, processes, systems, performance measurements, and sometimes culture, which can disincent individuals from working together in a way that supports enterprise-wide transformation toward a harmonized customer journey.

I recently had to return a defective product that I ordered on Dell.com. I tried using their customer service chat, but after some back and forth with the agent, he nicely explained that my order had been routed to and fulfilled by the Small and Medium Business group at Dell; however, *he* was with the Small Office/Home Office group, a totally different team. Therefore, he could not access my order. I asked whether there was a different chat link for the "Small and Medium Business Group," but he explained that *that* group does not have chat, so I'd have to call them.

Ok, so Dell has a different group to support "small offices" versus "small businesses," and even though both take orders from Dell.com, you have to know which one received your order and communicate with them using the systems and touchpoints specific to that silo. Undoing all this tangle is part of the challenge of digital transformation.

In my consulting, I *often* come across these types of siloed enterprise structures, as well as other policies or behaviors that, by any reasonable external standard, seem ridiculous and inefficient. Usually, the people working at the company, including the executives, will also acknowledge that they are indefensible. And yet they persist. Why not just get rid of them?

Every summer, my family rents a house on the Jersey Shore. One year, we had a property that directly overlooked a beach. The tide would come in and out throughout the day. I noticed that when I woke up early in the morning and sat out on the porch looking at the ocean, there would be a ripple pattern in the sand from the waves and there'd be a lot of seaweed on the beach. The company that managed the beach would come by around 7 a.m. each day with a tractor and a sort of rake they dragged off the back of it. The seaweed would get scooped up and the sand would become smooth. But the tide would come in, and a couple hours later, if you looked back at the beach— ripples and seaweed. The tractor would come back late morning, fix it all, then ripples and seaweed again a few hours later, then tractor again. I observed this cycle repeat over and over each day for the week I was there.

I've often started working with a new client and observed processes or structures that seem undesirable, like seaweed all over a nice beach. But I've learned that before I just fire up my tractor and start fixing them, it's important to try to understand what the *force* is that's keeping them that way. In all likelihood, smart people have been there before me and tried to scoop up the seaweed, but it reappeared. Someone is benefiting from this status quo, even if it's harmful in the big picture, or some other force is keeping it in place. Start by trying to understand those forces because if you don't solve the issues at that level, you'll be waking up early every morning to scoop up more seaweed.

Reason Number 6:
ADDICTION TO A LEGACY BUSINESS MODEL

Real success in digital usually requires a shift in business model. Google invented a totally new sales system in programmatic advertising. Companies like Uber and Airbnb leverage the "gig economy" to build businesses that are totally different from competitors. Great legacy brands can do it, too. NBC and Fox came together over ten years ago to offer the same broadcast content that they normally monetize through advertising on a subscription platform they called Hulu, a very unusual model at the time for broadcasters. Hulu today is worth over $15 billion,[9] about half of what all of NBC-Universal is worth, including their television, film and theme park divisions.

Companies that successfully "cross the chasm" to digital often discover they need to provide for free what they used to charge for, sell as a subscription what used to be "a la carte," monetize via advertising things that used to be paid for in other ways, and generally rethink how they derive revenue from the value that they create. Those that do so flexibly often find that they can achieve more scale, revenue, and profit than they did using the legacy approach. But achieving an effective digital strategy takes experimentation, an assumption of risk, and—to be blunt—some failure along the way.

As in the example of Blockbuster's candy fixation, companies can become addicted to a certain business model or revenue streams. Apple readily created the iPhone despite the fact that it would inevitably cannibalize iPod sales, but many companies would not take that risk. As discussed throughout this book, digital transformation often requires a shift in business models, but it's not always possible to determine that there will be no disruption in revenue during the transition. For many companies, this is the hardest bridge to cross.

Reason Number 7:
LACK OF LEGAL FLEXIBILITY

Many innovative ideas require a willingness to operate in areas not yet well-defined legally. For example, Uber and Airbnb were not at all certain whether their businesses were legal in many municipalities when they started operating. In other markets, it was pretty clear that what they were doing really *wasn't* legal, based on local codes and regulations that were written before the age of digital.

When Google first started indexing the web, it was unclear that they had the legal right to "spider" other companies' sites;[10] some complained and threatened legal action at the time. (Of course, today those "complainers" are engaging top dollar SEO firms to get Google to spider them as much as possible.)

Large companies tend to be very conservative legally, making it difficult for them to pursue innovative opportunities that smaller companies would seize. The truth is that:

Had Google started as a project within a large media company, it may very well have been shut down at the first legal challenge.

Reason Number 8:
INVESTOR EXPECTATIONS

Investors in mature companies have certain financial expectations of quarterly profit and dividends that may not be consistent with major new digital investments. CEOs who see their net revenue drop even for a single quarter may soon see a corresponding drop in share price and shortly thereafter find themselves with far more time to "spend with their family."

In other words, it can feel like their hands are tied when wanting to invest in the future. In contrast, investors in digital startups expect that it will take years for the company to make a profit or, in some cases, even generate revenue.

Bottom line, for large enterprises, it can be challenging to get "permission" to change the game and invest in their own future at the level necessary to win.

Reason Number 9:
LACK OF ALIGNMENT AROUND THE SOLUTION OR EXECUTION

Of course, one reason why people resist change is that they just don't agree with its direction. Once you have gotten someone to agree that change, in general, is needed, you still need to persuade them to align to a *specific* change, and good people can disagree on the best direction. Because the changes we are talking about can seem profound and existential, it can be hard to "compromise" if you just aren't feeling the correct vision has been identified. Sometimes this disagreement leads to paralysis.

HOW TO OVERCOME ORGANIZATIONAL RESISTANCE TO CHANGE

That's a lot of reasons why people resist change! And you may face multiple of them, maybe even *all* of them, as well as others *not* on this list. But change is essential to survival, especially in this digital era; so how do you drive change despite these obstacles?

Be prepared for a rocky road.

If you value corporate tranquility above all else, digital transformation is not for you.

< wdc.ht/TRANQUILITY

But there are many strategies that you can employ to help overcome the resistance, and if you've been following the approach outlined in this book, you also have some assets you can leverage. Here are some specific tactics that have worked well in transformations that I've been a part of.

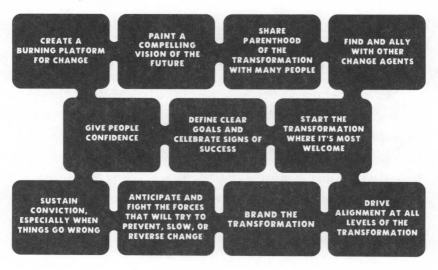

Tactic 1:
CREATE A BURNING PLATFORM FOR CHANGE

It's critical to have a strong story around why change is essential and to back it up with data. The story should also connect with people emotionally. Your "current state" customer journey maps can help bring to life what is unsustainable about today's customer experience.

You may also be able to leverage some of the anecdotes and statistics about why change is essential in Chapter 3, as well as other parts of this book.

BONUS TOOL: *As we mentioned earlier, we've compiled a range of relevant statistics to help support the need for digital transformation and put them into a periodical called* Digital Stats Quarterly. *A one-year subscription is included with your book purchase, so just head to the book website where you can download persuasive stats as PowerPoint slides, and tailor them for your own decks. We will update them over time, so make sure to check back when you need the most up-to-date data.*

 wdc.ht/DSQ

Tactic 2:
PAINT A COMPELLING VISION OF THE FUTURE

It's essential to pitch the transformation vision in such a way that you inspire people to want to participate. Having a compelling vision and method of communicating it is critical to achieving this.

The *future* state customer journey you created in Chapter 11 should describe that inspiring vision. The prioritized business rationales for the various components of the transformation discussed in Chapter 11 combined with the broader business case for change discussed in Chapter 3 should provide a compelling *financial* vision to top executives, board members, and investors.

Tactic 3:
SHARE PARENTHOOD OF THE TRANSFORMATION WITH MANY PEOPLE

If only we could channel all of the individual and organizational resourcefulness that's being applied to *resisting* change into making it successful, we'd be well on our way to victory. Can we perform some sort of psychological jujitsu?

Yes. Because there's a second half to the axiom that people resist change. Something I learned long ago from my friend and colleague Rob Evans at the Capgemini Accelerated Solutions Environment.

PEOPLE RESIST CHANGE, BUT THEY SUPPORT THE CHANGE THAT THEY CREATE.

 wdc.ht/CREATE

You've probably encountered teams, departments, or whole companies who seem to reject any ideas that are "NIH" (not invented here). And you've probably also seen cases where individuals or teams fall in love with their own ideas and defend them, no matter what.

It turns out that there is a loophole in the evolutionary programming discussed earlier. Humans instinctively fear change, but they support the change that *they initiate*.

Consider that the *ultimate* change to one's life—having and raising a child—is something that many people pursue as a primary goal in life. Babies are the loophole.

And usefully, that loophole that encourages people to support the success of their *offspring* also applies to their *ideas*. There's a deep psychological reason why people often talk about someone's idea as their "baby."

If you have an idea for an innovation, you probably need the support of a group of people to take it to the next level. You want Finance solidly behind its business case, Marketing engaged and thinking about the brand and positioning, product designers enthusiastic, and Manufacturing motivated to research the most efficient method of production. But *your* idea isn't *their* idea, so they have no emotional reason to support it and, as outlined earlier, if it drives change, they may have many reasons to resist it. How do you get people to develop ownership over ideas that are not originally their own? How do you make *your* idea *their* "baby"?

One tactic that we utilize frequently to accomplish this is conducting workshops for ideation, prioritization, and action planning. When we think about who to invite, we consider not only the people who will have the *best ideas* but also the people whose *support* will be needed to make the initiative successful.

Then, in the workshop, it's sometimes useful to take a few steps back from the identified "solution" in order to foster shared ownership. You may already believe you have the "right answer." However, by bringing together a group with the right background information and asking *them* to brainstorm solutions, you may find that you can get that *group* of people to ideate something very similar to your initial concept, to "rebirth" your idea in a collective fashion, so to speak.

In fact, you *may* find that the right participants, provided with the key objectives information and context, will invent an *even better* version of your idea. This is superior not only on the merits but also because you will have more support in the long run if the whole group takes ownership. And frankly, even if you think the group's collective idea isn't *quite* as "good" as your original concept, you are probably still ahead of the game.

*If a group "rebirths" an idea that is only 80%
as "good" as the original idea but has wide alignment,
you are better off than with a more "perfect" idea
that only you feel ownership over.*

There may be cases where you'd say, "That ship has sailed. We already announced that we intend to launch product XYZ. We can't go back and ask people to 'reinvent it.' They'll see right through that."

In such a scenario, you may be able to focus the collaborative innovation on the "idea pyramid" *below* the core vision (discussed in detail in Chapter 13). Briefly restated, the success of a given innovation isn't really one idea—it's a hierarchy of ideas. The first idea might be the recognition of a previously unseen customer need. The second level might be a concept for a new product to address that need. The third level might be a business model for bringing it to market, and the fourth might be its naming or packaging—and so on.

A successful initiative, especially one that breaks new ground in a significant way, often needs a vast network of new ideas. Each round of these new ideas is an opportunity to bring together a fresh team of people and ask them to invent the solution for the next layer—bringing them into the fold of fellow "parents" of the effort.

Tactic 4:
FIND AND ALLY WITH OTHER CHANGE AGENTS

Does everyone in a company resist change and do so with the same ferocity? No. In any given enterprise, there are *certain* people, even if a minority, who are hungry for change. For example, the majority of CEOs of large enterprises recognize that transformation is essential to their company's success and, consequently, their continued tenure as CEO. Why? A CEO's job is to *grow* a company so that the overall value and stock price rise. Transformation is key to that, especially today. But CEOs are not kings, and their desires do not automatically become results.

Also, entry-level employees at a given company tend to be *relatively* more open to change—often younger and more enthusiastic about innovation, as well as less tolerant of their company being "second rate" in the digital world. They also don't have as much to lose. Of course, it depends on the type of transformation (nobody likes to feel their livelihood is threatened).

And, as we discuss in more detail in the next chapter, you can find "innovation heroes" at all levels—people whose DNA bucks the trend of evolutionary psychology and who will be ready to get on the transformation bandwagon. They are a minority to be sure, but they are out there. Identify them and bring them onto your team.

Tactic 5:
GIVE PEOPLE CONFIDENCE

One reason people fear change is that they worry it will fail—wasting time and money and possibly creating embarrassment. These fears can become a self-fulfilling prophecy. Leaders need to demonstrate the confidence that will empower the organization to deliver at its best.

Of course, nobody can predict with absolute certainty the outcome of any given initiative, but people need to feel *certainty in order to be confident. And it's a leader's job to provide it.*

‹ wdc.ht/CERTAINTY

Executives leading change need to express certainty of victory not only with their words but with their nonverbal communication. Nonverbal communication basically means your tone of voice and the way you use your body—your posture, energy, and physical expressiveness. We've all listened to people whose words were saying one thing and their nonverbal communication was saying something different. They tend to not be believable and definitely not inspiring.

It's lot harder to lie with body language than with words, so the easiest and best way to get your "nonverbal" communication right is simply to be fully sincere in what you are telling people. In order to do that, though, you have to really believe that the company *will* succeed or at least has an outstanding chance. Of course, confidence in success doesn't mean you think that nothing could go *wrong*, but only that when it does the team will *still* find a way to succeed.

If you don't believe that, you may not be ready to lead. To remedy this problem, you can use the techniques in this book to look to your own limiting beliefs and work to overcome them. Or else, if you think you're not set up for success, maybe find another job and let someone who *does* believe take yours.

Once your mindset is right, it can be helpful to video yourself giving presentations to evaluate your own nonverbal communication and to work with a communications coach who can support you in being sure you are expressing what is in your heart as effectively as possible with your whole voice and body language.

In addition to expressing *that* you are confident, describe to the team *why* you are certain that the organization is capable of achieving the goals of the transformation. What are the reasons to believe? The details will vary situationally, but here are some good topics to cover:

- **THE COMMITMENT** the organization has to the program, including the resources and budget that have been allocated. It helps greatly if the CEO frames the transformation as a top priority and empowers the transformation's leader through a public endorsement and expression of confidence.

- **THE SPECIFIC ASSETS** the organization has and can leverage to set them up to win. This may include the experience of individual leaders or teams, unique products or patents, strong brands, customer loyalty, existing partnerships, or acquisitions—anything that gives the company an "edge" in the marketplace.

- **THE HISTORY** the organization has of past success. All large companies have past victories, even if recent years haven't been as glorious. We once worked on a transformation at a struggling company that had been a major pioneer and innovator at far earlier points in their long history. Pick up on those themes even if they've been forgotten. Remind people that the heritage of the company includes innovation and transformation. If the company could do it *then*, it can do it now.

- **RECENT SUCCESS:** If the company has recently had a major success, even if it is of a totally different nature, leverage that as another reason for confidence. For example, an insurance company whose team pulls together to process ten times the number of typical claims during a major hurricane has shown a level of grit and resourcefulness that can then be highlighted when outlining the reasons they will be successful at a major technology transformation.

- **ANALOGOUS SUCCESS:** Sometimes people feel that the transformation challenge is too great to overcome. There are many inspiring stories of football teams that came back from a demoralizing first half, mountain climbers that made it to the top of Everest despite horrible storms, and "underdog" military victories such as George Washington's "against all odds" defeat of the British in the American Revolutionary War. Remind teams that the challenge you face is not nearly as significant as those which others have overcome, and that the greatest satisfaction comes from a difficult mission accomplished.

Tactic 6:
DEFINE CLEAR GOALS AND CELEBRATE SIGNS OF SUCCESS

Everyone likes to feel like they are part of a winning team and program.

The sooner you can start to prove the transformation is working, the faster you will bring more people on board. One way to show quick progress is to begin by tackling some of the easier parts of the transformation. In Chapters 17 and 18, we talked about optimization, which enables you to quickly find points of pain that can be fixed for rapid, measurable impact. Be sure to measure that impact and communicate it broadly.

Also, lay out the timeline and anticipated early indicators of success of the broader transformation in advance so that when you hit those milestones, you can promote them as promises kept and goalposts crossed.

For example, it might take quite a while for a new digital product to be a financial success, but you could telegraph as you begin development, a key goal of 1,000 paid users in the first six months. That can then become a specific line of victory that the team can see growing closer and can celebrate when realized.

Once those interim victories occur, make the most of them. Parties, bonuses (even if small), and shared recognition re-energize the team for the next day's challenges.

Tactic 7:
START THE TRANSFORMATION WHERE IT'S MOST WELCOME

When it comes to more ambitious transformation, it can be strategic to prioritize your initial efforts in areas of the company that are most welcoming to change and where the barriers are the lowest. That way, you can demonstrate that not just optimization, but *true* transformation (even within just one area of the business) is possible, beneficial, and even rewarding. Once you have a few inspiring examples, it will be easier to win over the more intransigent areas.

Tactic 8:
SUSTAIN CONVICTION, ESPECIALLY WHEN THINGS GO WRONG

There will be tough times. Know in advance that they will come. Then when they do, you must maintain your confidence and commitment, as well as remind stakeholders of the *reasons* the organization must sustain *its* commitment.

When initially pitching and then announcing transformation, publicly predict and communicate that those tough times *will* come as an inevitable part of the journey—it won't be a straight path to success—and you will need everyone's support and commitment to get through them. That way, when those times *do* come, you can remind everyone that this was an expected part of the process.

There are many stories of transformations that did not progress in a straight line but eventually achieved major success. These types of anecdotes can be powerful reminders that setbacks do not equal failure unless you give up.

For example, many well-known "tech" successes like Skype and Airbnb spent years "spinning," trying different approaches to drive growth. Edison famously had to try over 3,000 materials to find the right filament for his light bulb. Apple went through bleak periods where its existence was uncertain. Yet all sustained their commitment and emerged victorious.

BONUS TOOL: *On the book website, we've posted a slide deck of some inspiring stories that depict transformational efforts that struggled but ultimately succeeded. Pick a few of those stories and share them with your teams.*

 wdc.ht/INSPIRE

Tactic 9:
ANTICIPATE AND FIGHT THE FORCES THAT WILL TRY TO PREVENT, SLOW, OR REVERSE CHANGE

Even when things are going well—or *especially* when they are going well and the "threat" of successfully transforming the organization is increasing—there will be forces trying to derail the progress for their own benefit. Keep an eye out for these forces and recognize that half of your job as a transformation leader is dealing with the politics of sabotage and subversion. Since there are so many different flavors of obstruction, it's difficult to provide concrete advice about what to do in every case, but forewarned is forearmed.

Tactic 10:
BRAND THE TRANSFORMATION

There's a reason countries have flags and rallying cries like "Give me victory or give me death," or "Make America great again." They work. Create an inspirational brand—a slogan and visual identity for the transformation effort that reflects the aspirational vision.

Simon Sinek's blockbuster book *Start With Why* describes how teams are inspired not just by what you intend to *do* but by sharing the emotional impact it's going to have on people. Be sure your brand incorporates a sense of greater meaning and purpose than raising the stock price or hitting a revenue goal.

Tactic 11:
DRIVE ALIGNMENT AT ALL LEVELS OF THE TRANSFORMATION

Sometimes people are ready to change, but they just don't agree with the current plan.

Transformation efforts almost always need diverse teams participating in conceiving, designing, building, testing, marketing, and selling a solution. But at the beginning, transformation can seem wide open, with everyone possessing a different perspective about what should be done.

One group may want to change the form of the product, another wants to focus on its features, and yet another on its pricing model or distribution methods. Discord can emerge, especially when people feel invested, making it imperative that your team has a go-to method for resolving conflict and fostering alignment.

Sometimes disagreements are easy to solve by simply laying out the decision criteria and the facts and collaborating to determine the best path.

Remember that while it's important not to dilute the core vision too much, it's also smart to "pick your battles." For your colleagues to sustain a feeling of ownership, they need to be given wins along the way in terms of their role in shaping the result. Alignment is more important than perfection. Small compromises may be strategic.

But at other times, disagreements can crop up that are more stubborn. You have a series of meetings that seem to be going nowhere. The process is "spinning." This can have a huge impact on team morale, especially if the disagreements are between leaders.

We used to struggle with this issue at our clients, but then we developed a simple tool that usually gets things moving. The tool is called "The 5 Tiers of Solution Alignment."

What we realized is that there are different "levels" of decision-making in business, as outlined below, and disagreements can occur at any of the levels. When discussions are not progressing, it's usually because the *discussion* is not really occurring where the level of *disagreement* is.

By using the pyramid, we determine first on what *tiers* the disagreements exist on. Then we focus discussions solely on the *lowest* tier of disagreement and only move up the pyramid when everyone is aligned on the lower tiers.

The 5 Tiers of Solution Alignment

wdc.ht/5TIERS

The disagreements may not be *easy* to overcome, and compromise might be needed, but you can finally start to make *progress* when you are actually talking about the issue at the right level.

If you have a group that isn't aligned, try to figure out on which tier they're disagreeing.

- Are they really trying to achieve different outcomes? Then focus on debating what the *objectives* should be.

- Do they agree on the goal or objective but disagree on where there are *gaps* in the current experience—which problems are the most critical? Then focus on alignment around the gaps.

- Does everyone agree, for example, that a product that lasts longer is what is needed but disagree on the *method* that will achieve that goal? That's a *solution* disagreement.

- Does everyone agree on the basic solution but disagree on whether it should be, for example, manufactured internally or outsourced? That's an *implementation* disagreement.

- Do you agree on the product and how to build it but remain divided on what's a reasonable measure of sales success for the first year? That's an example of a *metrics and accountability* disagreement.

And most importantly, remember:

DISAGREEMENT IS NOT INHERENTLY BAD. IN FACT, IT'S **WILDLY VALUABLE** WHEN RESOLVED IN AN EFFECTIVE MANNER.

‹ wdc.ht/DISAGREEMENT

The process of debating alternatives and working through differing perspectives helps drive much better decisions *and* develops teams that are more invested in the results.

BONUS VIDEO: *We've provided a video about how to use this pyramid, as well as a PowerPoint deck that walks through the levels of the Solution Alignment Pyramid, which can be helpful for facilitating group decision-making.*

▶ wdc.ht/LEVELS

371

. . . .

*For all this gloom and doom about disagreements and
resistance, transformational change absolutely can and does
happen. It happens when a leader inspires teams across an
organization, aligns them around a clear vision, gets the
resources and political support to make it happen, and then
anticipates and proactively strategizes how to avoid the
potholes along the way. In the next chapter, we'll focus on
the types of qualities required to be that inspiring leader.*

CHAPTER TWENTY

LEAD THE CHANGE

TRANSFORMATIONAL LEADERS & TEAMS

I n the aftermath of World War II, Japan was decimated. Much of their infrastructure was damaged, their economy was in ruins, and, perhaps most critically, their confidence was destroyed. One of the national projects undertaken as Japan pulled out of the rubble, physically and spiritually, was the rebuilding of the country's train system. The Japanese sought not only to restore their rail network but to do so in a way that would dramatically improve the speed of transport across the country, both to boost the economy and to inspire national pride.

The first 10 years of the program consisted of incremental improvements on pre-existing 19th-century steam locomotive technology—new lubricants, ball bearings, and other engineering optimizations. These changes succeeded in enhancing the speed of trains somewhat. However, the impact was not transformational.

Enter Hideo Shima, a visionary leader, who was then appointed to take charge of the critical train line between Osaka, Tokyo, and Nagoya.[1] Prior to Shima's appointment, the preexisting plans for rebuilding

the route had called for con-
tinuation of the steam-engine
approach, but Shima pushed a
transformational vision of high-
speed rail or "bullet trains," as
they became known. He used a
combination of charisma, confidence, and engineering science
to demonstrate to the government and his teams that this
bold way of thinking about rail
transport was possible.

It took almost 10 years to launch the first of Shima's new lines,
which operated at nearly 200 miles per hour and cut the six-hour trip
from Tokyo to Osaka down to around three hours.

Achieving this transformational speed required removing constraints that had previously been considered "fixed." Fossil fuels were
difficult and expensive for Japan after World War II, so Shima's trains
used electricity. He shifted from the traditional "wheels-on-steel" car-
riage that seemed inherent to the very idea of a train, to magnetic
levitation, massively reducing friction. He rethought the idea that a
locomotive should pull a train, instead putting power in the wheels
of every car—generating far more speed. And in mountainous Japan,
trains often had to slow down to go around or over rocky terrain, but
Shima used new technology to tunnel straight through the mountains, creating a more direct route.

In the end, he delivered a true transformation that had a massive
impact on the economy of Japan, as well as its national pride.[2]

But Shima influenced far more than Japanese rail. I was first
introduced to this story by my client, Bryan Sander, who is in charge
of Customer Experience for AAA Motor Club and who used it very

effectively to inspire the leadership of a 21st-century transformation there.

Sander learned it when he worked for Steve Bennett, the CEO of Intuit, where Shima's story became a rallying cry for bold change at the $5-billion software company. Bennett, in turn, had learned it working for Jack Welch, the legendary CEO of General Electric. Welch had gone to Japan in the '80s to learn from the Japanese and, upon his return, evangelized Shima's story and decreed that every division of GE needed to identify "bullet train" level opportunities.

So not only do transformational leaders need to paint a bold, exciting vision, as Shima did, but they can also leverage parables of past innovation successes, like Sander, Bennett, and Welch did when they inspired their organizations with Shima's story.

This is only a small part of what it takes to *be* the leader of the types of massive transformations that are required to re-make great legacy companies to be relevant in this new digital age.

. . . .

YOUR INNOVATION HERO

Who will lead digital transformation at your company? Who will be *your* Hideo Shima? Based on the metaphors we have articulated in this book, it would you appear you need someone who can carve an entire iceberg, shift a planet's orbit, tunnel through mountains and make trains levitate.

This doesn't sound like a job for an ordinary mortal but rather something you'd see Superman do in a movie. In fact, what we have observed is that legacy companies that achieve real success at transformation are able to do it, at least in part, because they *have* what we call an "innovation hero." This is someone who has the vision and tenacity to make it their personal, 24/7 mission to drag their enterprise toward digital excellence, no matter how challenging or how much resistance they face. Even if it costs them their job.

Who is the innovation hero and why is he or she necessary? Well, why was Batman or Superman necessary? Metropolis and Gotham City both had perfectly capable police forces to fight crime, but those police forces were built for ordinary day-to-day criminals. They were not structured to deal with a super-villain transforming the town's power plant into a galactic death ray or a half-man, half-reptile monster hypnotizing the entire population of a city into zombies. For these types of threats, someone outside the system is needed—someone who doesn't follow all the rules, someone who does whatever it takes, for whom failure is not an option—that's the superhero.

Similarly, enterprise brands have been adapting to new competitive threats and shifting consumer preferences for many decades. But these changes were of a more ordinary pace and range. Today's digital threat is more on the scale of a super-villain. Accordingly, the methods and processes most large brands have established to evolve their offerings and customer interactions are as inadequate for digital transformation as the street cop's baton is against the Joker's laughing gas.

So how can you find the innovation hero who can save your company? Comic book superheroes often emerge from humble backgrounds, yet other times they're millionaires. Some have an inner drive, while others are chosen by a higher power.

Before my career in consulting, I was trained in the theatre. I've made it this far in the book without a single Shakespeare quote, but that ends right now with this classic line from *Twelfth Night:*

"SOME ARE BORN GREAT, SOME ACHIEVE GREATNESS, AND SOME HAVE GREATNESS THRUST UPON 'EM."

< wdc.ht/GREAT

At your company, the innovation hero might be your CEO, CIO, or CMO, or it might be someone who starts a few levels down. Perhaps it's you? In any case, the innovation hero inevitably winds up acting well beyond their assigned purview. This is because no matter the level, the demands of digital innovation and transformation cut broadly across an organization and, other than perhaps the CEO, nobody has the breadth of authority to cover it all.

What are the innovation hero superpowers that this individual will have to bring to the table? Wonder no more; they are shown below.

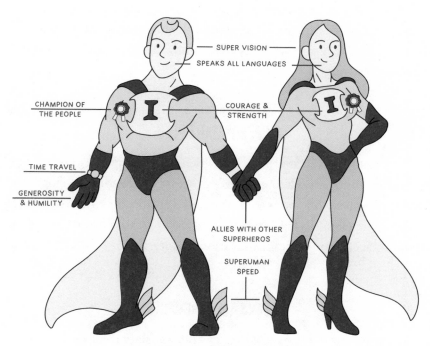

The Superpowers of an Innovation Hero

‹ wdc.ht/SUPERHERO

Superpower 1:
SUPER VISION

Innovation heroes see threats to the business clearly and can envision how transforming customer experience, technology capabilities, and the organization itself will enable it to meet the opportunities of the future.

Superpower 2:
COURAGE AND STRENGTH

There will be battles, and there will be injuries along the way. Innovation heroes are not focused on "covering their butts" or deterred by setbacks. They persist. They fight. They take their licks and come back even stronger.

Superpower 3:
SUPERHUMAN SPEED

Digital moves at a pace for which most organizations are not prepared. Innovation heroes utilize processes like Agile Development and immersive workshops to drive rapid decision-making. They push for flexible, cloud-based solutions and other technologies that allow them to accelerate digital innovation and iteration.

Superpower 4:
SPEAKS ALL LANGUAGES

Innovation heroes can convey and translate their message into the languages of business, IT, marketing, finance, legal, and user experience. They may not be the top experts in all or any of these areas, but they can bridge them and create a common understanding.

Superpower 5:
IS A CHAMPION OF THE PEOPLE

Innovation heroes drive business success by prioritizing the needs of the company's *customers,* as well as its rank and file employees—making sure their needs are understood and that they are truly taken care of.

Superpower 6:
TIME TRAVEL

The Innovation hero focuses both on driving the multi-year "big picture" and on executing the near-term wins that demonstrate success—helping fund future transformation.

Superpower 7:
GENEROSITY AND HUMILITY

The innovation hero is looking to drive a glorious outcome, but not to achieve personal glory. He or she lives by a memorable quote from the only U.S. president to share my initials:

"IT IS AMAZING WHAT YOU CAN ACCOMPLISH IF YOU DO NOT CARE WHO GETS THE CREDIT."
– HARRY S. TRUMAN.

Superpower 8:
ALLIES WITH OTHER SUPERHEROES

Digital transformation requires many parts of the organization to work together to win. Innovation heroes persuade leaders across different departments and divisions to come onboard and be part of a super-team, driving victory.

Remember, superheroes don't have to be perfect. In fact, comic book heroes are *always* flawed in one or several ways, but their inner strength, sincerity of purpose and persistence ultimately cause them to triumph. As you embark on digital transformation, these heroic qualities are essential to seeing it all through.

· ·

YOUR SUPER TEAM

Of course, no superhero does it alone. Batman has Robin, and, for the really serious battles, whole teams of superheroes band together. People are inspired when they see this happen, as evidenced by the fact that Marvel's *Avengers: Endgame*, in which over 20 major super-heroes band together to save the universe, has now become the most financially successful film of all time, grossing almost $3 billion.[3]

While all superheroes embody certain *common* characteristics as described above, each also has their specializations. Aquaman can control sea creatures. Wonder Woman has her golden lariat, and Spiderman can swing from buildings.

As a leader, a key part of your job is assembling a leadership *team* of superheroes, all of whom embody core characteristics, but each of whom can bring a special area of strength.

Here are the types of specialization you'll need to bring together:

The Members of Your Super Team ‹ wdc.ht/SUPERTEAM

BONUS EBOOK: *For more details on the best way to structure your Super Team, check out our short eBook,* Structuring a Digital Team. *The eBook expands on this section to give a more complete overview of who you need on your side to make transformation happen.*

wdc.ht/TEAM

TEAM SYNERGY

The clarity of each leader's vision builds on the others. Without a business vision, the product leader is adrift. Designers trying to lay out digital user experiences without clear product requirements are likely to fail, and so it goes on down the list. But if provided strong direction from their partners, the leader in each role then has the clarity to do their very best work.

Success also requires a culture of collaboration between *all* the different types of leaders, as well as tight iterative cycles for high productivity. Your product leader may raise questions to the business leader that causes the business vision to be adjusted with input from the technology leader. It's essential that the owners of each part of vision have the independence to "own" their area of focus *and* maintain continuous communication and positive regard amongst the entire leadership team so as to benefit from the talent, knowledge, and ideas of the entire group. Each of these roles is critical, so select them with care.

It may be that initially one person will wear many of these hats, but in that case, it's important that each leader clearly understands the scope of their responsibilities across multiple domains. Longer term, successful digital organizations at scale generally have strong and separate leaders in each of these roles.

BONUS EBOOK: *Getting the mandate to bring in or assemble this array of talent, as well as the funding to support their teams, requires a lot of organizational buy-in. On the book web site, we've provided an entire supplemental eBook on* How to Pitch Digital Transformation to Your Organization. *This may be one of the most valuable bonuses we have provided (of many) because getting executive buy-in and funding is usually central to getting started on any significant transformation.*

wdc.ht/PITCH

CHAPTER TWENTY-ONE

THE ROAD AHEAD: YOUR 90-DAY ACTION PLAN

O ne of the greatest innovators of the 4th century was Aristotle, who said, "Well begun is half done." [1] Congratulations for making it to the end of the book!

We've defined digital transformation, outlined what it looks like, and demonstrated why it's essential. We've explained that the key to success in this digital age is driving customer behavior and provided you with a large number of tools for *understanding* your customer and mapping their current *experience*.

We've laid out how to define a high-level future state journey, as well as how to leverage Design Thinking 2.0 to iteratively create the new products and services that will bring that journey vision to life.

We've also presented tactics for achieving quick wins by optimizing current touchpoints, overcoming resistance to change within your organization, building your leadership team, and crafting your pitch to gain executive support. (Don't forget to download that bonus eBook! ↷ wdc.ht/PITCH.)

Along the way, we've touched on issues of technology, data, business process, and business models—all in the context of a five-part approach for digitally transforming to achieve customer love.

The Customer Love Digital Transformation Formula

I admit, it's a lot. You don't have to master it all in order to get started. I'd love to tell you *exactly* where to start, but it depends on your situation. The good news is that there are many "right" answers. Here are a few possible starting points that have worked well for some of my clients:

1. Start by assembling an informal digital transformation leadership team. Find those "innovation heroes" who are committed to making a difference, whether it's part of their job description or not. Maybe get them all a copy of this book and plot a course together. (Bulk purchases of this book are available ↶ wdc.ht/BULK.)

OR...

2 Start by commissioning research to map out the current customer journey, its points of pain, and the opportunities it presents to make a difference through transformation. Then use that to build your burning platform for change. By the way, my company can help you with this if you like. Learn more at ∞ wdc.ht/JOURNEY.

OR...

3 Start with a specific new product that needs innovation. Focus on just that one area and apply the principles of Design Thinking 2.0 to prove that it can work. Then expand to more areas of the product and services portfolio. My company works in this area, as well. Learn more at ∞ wdc.ht/DT.

OR...

4 Administer the Digital Transformation Index (available free at ∞ wdc.ht/DTI) to a sample of employees across functions and lines of business at your company. See where you are strong and where you are weak. Then use that as a starting point.

OR...

5 Just pick any random chapter of this book and start there. Starting any place is better than waiting.

I also encourage you to utilize all the bonus online resources available with this book at ∞ WDC.HT. Each chapter has templates, links to additional resources, infographics, and other materials to support you in putting the book's content into action. There are also short PowerPoint decks on the content of each chapter. If you see a concept in the book that you'd like to present in a meeting, odds are there are already a few slides to get you started. The website also allows you to post questions specific to any topic in the book. I will try to respond there, or others in the community who are in a similar situation may provide you with even better answers.

As mentioned, my company, FROM, The Digital Transformation Agency, also provides consulting around all these issues including digital strategy, customer research, design thinking, and the other topics covered in this book, so if we can be of help to you, our contact info is available on the book website, or at ∞ FROM.DIGITAL. Alternatively, seek out *another* source of expertise. Most companies engaged in transformation find having the help of outside experts is invaluable. Consultants and agencies cannot do it *for* you (unfortunately), but they can do it *with* you in a way that reduces the risk and increases the pace.

WARTIME LEADERSHIP

I want to leave you with a final metaphor. I am an avid reader of books about leadership, and I am especially interested in biographies of those who were challenged to lead organizations or countries in moments of crisis, like wartime.

When you take up the mantle of a leadership role in digital transformation, you may feel that you have the weight of your company's future on your back, and, in fact, this may well be true. The times we live in are changing fast. Companies are rising and falling at a rate that may be unprecedented—I've certainly not seen it in my lifetime. We are all leading in times of crisis. While you may not literally be at war, there is much to be learned from those who have had to lead during battle. Here are some distinctions between peacetime and wartime leadership. Consider which approach is most appropriate for your leadership style and role within your company's digital transformation.

Peacetime vs. Wartime Leadership

PEACETIME	WARTIME
Relaxation	Urgency
Technology is a helpful enabler.	Technology is life or death.
There's time for contemplation and philosophizing.	There's one crystal-clear goal: to win.
Competing teams go in various directions.	Everyone must row together.
Allies are nice but not essential.	Allies are critical; find them wherever you can.
Heroes are not necessary or even appreciated.	Heroes are needed to save the day.
Opportunity to prosper is present but moderated.	Spoils of war can be enormous.
Risk of death is low.	Risk of death is high.

. . . .

And most of all, as you develop your plan to move forward, be ready to be nimble. As one of the most objectively successful wartime leaders in modern times observed:

"NO PLAN SURVIVES CONTACT WITH THE ENEMY."
— NAPOLEON BONAPARTE

 wdc.ht/NOPLAN

WAIT!

If somehow you have made it this far without accessing the book website, be sure to do so since it contains extensive resources to support you in applying the content from this book, including:

- Over 20 training videos
- PowerPoint slides summarizing each chapter of the book
- Updated statistics to support building your case for digital transformation
- Templates for many of the deliverables discussed in this book
- Team exercises not printed in the book
- Links and recommendations to other valuable resources
- Bonus eBooks about pitching digital transformation, putting together your transformation superteam, and conducting customer research

Go now to WinningDigitalCustomers.com and use the passcode

CustomerLove

To create your FREE account and access all the bonus material

Also be sure to connect with me on ⓘn LinkedIn.com/in/Tiersky or follow me on 🐦 Twitter @Tiersky.

We also appreciate Amazon reviews and you can follow my author page at ↺ wdc.ht/AMAZON.

ACKNOWLEDGEMENTS

I wish to express my deep gratitude to all those who have supported and encouraged my journey, not just of writing this book but of studying the world of "digital" over these last 20+ years.

My wife, Lana is not only the love of my life, but a fantastic sounding board for ideas related to human psychology, which is so core to everything we do in digital transformation, whether influencing customers or our own organizations.

My children, Rachel, Jessica, Foster, Samantha and Joseph, who range in age from 7 to 18, are a never-ending source of inspiration, as well as a fascinating longitudinal ethnographic study on how the new generation is weaving digital into every aspect of their lives.

My parents, Martin and Ethel Tiersky, have always been incredibly supportive of all my undertakings, and an extra thank you to my mother for the proofreading.

I wish to thank my clients over the years such as Neal Zamore, Dawn Zier, Renee Jordan, Bryan Sander, George Vega, Jonathan Hills, Matt Holt, and so many more who have entrusted my team and I with some of their most critical strategic endeavors. I am honored by their confidence and appreciative of all the opportunities to learn and grow, which has directly led to the insights that make up this book.

I'd like to *especially* express my appreciation to my long standing client and friend Michelle McKenna, the CIO of the National Football League, for her many years of partnership on projects at companies like Universal Studios and Constellation Energy, as well as for writing an awesome foreword to this book.

I've also learned an immeasurable amount over the last 15 years from Tony Robbins and the entire Tony Robbins community, including the staff, coaches, crew, senior leaders, and trainer family. Many themes of Tony's work are woven into the approaches I describe here.

I received a fantastic education in organizational change, ideation and group dynamics from my time working with the Ernst & Young and then Capgemini Accelerated Solutions Environment team, trained by Matt and Gail Taylor and led by Rob Evans, Chip Saltsman and many other talented individuals. I've credited Matt Taylor's work in one or two places in the book, and no doubt I have conveyed ideas inspired by his principles in many additional places without direct attribution. My prior education in the theatre has proved an invaluable foundation for a wide range of seemingly unrelated pursuits. I owe a debt of gratitude to Bob Johnson, Cindy Philbin, and the NYU Tisch School of the Arts as well as its Experimental Theatre Wing for lifelong lessons in leadership, storytelling and personal presence.

My team at FROM, The Digital Transformation Agency has taught me a great deal about so many facets of design, strategy and technology as we have worked side-by-side for many years discovering solutions to novel problems for our clients. They have also been extremely supportive of this book, including working on the editing, diagrams, research and many other tasks necessary to pull it together. I'd like to specifically thank Connor Gundersen, Juan Diaz, Lubov Babaeva, Natasha Jaime, Sam Kang, Ginna Cortese, David Franklin, and Marilyn Freedman for their work directly on the book. And I'd like to thank my leadership team at FROM, all of whom I have worked with for more than 10 amazing years and who include Janet Buckles, Anis Dave, Debbie Neuman, Bob Taylor, and Heidi Wisbach.

Lastly, I'd like to thank YOU for reading this book all the way to the end and even the acknowledgments. You are a real trooper! But more importantly, thank you for the work you do every day to improve the experiences of your customers and team members. While critics may point out downsides of our digital world, and there are some, I am thrilled to have had the opportunity to be alive during this incredible time of change. I see today's wave of digital transformation as a massive force for good in the world. Thank you for your role in it.

ABOUT THE AUTHOR

Howard Tiersky has been named by IDG as one of the "Top 10 Digital Transformation Influencers to Follow Today." As an entrepreneur, he has launched two successful companies that help large brands transform to thrive in the digital age: FROM, The Digital Transformation Agency and Innovation Loft. His dozens of Fortune 1000 clients have included Verizon, NBC, Viacom, Avis, Universal Studios, JPMC, Crayola, Morgan Stanley, Conde Nast, the NBA, Visa, and digital leaders like Facebook, Spotify, and Amazon.

Prior to founding his own company, Howard spent 18 years with Ernst & Young Consulting, which then became part of Capgemini, one of the world's leading global consulting firms, where he helped launch their digital practice.

Howard speaks regularly at major industry conferences and is proud to have served on the faculty of the NYU Tisch School of the Arts, his *alma mater*.

Howard can be reached at LinkedIn.com/in/Tiersky or via email at Howard_Tiersky@From.Digital.

ENDNOTES

All of the sources cited throughout the book can be easily found online by entering the URLs that are listed after the citations here.

CHAPTER ONE

1 "Number of smartphone users in the United States from 2010 to 2023 (in millions)*," *Statista*, 2019. ⊘ wdc.ht/1.1

2 "Trends in Consumer Mobility Report," Bank of America, 2015. ⊘ wdc.ht/1.2

3 Julio Bezerra, Wolfgang Bock, François Candelon, Steve Chai, Ethan Choi, John Corwin, Sebastian DiGrande, Rishab Gulshan, David Michael, and Antonio Varas, "The Mobile Revolution: How Mobile Technologies Drive a Trillion-Dollar Impact," BCG, January 15, 2015. ⊘ wdc.ht/1.3

4 Ibid. ⊘ wdc.ht/1.4

5 Ibid. ⊘ wdc.ht/1.5

6 Ibid. ⊘ wdc.ht/1.6

7 "Survey Analysis: CIOs Must Help Close the Gap Between CEOs' Digital Ambitions and Consumers' Digital Perceptions," Gartner, 2018. ⊘ wdc.ht/1.7

8 "Global Transformation Study 2016," KPMG, 2016.

9 "Why 84% of Digital Transformations Fail," *Forbes*, 2016. ⊘ wdc.ht/1.7

10 "Digital Transformation Review – 12th Edition," Capgemini, 2019. ⊘ wdc.ht/1.8

CHAPTER TWO

1 Jessica Young, "US ecommerce sales grow 14.9% in 2019," *Digital Commerce 360*, February 19, 2020. ⊘ wdc.ht/2.1

2 "How Skype Makes Money," *Investopedia*, June 25, 2019. ⊘ wdc.ht/2.2

CHAPTER THREE

1 Scott Allison, "The Responsive Organization: Coping With New Technology And Disruption," *Forbes*, February 10, 2014. ⊘ wdc.ht/3.1

2 Adam Lashinsky, "How Dollar Shave Club got started," *Fortune*, March 10, 2015. ⊘ wdc.ht/3.2

3 CNBC Make It Staff, "This CEO sold his company for $1 billion—here's how he finds work-life balance," *CNBC*, February 6, 2019. ⊘ wdc.ht/3.3

4 Warren Shoulberg, "Harry's Is Selling To Owner Of Schick Razors, The Latest Example Of Disrupter Joining Disruptee," *Forbes*, May 9, 2019. ⊘ wdc.ht/3.4

5 Ameena Walker, "In NYC, 139 prized yellow taxi medallions will hit the auction block," *Curbed New York*, June 11, 2018. ⊘ wdc.ht/3.5

6 "Digital hits the road," Accenture, 2016. ⊘ wdc.ht/3.6

7 "State of the Connected Customer: Second Edition," Salesforce Research, 2018. ⊘ wdc.ht/3.7

8 David Clarke and Ron Kinghorn, "Experience is everything: Here's how to get it right," PwC, 2018. ⊘ wdc.ht/3.8

9 Ibid. ⊘ wdc.ht/3.9

10 Andrew Tenzer and Hanna Chalmers, "When Trust Falls Down - How brands got here and what they need to do about it," Trinity Mirror Solutions & Ipsos Connect, 2017. ⏎ wdc.ht/3.10

11 The *Learnbrite* Team, "Millennials in the Workplace, Are You Ready?", *Learnbrite*, 2018. ⏎ wdc.ht/3.11

12 Steve West, "Meeting Millennial Expectations In These Four Areas Of Technology," *Forbes*, June 28, 2018. ⏎ wdc.ht/3.12

13 Ibid. ⏎ wdc.ht/3.13

14 "Aligning the Business Around a Customer," Aberdeen Group, 2016. ⏎ wdc.ht/3.14

15 George Westerman, Maël Tannou, Didier Bonnet, Patrick Ferraris, and Andrew McAfee, "The Digital Advantage: How digital leaders outperform their peers in every industry," MIT Sloan and Capgemini, 2017. ⏎ wdc.ht/3.15

16 Ragu Gurumurthy and David Schatsky, "Pivoting to digital maturity," Deloitte Insights, March 13, 2019. ⏎ wdc.ht/3.16

17 Marco Iansiti and Karim Lakhani, "The Digital Business Divide," *Harvard Business Review*, 2017. ⏎ wdc.ht/3.17

18 George Westerman, Maël Tannou, Didier Bonnet, Patrick Ferraris, and Andrew McAfee, "The Digital Advantage: How digital leaders outperform their peers in every industry," MIT Sloan and Capgemini, 2017. ⏎ wdc.ht/3.18

19 "No Normal is the New Normal: 2018 Global Consumer Executive Top of Mind Survey," KPMG International, 2018. ⏎ wdc.ht/3.19

20 George Westerman, Maël Tannou, Didier Bonnet, Patrick Ferraris, and Andrew McAfee, "The Digital Advantage: How digital leaders outperform their peers in every industry," MIT Sloan and Capgemini, 2017. ⏎ wdc.ht/3.20

21 Rick Parrish, "Does CX Quality Affect Stock Performance? Yes, But...", Forrester, February 28, 2018. ⏎ wdc.ht/3.21

CHAPTER FIVE

1 Quentin Hardy, "At Kodak, Clinging to a Future Beyond Film," New York Times, March 20, 2015. ⏎ wdc.ht/5.1

2 John Paczkowski, "Breaking Down Apple's Retail Distribution Strategy," AllThingsD, October 3, 2012. ⏎ wdc.ht/5.2

3 John Laposky and Alan Wolf, "Sony Phasing Out Its Retail Stores," AllThingsD, March 4, 2015. ⏎ wdc.ht/5.3

CHAPTER SIX

1 Rodney Page, "First time on the course and golfer hits a hole-in-one," *The Norwegian American*, March 17, 2009. ⏎ wdc.ht/6.1

2 Rob Wengel, "How to Flip 85% Misses to 85% Hits: Lessons from the Nielsen Breakthrough Innovation Project," Nielsen, June 24, 2014. ⏎ wdc.ht/6.2

CHAPTER SEVEN

1 Dave Davies, "Meet the 7 Most Popular Search Engines in the World," *Search Engine Journal*, January 7, 2018. ⏎ wdc.ht/7.1

2 "Outliers' Puts Self-Made Success To The Test," *NPR*, November 18, 2008. ⏎ wdc.ht/7.2

CHAPTER EIGHT

1 "The Story of One of the Most Memorable Marketing Blunders Ever," The Coca Cola Company, 2020. ⟲ wdc.ht/8.1

CHAPTER NINE

1 Greg Brenneman, "Right Away and All at Once: How We Saved Continental," *Harvard Business Review*, September-October, 1998. ⟲ wdc.ht/9.1

2 "Management Advice From the Former CEO Who Saved Continental Airlines," CO— by *U.S. Chamber of Commerce*, 2019. ⟲ wdc.ht/9.2

CHAPTER TEN

1 Howard Tiersky, "Macy's CEO credits 'customer journey mapping' as the foundation of their turnaround," *CIO*, April 3, 2018. ⟲ wdc.ht/10.1

CHAPTER TWELVE

1 Gregory Garrett, "Cyberattacks Skyrocketed in 2018," *Industry Week*, December 13, 2018. ⟲ wdc.ht/12.1

2 Nick Ismail, "Worldwide, targeted cyber attacks are on the rise — SonicWall," *Information Age*, March 26, 2019. ⟲ wdc.ht/12.2

3 "2018 Cost of a Data Breach Study," IBM Security & The Ponemon Institute, 2018. ⟲ wdc.ht/12.3

4 Dan Farber, "Analog dollars for digital pennies," *CNET*, July 23, 2013. ⟲ wdc.ht/12.4

CHAPTER THIRTEEN

1 Hayley Tsukayama, "How Samsung moved beyond its exploding phones," *Washington Post*, February 23, 2018. ⟲ wdc.ht/13.1

2 NMAH, "Build a better mousetrap," National Museum of American History, January 26, 2011. ⟲ wdc.ht/13.2

3 Nicholas Jackson, "Mousetraps: A Symbol of the American Entrepreneurial Spirit," *The Atlantic*, March 28, 2011. ⟲ wdc.ht/13.3

4 "Victor Choker Mouse Trap," National Museum of American History, 2020. ⟲ wdc.ht/13.4

5 EntreVersity, "Buckminster Fuller: The first author in design thinking," *EntreVersity*, September 6, 2018. ⟲ wdc.ht/13.5

6 "Design Thinking History," IDEO, 2020. ⟲ wdc.ht/13.6

7 Rikke Friis Dam and Yu Siang Teo, "Design Thinking: Get a Quick Overview of the History," Interaction Design Foundation, 2020. ⟲ wdc.ht/13.7

CHAPTER FOURTEEN

1 Jennie Cohen, "Human Ancestors Tamed Fire Earlier Than Thought," *History*, April 22, 2012. ⟲ wdc.ht/14.1

CHAPTER FIFTEEN

1 "Innovation & Brainstorming," MIT, 2015. ⟲ wdc.ht/15.1

2 "Convergent Vs. Divergent Thinking: Know the Real Difference," *PsycoloGenie*, 2014. ⟲ wdc.ht/15.2

3 Snowy Range Reflections Staff, "Mining Techniques of the Sierra Nevada and Gold Country," Sierra College, Spring, 2009. ⟲ wdc.ht/15.3

4 "Wallpaper Design," LG, 2019. ⟲ wdc.ht/15.4

5 "Whether You Believe You Can Do a Thing or Not, You Are Right," *Quote Investigator*, February 3, 2015. ⟲ wdc.ht/15.5

6 Tim Bajarin, "How Corning's Crash Project For Steve Jobs Helped Define The iPhone," *Fast Company*, November 11, 2017. ℃wdc.ht/_{15.6}

7 Fred Vogelstein, "The Untold Story: How the iPhone Blew Up the Wireless Industry," *Wired*, January 9, 2008.℃wdc.ht/_{15.7}

CHAPTER SIXTEEN

1 "Minimum Viable Product (MVP)," Agile Alliance, 2017. ℃wdc.ht/_{16.1}

2 Jini Maxin, "To Prototype or Not To Prototype...Ask Leonardo Da Vinci," *Openxcell*, June 24, 2015. ℃wdc.ht/_{16.2}

3 "Sculptors at Work," *Italian Renaissance Learning Resources*, 2013. ℃wdc.ht/_{16.3}

4 "Virtual reality with real benefits," Airbus, September 25, 2017. ℃wdc.ht/_{16.4}

CHAPTER SEVENTEEN

1 Dan Zarrella, "Don't 'Submit' To Landing Page Button Text," *HubSpot*, October 8, 2010.℃wdc.ht/_{17.1}

2 Hara Estroff Marano, "Our Brain's Negativity Bias," *Psychology Today*, June 20, 2003.℃wdc.ht/_{17.2}

CHAPTER NINETEEN

1 Christopher Harress, "The Sad End of Blockbuster," *International Business Times*, December 5, 2013.℃wdc.ht/_{19.1}

2 Nathan McAlone, "This man invented the digital camera in 1975 — and his bosses at Kodak never let it see the light of day," *Business Insider*, August 17, 2015. ℃wdc.ht/_{19.2}

3 David Usborne, "The moment it all went wrong for Kodak," *The Independent*, January 20, 2012. ℃wdc.ht/_{19.3}

4 Elizabeth Nix, "Who Invented Sliced Bread?", *History*, January 16, 2015. ℃wdc.ht/_{19.4}

5 Lucas Reilly, "The Time the U.S. Government Banned Sliced Bread," *Mental Floss*, January 3, 2019. ℃wdc.ht/_{19.5}

6 Daniel Ionescu, "Apple's iPhone 4 Antennagate Timeline," *PCWorld*, July 17, 2010. ℃wdc.ht/_{19.6}

7 Nilay Patel, "Wrong turn: Apple's buggy iOS 6 maps lead to widespread complaints," *The Verge*, September 20, 2012.℃wdc.ht/_{19.7}

8 Dan Nielsen, "Leadership: Success is a Lousy Teacher," *The Journal of Healthcare Contracting*, 2014. ℃wdc.ht/_{19.8}

9 Kristen Korosec, "Hulu buys back AT&T's minority stake in streaming service now valued at $15 billion," *TechCrunch*, April 15, 2019. ℃wdc.ht/_{19.9}

10 Brendan Gibbons, "Search Engines, Indexing and Copyright Law," *PracticalEcommerce*, December 14, 2009. ℃wdc.ht/_{19.10}

Dustin Smith, "Nonverbal Communication: How Body Language & Nonverbal Cues Are Key," *Lifesize*, February 18, 2020. ℃wdc.ht/_{19.11}

CHAPTER TWENTY

1 The Editors of Encyclopedia Britannica, "Hideo Shima," *Encyclopedia Britannica*, 1998. ℃wdc.ht/_{20.1}

2 "Hideo Shima, a Designer of Japan's Bullet Train, Is Dead at 96," *New York Times*, 1998. ℃wdc.ht/_{20.2}

3 Alex Abad-Santos, "Avengers: Endgame finally beats Avatar to become the biggest movie of all time," *Vox*, July 22, 2019. ℃wdc.ht/_{20.3}

CHAPTER TWENTY-ONE

1 "Well begun is half done," *BrainyQuote*, 2001.℃wdc.ht/_{21.1}

DIGITAL INDEX

The index for Winning Digital Customers can be found on the
book website at

```
🔗 wdc.ht/INDEX
```

You can access it from your computer or mobile device.

Search for any word or phrase in the book and be referred to the
page numbers that address that topic. For each instance, you will
also see snippets of the text around the term. We hope you will
agree this is a better experience than a printed index and also
saves a few trees. Happy searching!